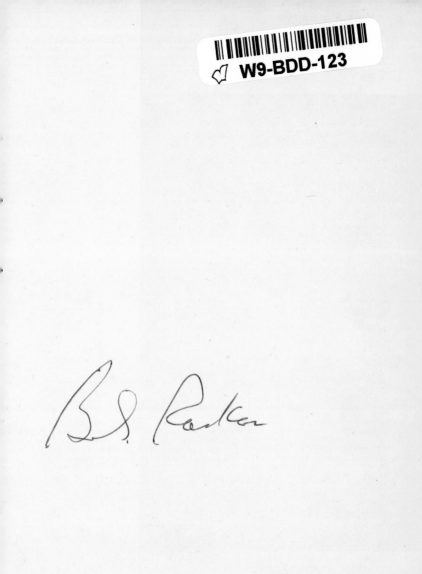

A THOUGHT FOR EACH DAY
OF THE JEWISH YEAR

# HEART
# OF
# WISDOM
## Book II

*by*

*Bernard S. Raskas*

THE BURNING BUSH PRESS
NEW YORK

To Laeh

in gratitude

ראה חיים עם אשה אשר אהבת

It is my privilege and pleasure

# Foreword

In 1962, the National Academy for Adult Jewish Studies and The Burning Bush Press broke fresh ground in sponsoring Rabbi Bernard S. Raskas' pioneer volume *Heart of Wisdom*. Previous United Synagogue adult publications had, in large measure, begun with the Text and then proceeded to intensively expound Jewish ideas. *Heart of Wisdom* represented a new direction in the work of the National Academy. Organized around the Jewish calendar and dealing with the varied problems of modern men and women, it offered, for their resolution, the insights of a tradition of four milennia presented in capsule form. Beginning in each case with a human concern, it drew upon Jewish sources via anecdote, folklore and direct quotation from writings ancient, medieval and modern.

Over the years, *Heart of Wisdom* has attracted a large and devoted following. Many of its messages have been widely quoted; they have found their way into anthologies and have been presented over radio and television. At long last, in response to popular demand, Rabbi Raskas has prepared this sequel volume. It is our hope that this collection may stimulate the reader to intensive and systematic study of the rich literature of Judaism.

It is my pleasant task to express our appreciation to Rabbis Morris S. Friedman, Murray Levine and Amos W. Miller who served as readers of the original manuscript and who offered a number of helpful suggestions. Thanks are also due to Dorothy Sachs for preparing the text for the printer and to Dorothy Nathan for secretarial assistance.

v

May *Heart of Wisdom II* bring the many nearer to Torah and may they be privileged to say with the Psalmist (19;8-9), "The teaching of the Lord is perfect, renewing life; the decrees of the Lord are enduring, making the simple wise. The precepts of the Lord are just, rejoicing the heart; the instruction of the Lord is lucid, restoring strength."

*Marvin S. Wiener*

SIVAN 5738
JUNE 1978
New York City

# Preface

*Heart of Wisdom II* is a reader for the individual who wishes to have a daily spiritual message that is rooted in Jewish tradition. The book has been written with this in mind and it provides a thought for each day of the year.

Contemporary human beings, even as human beings in every generation, n. contact with a source that is traditional as well as relevant. In this way the individual finds the meaning of life enhanced and also develops a feeling of rootedness in a faith that provides stability and security. As a congregational rabbi and as one who has worked with Jews who possess many approaches to life, with individuals of all ages and many generations and, generally, with human beings representing many faiths and walks of life, I have seen the need for such a book. On many occasions, works such as this have been most helpful in situations of stress as well as of human happiness.

I would like to thank Cecelia Rose Waldman for her help and good advice in the preparation of this book. Sheila Kaufman's efforts were most useful in the editing. Lucy Cook added immeasurably to the final form. Rabbi Marvin S. Wiener, Director of the National Academy for Adult Jewish Studies of the United Synagogue of America, served as editor with exceptional devotion and competence. I am most grateful for his sustained interest which helped bring this book to publication.

This work was conceived with the traditional purpose of devotional literature, which is to teach that the Torah continues to be meaningful today as it was yesterday. It seeks to give a sense of the present to the timeless. It is an attempt to fulfill the prayer:

> "We shall rejoice in the words of Your Torah and in Your Commandments now and forever, for they are our life and the length of our days and we shall meditate upon them day and night."

If the reader will be helped to do this, then the purpose of the book will be fulfilled.

*Bernard S. Raskas*

IYAR 5738
MAY 1978
Temple of Aaron
St. Paul, Minnesota

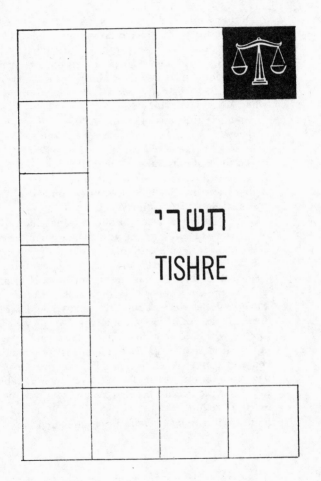

תשרי

TISHRE

# A New Beginning

During the ordinary course of the year, we rarely stop to ask where we are or in what direction we are traveling; we just travel. But intelligent people know that whether we are steering or drifting depends on knowing our present position and our destination and then adjusting the course between them. And the first step is really knowing our position— where we are and who we are.

An interesting analogy can be found in a news story which would be funny if it were not so foolish. The skipper of a sinking pleasure boat near Chesapeake Bay radioed repeatedly and frantically for help. "We're on our way," the Coast Guard replied. "What is your position?" The yachtsman answered, "I'm Executive Vice-President of the First National Bank. Please hurry!"

Most of us are prisoners of our set minds and captives of our status symbols. We are governed by what our friends say and what our neighbors think.

But then comes Rosh Hashanah, the beginning of the New Year, and it asks, "Where are you going?" Conformity says our present way of life is comfortable, but Rosh Hashanah asks: Is it correct? Status drives tell us our goals for today are desirable, but Rosh Hashanah asks: Are they sensible for tomorrow? Public morality dictates a view on a given issue, but Rosh Hashanah speaks to the privacy of the individual conscience and asks: Is it right? For the focus of this holy day is not on the passing hour, but on the honorable position. With the coming of a New Year we are given the opportunity to rethink our positions in life and then to lift the levels of lives to new heights of meaning and purpose.

*A new year has begun, reminding us of the eternal possibility of renewal.*
EUGENE KOHN

# The Dawn Of Conscience

Often the question is raised, if the earth is more than four billion years old why, then, is Rosh Hashanah, the beginning of the Jewish New Year, referred to as "the day when the world was created"? Since the Jewish calendar is less than 5800 years old, the explanation is that Jews celebrate on Rosh Hashanah the time when *recorded* history began, about 5800 years ago.

Though the earth is of a far greater age, man's career as a food gatherer began only a half million years ago; then some 50,000 years ago man began to live in caves, but not until the last five-and-a-half millenia has man demonstrated a sense of responsibility to his fellow man. So it is that on Rosh Hashanah, appropriately enough, we celebrate the anniversary of the dawn of conscience.

In fact, the first episode in the Bible which highlights clear moral choice and man's accountability for his actions is the Cain and Abel story in which God asks Cain, "Where is Abel your brother?" Cain's reply is: "Am I my brother's keeper?" The answer of the Bible is that we *are* our brothers' keepers, for God's reply is: "The blood of your brother is crying out to Me." This phrase represents the first statement of conscience, and with it begins the history of civilization.

What all this is really telling us is that the way to lessen our anxiety is to accept moral responsibility. Biblical history specifically, and history generally, demonstrate that when man had faith in himself and lived by a set of moral values, he sustained himself and survived. For it is man's humanity to man that can abolish our mutual anxieties. The Jewish conviction is that only conscience can save and secure a civilization.

*Conscience is like charity, a Semitic importation. Israel introduced it into the world.*    ANATOLE LEROY-BEAULIEU

# Tune-Up Time

The Hebrew word for "repentance" is *teshuvah*. But it is also interesting to note that, literally, *teshuvah* means "return." This teaches us that atonement in Judaism implies returning to the right direction in life.

An automobile often needs a wheel alignment to keep it going in the right direction. The steering mechanism goes out of line through constant use, and the car begins to wobble. Just as often a human being begins to wobble morally and needs a new direction and sharper reading of the signs on the road of life.

How is it that we need our guidance system corrected? Some of us are too far-sighted, and we neglect to see those near and dear unto us. Some of us are too near-sighted, concentrating on ourselves alone and ignoring those who are distant from us. We must make sure that we are concerned with our whole community and the whole human race; and that they, too, are included in the range of our vision. Some of us are at the age when we need bifocals so that we can read the signs of the time. But if we want to have the correct vision we can always turn to the right path.

A Hasidic *rebbe* once asked, "If you are going East and suddenly you want to travel West, how far do you have to go?" His congregants gave many complex answers, but the *rebbe* himself answered his own question in this way. "If you are going East and suddenly you want to go West, all you have to do is turn around. It is as simple as that."

To return to Judaism requires only one turn. To return to reasonable living takes but one turn. To return to a society that is sane and sensible takes but the right turn.

*The gates of prayer are sometimes open, sometimes closed; but the gates of repentance are open forever.*

DEUTERONOMY RABBAH 2:7

# The Greatest Day Of Your Life

Which day is the greatest day of your life? Think about it for a minute. This question was asked of several people.

A young boy answered: "The day I was born."

A groom in the presence of his bride said: "The day I met her."

An elderly Jew replied: "The day I arrived in America."

We would all agree that these are very significant days. But some people live as though the greatest and most important day of their lives is tomorrow!

"Tomorrow is the day I am going to spend with my family."

"Tomorrow is the day I am going to begin to read a good book."

"Tomorrow is when I am going to plan a vacation."

But do they really do these things tomorrow? For tomorrow rarely comes in the way we expect it today. That is why worrying about tomorrow is really useless. For whatever we worry about seldom happens. What really occurs is usually the thing that we never even thought about. In one sense, tomorrow exists only in our minds. What we truly experience is really a succession of todays.

So we have come to the answer to our opening question. Yesterday is past; tomorrow does not exist. So, what is obviously the greatest day in one's life? The answer is, "Today." Every hour, every day in one's life has the potential of becoming the greatest time to have lived. Every second has its meaning. Every minute has its message. Every moment has its opportunity. Every tick of the clock, every beat of the heart has its wonder, its challenge, its hope.

*Every person has his or her hour as everything has its place.*
                                                              AVOT 4:3

# Man And Animal

It was the practice of Israel's Canaanite neighbors to muzzle an ox while it was working the fields so that it might not eat. But because binding an animal while it is working near food is an act of great cruelty, we find in the Bible a commandment forbidding this practice and expressing compassion for the beast of burden: You shall not muzzle an ox while it is threshing (Deuteronomy 25:4). This text reflects the deep sensitivity of Jewish tradition not only for the pain and anguish of human beings but for the hurt of animals.

In the Talmud, these feelings are further amplified in the teaching that one should feed an animal before one has fed one's own children, because children can ask for food when they are hungry but an animal cannot articulate its needs.

Those who have come to love and care for animals learn a great deal, for there is a natural wisdom in the animal kingdom that we sophisticated human beings often lack.

An illustration of this notion can be found in the life of Glenn Cunningham, a world-famous athlete, who retired in his middle years and devoted the rest of his life to rehabilitating wayward youths. He would take some of them to his ranch in Kansas, where he assigned them to care for animals. By learning to care for animals, they discovered the meaning and the value of life. And working to preserve animals, they were taught to preserve their own sense of humanity.

This wonderful concept of rehabilitation is to be found in the Biblical sensitivity to the feelings and needs of animals. For those who care for the lives of others find the meaning of their own lives greatly enhanced.

*A righteous person is also concerned for the life of an animal.*
                                                    PROVERBS 12:10

# Sooner Or Later

Most of the year we go about our frivolous ways, indifferent to the condition of our conscience, oblivious to our soul. But on the *yamin noraim*, the Days of Awe, we are summoned to render an accounting for our lives. On the High Holy Days, each of us must face the Supreme Judge.

This brings to mind the following story: A man who was arrested for vagrancy was brought to appear before the judge. When questioned as to when he worked, the man replied, "Now and then." When asked what he did for a living, the reply was, "This and that." The last question by the judge was, "Where do you live?" to which the man replied, "Here and there."

"Young man, you are going to jail," the judge said, thoroughly exasperated. "When do I get out?" asked the vagrant. "Sooner or later," replied the judge.

Sooner or later we appear before the holiest of judges, and we are tried at the bar of conscience. But we act as our own judge, we try ourselves through the recitation of the hallowed High Holy Day words.

One may ask, what are words? Words evaporate in the air. But do they really? What was the Declaration of Independence? Just a group of words, but they changed the destiny of a nation. What was the Magna Carta? Just a group of words, but they redirected the course of a civilization. And what were the Ten Commandments? Just 72 words and they altered the destiny of mankind. During the Days of Awe we recite words, meditate on words, and even offer up unspoken words. If we take these words seriously and if we judge ourselves honestly, we can alter our lives for the good.

*The great trumpet is sounded; a still small voice is heard; fear and trembling seize the angels as they proclaim: Behold the Day of Judgment.*     LITURGY OF THE DAYS OF AWE

# Creative Pauses

The seventeenth verse of the thirty-first chapter of Exodus is usually translated as "And on the seventh day God ceased from work and rested." Actually, the Hebrew word here for rest is *vayinafash* which means more than "rest." The most accurate translation would be "and He restored His soul."

The meaning is that Sabbath is much more than cessation from work: It is rather creative thought. The real purpose of the Sabbath is to teach us that a human being has a soul, that indefinable something that makes each person precious and unique.

But, if we rush and we push and we hurry all week long, how are we going to discover our souls? We will pass ourselves up in the effort to move ahead.

But, what really is ahead? That is what *Shabbat* seeks. Ask yourself, "What's happening to my soul? In what way am I unique and, therefore, precious?" *Shabbat* gives us the regular weekly chance to scrutinize our souls.

Arthur Schnabel, the world renowned concert artist, was once asked for the "secret" of his superb piano playing. "How do you handle the notes as well as you do?" inquired a student.

"The notes I handle no better than many pianists," Schnabel replied. "But the pauses between the notes—ah, that is where the art resides!"

Yes, it is in the refreshing pause that the art of living is found.

*The Israelite people shall keep the Sabbath, observing the Sabbath throughout the generations as a covenant for all time: it shall be a sign for all time between Me and the people of Israel. For in six days the Lord made heaven and earth, and on the seventh day He ceased from work and was refreshed.*                                EXODUS 31:16-17

# Befriend Your Enemy

We are taught in all religious traditions that one of the ways to blunt the force of evil is to treat it with understanding and even with kindness. At first, this sounds like a pleasant irrelevancy, but upon deeper thought we see that it may be a hard fact. For the only way to destroy an enemy completely is to make him your friend.

During William McKinley's campaign for President, one of the reporters assigned to cover him represented a newspaper that was violently opposed to McKinley. The reporter was to travel on the train with the candidate and send back negative stories at every opportunity. At first he did; and McKinley knew what was happening, but said absolutely nothing. One bitterly cold afternoon the reporter fell asleep huddled on the seat of the unheated car. McKinley came by, stopped, and spread his overcoat over the man. When the reporter awoke and discovered what had happened, he sent a telegram resigning from his job. He could not go on maligning a man compassionate enough to answer his criticisms by befriending him.

This is the ultimate truth of religious teaching. Friendship breeds fellowship and nothing in the world is stronger than that. We do not advance by competition, we move forward by cooperation. It is simply not true that pressure always moves people. Politeness is much more effective. Aggression may achieve a goal, but in its wake it leaves the memory of many hurts. Kind actions may bring us to our goals a little bit later, but they create an enormous reservoir of good will. For every angry force there will be a force in reply, and for every act of kindness there will be a kindness returned.

*Who is truly mighty? He who can convert an enemy into a friend.*                    AVOT DE-RABBI NATHAN 23

# Promises! Promises!

It is essential to Jewish theology that on *Kol Nidre* night we emphasize the concept of "vows." But we ought to emphasize less the negative idea of broken promises and stress more the positive thought of the renewal of vows. This is the time to remember our marriage vows. The remembered beauty of the love of our younger years can strengthen our more difficult later years. This is the time to remember our vows made to fulfill our personal values. The shining splendor of our earlier aspirations can still bring light and hope to our lives as we determine to carry them forth. This is the time to remember the vows we made to Judaism. The re-identification with our Jewish experiences, our Jewish traditions, our Jewish loyalties can still give us strength as we face the future.

Life is hard, responsibilities wear us down, situations tempt us. Sometimes we resist, sometimes we give in. Why judge others harshly? After all, we are all human. And to be human is to make excuses. But let us not use our excuses to justify a sense of cynicism, for a cynic knows the price of everything and the value of nothing. *Kol Nidre* says: Don't be a cynic, be a child of God. Give yourself a chance to start anew. Give others a chance to begin again. The essence of Jewish thought is the belief that we are not animals doomed only to be born, reproduce, and die. We can rise above the animal functions of sleeping and eating and snarling.

Someone once told Rabbi Pinchas Koretzer that the philosopher Spinoza asserted in his works that man has the same nature as animals and stands no higher than them. The Rabbi laughed and said, "If this is the case, one should ask him why the animals haven't yet produced a Spinoza."

We are all capable as human beings of producing more, doing more, and loving more.

*The righteous promise little, but do much.*  BAVA METZIA 87a

# Yom Kippur! Yom Kippur!

A lively and very popular Israeli singer represented her country at an international film festival held serveral years ago in Moscow. She sang Hebrew folk songs, a Yiddish number, and a Russian lullaby which she had memorized without understanding the meaning of the words. She was received with tumultuous applause. After the performance, as she was on the way to her hotel, a young man approached and told her in Russian how impressed he was with her presentation of the Hebrew songs. She sensed what he was trying to convey and tried to answer in simple Hebrew accompanied by gestures. The conversation came to a halt and it was obvious that the young man felt that he had been unable to communicate clearly that he himself was Jewish. In desperation, he caught her hand, pressed it hard, and uttered the only Hebrew words he could remember: "Yom Kippur! Yom Kippur!" The young singer overcame her tears and answered: "Yom Kippur! Yom Kippur!"

This happening is a striking expression of the power and meaning of Yom Kippur, the Day of Atonement. Divided by continents, estranged by cultures, these two Jews nonetheless found a method of communication through the bridge of Yom Kippur. But, even more, this is an expression of the simple and singular commitment that a Jew must make toward other Jews. All Jews, no matter how different their customs, how disparate their concerns, are part of us. The young Jewish radical, the alienated Jew, the culturally conflicted Jew are still part of Jewish life. It is our responsibility to draw them into the Jewish community and accept them. We are all part of the Jewish experience.

*Jewishness is exacting but inspiring, exhausting but always an adventure.*    ABRAHAM L. FEINBERG

# Continuity

At the conclusion of Yom Kippur it is customary to place into the ground the first stake of the *sukkah*. This ritual demonstrates the seriousness and the purpose of our pledges to be Jewish made on this most sacred of days.

This is a way of making certain that Yom Kippur was for us a meaningful experience that in some way has changed our lives; and when we are changed, our world is changed. This affirmation is not the end of a great spiritual commitment; it is only the beginning. And the real way to begin is to continue—continue to do all that makes life worthwhile.

In keeping with this thought, would it not be a wonderful thing if the next act we did would be a simple but effective sign of how we mean to begin a commitment that we will continue:

To take your pen and register for that adult education course you have been putting off taking.

To pick up your telephone and call someone to whom you may have spoken a harsh word and simply apologize to him or her.

To take a piece of bread and say a blessing and then realize that we ought to say a blessing of thanksgiving for every piece of bread we taste, for every article of clothing we wear, for every act of good fortune that comes our way, for everything that is truly beautiful and wonderful in God's world.

Finally, the real way to begin is to continue; to continue to carry forth the excellence and moral purpose of Judaism.

*The beginning will bear witness to the end, and the end will at long last bear witness to the beginning.*    LEO BAECK

# For Goodness Sake

It is important as we consider the many problems that beset our community to keep in mind that those who do the most significant work are not the critics but the creators. Those who truly serve God and humankind are not those who seek out the flaws, but rather those who find how to build, those who act out of compassion and a sense of justice, rather than out of fear.

Consider the story about the doctor who was talking to his patient and said, "You are a very sick man but you'll pull through." The patient was frightened and he said, "Please, Doctor, do everything you can for me. If I get well, I will donate $25,000 to the fund for your new hospital."

In the course of time, the patient recovered and the doctor met him on the street. He asked, "How are you?" The patient replied, "Marvelously well." "Good," said the doctor, "I have been meaning to speak to you about the money for the new hospital." The man said, as if surprised, "What are you talking about?" The doctor reminded him, "You said if you got well you would donate $25,000 to the fund for the new hospital." And the former patient exclaimed, "If I said that, I must *really* have been sick!"

Some of us seem to have the notion that we should only do things when we are threatened or filled with fear. This kind of motivation is negative and harmful. The real *mitzvah* is performed because it is the right thing to do and not out of fear or hope for reward. There are those who feel that we should help the poor because they fear riots and social upheaval. But rather shouldn't we do this because it is right to help every citizen achieve liberty and a good life?

*Let a good person do good deeds with the same zeal that an evil person does bad ones.*                THE BELZER REBBE

# Cultural Cousins

The establishment of enduring peace in the Middle East will be based on the fact that Jews and Arabs have learned how to live together creatively.

We must begin this process by understanding that Jews and Arabs are Semites, cultural cousins, if not blood brothers and sisters. Hebrew and Arabic are cognate languages, stemming from a common origin, and even today are closer to one another in structure than many other comparative languages. Isaac was one of the patriarchs of the Jewish people, and Ishmael, his brother, was the father of the Arab nations. In founding the religion of Islam in the seventh century, Mohammed mentions Jesus only four times in the early chapters of the Koran, while Moses is cited one hundred times.

On the other hand, the Jewish Golden Age in Spain was stimulated by Arabic culture. Medieval Jewish philosophy, grammar, and science has borrowed liberally from Arabic sources. Maimonides, the great Jewish genius, wrote his *Guide to the Perplexed* and even his commentary to the Mishnah in Arabic.

If Arab-Jewish encounters were so productive in the past centuries, could they not bear fruit again? Arabs have much to offer the Israelis in the arts, in natural resources, in a vast expanding economic market. Israel has health, education, welfare, and technological services readily available for Arab use. New Israeli techniques in solar heat, and desalination of water can benefit the whole Middle East. With the right attitude, this area of the world can become a model of mutual help.

*We have to remember that ultimately we are going to be the neighbors of the Arabs. And it is not only our duty to maintain law and order but also to create a form of good neighbor policy with them. So we have to look at them like a government looking at citizens.*                    MOSHE DAYAN

# A Measure Of Age

Since time is an arrow which flies in only one direction, it is inevitable that we must one day face aging and the concerns of the aged. Any real understanding of this question must begin with the realization that basic to all ages, but particularly old age, is the drive to survive.

President Dwight Eisenhower in his later years had about six heart attacks, several major operations and illnesses, and toward the end suffered greatly. Once when he was in the hospital, he asked a visitor, "Do you know who wants to live to 100?" The caller answered, "No, who?" Eisenshower grinned and said, "The guy who is 99."

The truth is that everybody wants to live—especially the aged. However, what must not be overlooked is the fact that growing old also brings with it the inevitable illnesses of aging. But recent research has shown us that many of the illnesses of the elderly can be helped through good medical care and, above all, a positive mental attitude.

Clearly, many old people would not be alive today if it were not for medical advances. Even more spectacular discoveries to prevent degeneration and slow senility are around the corner. But in all the aging studies, attitude is a decisive factor. We make a mistake when we think of the elderly as a homogeneous group. They are not. Some are rich and some are poor; some are sick and some are well. They also differ in their enthusiasm for life. The truth is that individuals who do not have a good attitude and a wholesome philosophy of life will find *every* age burdensome. The maxim still holds that "You are as old as you feel."

*You are as young as your self-confidence, as old as your fear; as young as your hope, as old as your despair.*

SAMUEL ULLMAN

# More Light And Less Heat

The roof of the *sukkah* must be made of leaves or branches, and the openings of the roof must be wide so that from the inside one can see the light of the sun by day or the stars by night. Think about this carefully: no heat but plenty of light. Perhaps this is a way of telling us that what we need is less heat and more light—less of the heat of quarrels, angers and tensions; more of the light of understanding and tolerance.

Tolerance is not an admission of weakness but a mark of strength. When a person is intolerant of other views, he is merely saying that he is afraid of exposing himself to the possbility that others might have some measure of truth on their side. When we are strong in our faith we have no need to be apprehensive of those who might disagree with us; indeed, we may even be able to say, "while my approach seems right for me, your way may be right for you."

On a flight across the Rockies, an airplane encountered considerable turbulence. One of the passengers looked out the window and noted the giant wings of the jet shaking under the stress of the violent winds. He fretted and frowned, but his seatmate leaned over clamly and said, "Don't worry. It is *because* the wings give and bend that they will be able to return to their original position. The strength of these massive aircrafts is to be found in their degree of tolerance."

So if we develop a tolerance and flexibility, we can take the stresses of conflicting views with serene confidence.

*A wise man's duty is to be scrupulously faithful to the religious laws of his country and not to abuse those of others.*      JOSEPHUS

# Share And Share Alike

The first tabernacle was erected during the forty-year trek through the wilderness on the way to the Promised Land. For this reason, everything had to be portable. Therefore, around the edges of the Ark, which contained stone tablets of the Ten Commandments, rings were created. Staves or poles could then be inserted in order to carry the Ark. Carrying the Ark was the responsibility of the people.

The lesson to be learned from this is that to carry the moral values of society is the responsibility of all people. There is a place for everyone to help carry the burdens of a community. In creating a healthy and happy city everyone must do his or her share.

There is a parallel to the story of the lifting of the Ark in an event that occurred many decades ago in our own country. The city of Richmond, Virginia, had commissioned a statue of General Robert E. Lee. On the day the statue arrived, the horses pulled it on a wagon from the train depot to the base of the hill upon whose crest it now resides. When the statue was removed from the wagon and placed on rollers, the people of the community of Richmond attached ropes to it and pulled it to the top. After it was set in place, the ropes were cut into pieces and distributed to the people. Years later, they treasured these mementos and upon displaying one's particular section of the rope one would say, "I pulled my share of the load, did you?"

That is the question each of us must ask. Are we pulling our share of the load, are we supporting the Ark of values, are we helping to lift the responsibilities of civic life?

*One who bears his or her share of the burdens of the community will also experience and enjoy its achievements.*

TAANIT 18a

# Every Little Tree

Emily Bronte once wrote: "Every leaf speaks bliss to me, fluttering from the Autumn tree." We can learn a lot from trees. It has been estimated that a typical apple tree will produce one hundred thousand leaves in its lifetime and an elm tree six million. What is marvelous, apart from the sheer number of these leaves, is that no two of them are exactly alike. An apple orchard of one acre will collect and discharge 480 tons of water a month. Just think how trees quietly contribute to the shaping of our natural world. One learns from this example that the most powerful forces in the world are not necessarily accompanied by noise and obvious change, but rather by silence and subtlety. Consider for a moment the following: Does love make noise or does it operate gently? Does responsibility come on with crashing cymbals or rather with calm and quiet inner examination? Does help come with harangue or rather with honesty?

We often talk about God and wonder where He is. Did He really create the world? What is His power? When these questions come to us we might, once more, think about trees. Is it possible that a tree with its simplicity and yet with all of its complexity could be an accident of nature? The world and all of its harmony, the change of seasons, the balances of nature, sunrise and sunset, surely cannot be the product of chance but rather of some divine power.

The tree speaks to us of God's handiwork in all the natural world.

*The power of nature is the power of God.*   BARUCH SPINOZA

# The Establishment Of Peace

It was the custom on the festival of Sukkot that the following rituals be included: On the first seven days seventy sacrifices were offered for the seventy nations of the world. On the last day of Sukkot, one sacrifice was offered for Israel. This was a symbolic way of saying that the sovereignty of humanity came before the sovereignty of a single people, even the Jewish people. With admirable sensitivity, our forefathers instituted within our very rituals the Jewish commitment to the welfare of all people.

And as we think of the sorry state of mankind today, we realize that this very peril may well provide the key to our salvation. If atomic warfare is potentially so destructive, perhaps our fear of this destructiveness will cause us to abandon warfare. For who wants to destroy, if he himself will be destroyed in turn? Who can rationally contemplate a struggle that is so wasteful of lives and resources? Consider this sobering accounting—the money spent in the course of World War II could have provided for every family in the United States, Canada, Austria, Britain, Ireland, France, Germany, the U.S.S.R., and Belgium: a $53,600 house, $21,200 worth of furniture and $86,000 in cash. In addition, every town of 200,000 population could have been given a cash donation of $100,000 for libraries, $100,000 for schools and $100,000 for hospitals.

Clearly, then, war is impractical, immoral, and irreligious; and so we must renew in ritual and in act our commitment to the vision of peace.

*The world is established only in peace.*

*ZOHAR LEVITICUS 10b*

# Thanks-Living

Religion reflects man's gratitude for the gifts of life and his desire to express his noblest instincts. When we look at Thanksgiving in this light we see that this festival is unique in being born not out of anxiety and fear but rather out of a desire to express gratitude through sharing and caring. The very verse for this day was found in the Book of Leviticus (23:39), "When you have gathered in the bounties of the land, you shall observe a festival of the Lord." And what is such a festival but the sharing of the bounties of nature with others in our homes and our communities. Then, how beautiful is the word "Thanksgiving," with emphasis on the "giving." If one could change it somewhat, it might be called "Thanksliving." A truly sensitive person will live a life of gratitude, not only on the fourth Thursday of November but every day of the year.

A revealing anecdote about bread, which is the essence of the meal, expresses this thought. An American who was traveling kept seeking the one thing he could not find— American bread. In vain the Europeans paraded their choicest bread products before him. Finally, one day in Florence, he came upon a restaurant run by Americans for Americans, where good, tasteless, crustless American sandwich bread was on display. In his joy, he carefully inscribed on a souvenir paper fan over his signature: "At last I have found, on European soil, a piece of American bread!" The souvenir fan was left in the restaurant. Before long, another American tourist came and added his comment in a bold hand: "Mister, if American bread means that much to you, why didn't you stay in Peoria, where all the bakeries carry it?"

*It is good to give thanks unto the Lord.*     PSALMS 92:2

# Look Up And See

When one enters the *sukkah,* one can look up and see the beautiful pattern of leaves and sky. For according to Jewish tradition, we are not permitted to cover the *sukkah* roof completely with foliage; space must be left to permit glimpses of the sky above.

A little story can help explain this custom. A small boy once asked his father, "How far can you see, Daddy?" The father replied, "Oh, I don't know. Twenty miles, maybe forty miles on a clear day. How far can you see?" And the child replied, "I can see a lot farther than that, because I can look up and see clear to the stars."

The openings in the roof of the *sukkah* are to teach us to broaden our vision and to cultivate a sense of wonder. To see twenty or forty miles is interesting; to see billions of light years all the way to the stars is wonderful.

One of the great problems of our age is that we have lost the art of vision. We live in a plastic age in which things come to us many stages removed from their natural states. When this happens we often end up believing that even the most valuable things are trivial. Violin music is nothing but horsehair scratching on catgut. Love is nothing but the activation of certain hormones. A sunset is nothing but light filtered through dust particles in the atmosphere. But this is a very partial and unsatisfying view, for music is enchantment, love is wonder and a sunset is beauty. And the person who can truly see each leaf and each blade of grass as a living miracle is blessed with vision and wonder.

*Learning is the raising of character by the broadening of vision and the deepening of feeling.*

MAYER SULZBERGER

# Save This

The seventh day of the festival of Sukkot is known as Hoshana Rabbah, which in Hebrew means "the great saving." According to Jewish belief, Yom Kippur is the great day of atonement. But so great is the compassion of God that if there are any sins left over to be forgiven they can be redeemed on Hoshana Rabbah. It is a way of saying that the gates of mercy are never closed. There is always one more opportunity to start over again.

The principle behind Hoshana Rabbah represents a very important insight into human nature. We do not suddenly get up one morning and turn over a new leaf. It takes time and patience to develop a new orientation and to withdraw from old habits. Hoshana Rabbah is highly realistic. It says to us: Never despair. If you took two steps forward yesterday and you fell one step back today, you are still ahead by one. A mistake is only a mistake, it is not the final defeat.

An irate employee went to the paymaster and carefully counted the money in his pay envelope. "It's one dollar short! What's the meaning of this?" The paymaster checked a record sheet and smiling broadly replied, "Last week we overpaid you a dollar. You didn't complain about the mistake then, did you?" "An occasional mistake I can overlook," answered the angry man, "but not two in a row."

In a sense, the spirit of Hoshana Rabbah is expressed in this story. We are just human beings. We do good and we do bad. The badness can be forgiven; the goodness must not be overlooked. In making judgments on others we should think in terms of Hoshana Rabbah. Like the Almighty, we must give everyone another chance to save himself or herself.

*Open the door of repentance only the width of the eye of a needle and God will open it wide enough for carriages and wagons to pass through.* SONG OF SONGS RABBAH, CHAPTER 5

# A Memorial Service

Originally, the memorial prayer was recited only on Yom Kippur, but since the eighteenth century it has also been included in services on the last day of Pesah, the second day of Shavuot and the end of Sukkot. The meaning of the prayer is to be found in the Hebrew word *yizkor* which opens the traditional prayer. The word comes from the root "to remember." In saying this prayer, the individual performs the important religious act of expressing reverence for the source of his or her being.

When the religious person speaks of reverence for the source of being, one calls to mind three basic elements, religious, social and personal: God, the Jewish heritage, and parents. In remembering the source of our being, we affirm the meaning of life and chart its true direction.

Although British Prime Minister Benjamin Disraeli was not well traveled, he read widely and possessed a vivid imagination. One evening, a famous explorer was recounting his experiences. The explorer was amazed at Disraeli's knowledge of the distant places to which he referred. He turned to the Prime Minister and said, "I have traveled extensively and I have seen more than I can remember, but where did you glean your information? Have you also traveled?" Disraeli replied, "No, I have traveled very little, but I can remember more than I have seen."

As we look about the world, we see a great deal. As we peer into our past, we have many memories. It is important to see and to remember, but it is most important to remember more than what presently meets the eye.

*The real message of the Yizkor Service is not that in the midst of life we are in death, but that in the midst of death we are in life; that memory is a living thing and makes us alive.*                    THEODORE H. GASTER

# An Expression Of Joy

Every person in his or her relationship with God should consider the moral law and religious observance not as a burden, but rather as a joy and an opportunity for fulfillment. Religion should not be a bore or a bar to creative living but rather a boon and a blessing to fulfill one's life. When we do not do what we should have done, we feel anxiety. But when we have fulfilled what was asked of us, or what we ask of ourselves, we feel relaxed and happy.

In talking of contributing to important causes, we often take a distorted view. We say, "Give until it hurts." What we should really say is, "Give until it feels good." For example, if we drive down the street and pass a hospital and remember that we made a contribution toward it, don't we feel good? After we have helped a person in distress, does there not come afterward the sensation of inner satisfaction? After we have offered something of ourselves for others in any humanitarian cause, does there not come a feeling of real inner spiritual pleasure? The message of religion in general and of Judaism in particular has suffered distortion. To walk upright does not imply ridigity, it expresses a steadfast relationship to the whole world. The world God has created is wonderful, and it moves us to awe and to delight.

An important passage in the writings of the Baal Shem Tov, the founder of the Hasidic movement, states this concept exactly: "It is the aim and essence of my pilgrimage on earth to show my brethren by living demonstration how one may serve God with merriment and rejoicing. For one who is full of joy is full of love for people and one's fellow creatures."

*You shall rejoice before the Lord your God.*
*DEUTERONOMY 16:11*

# More Than Meets The Eye

Two women were visiting an art museum. One of the women, obviously eager to get it over with and go to lunch, said as they were approaching a picture: "It looks just like a photograph." The friend responded, "Well, as long as we are here, let's look and see." They moved closer to the picture and the first woman stopped, examined it very closely for a few moments and then turned to her friend and noted, "You know, as you look at the detail there is really more here than meets the eye."

I wonder if this woman's comment does not in one way or another apply to all of us. We go through life seeing things as *we* are and not as *they* are. We do not see what is really there but rather what we have been conditioned to observe. Yet, in every situation there is more than really meets even the most trained eye.

For example, we go to the restaurant and we want immediate service. On occasion, we see the waiter or waitress as being curt or rude. Immediately, we respond in kind. But, we never stop to think perhaps the waiter is rushed and pushed or has a headache. Is it not possible that the waitress has a sick child at home or is under some strain? Are they really angry at us or is it that they are just upset? Should we not think before we react because there might just be a little bit more to it than meets the eye?

Actually, isn't this what we mean when we say "stereotype," which really implies "fixed thinking" or to quote Webster, "repetition of the same posture or form of speech"? Those who engage in stereotyped thinking fail to know, feel and see so much of the world. It is, indeed, their loss.

*Dive into the sea of thought and draw precious pearls.*
MOSES IBN EZRA

# You Have To Be Taught

Let us consider who are the people that we should honor first in our society. Should they be bankers or lawyers, doctors or ditch diggers, management or labor, men or women? Exactly who are the people who come first in our society?

It is interesting to note that long ago the Midrash *(Pesikta De-Rav Kahana, Piska* 15) wrestled with exactly this problem in the following way. In the third century it is recorded that two rabbis once took a trip to visit a very small Jewish community that was situated on the border of Israel at a great distance from the center of religious life in Jerusalem. The rabbis went to the center of the market place and said to the crowd, "Bring to us the guardians of your city."

The people went and quickly brought before them the city council. The visiting rabbis indicated that these were not the true guardians. Then in turn the villagers summoned the members of the local police force. But, again, the rabbis indicated that though these were very important, they were not the real foundation of the community.

Finally, in desperation, the villagers asked, "Then who are they?"

And the rabbis said, "Bring us the teachers, for they are the true guardians of the city who protect it day and night."

This is a great insight, for without our teachers our whole system of living and the continuity of our cultural heritage would collapse.

*Let reverence for your teacher be as your reverence for God.*
AVOT 4:12

# A Form Of Beauty

The description in the Bible of the sanctuary, its appointments and the vestments of the priests is filled with color, artistic skill and emphasis on beauty. The ancient sages spoke of *hiddur mitzvah*, "enhancing and beautifying the performance of a ritual or a good deed."

Dr. Burton L. White of Harvard University reported on exposing institutionalized infants to various forms of color in their surroundings. He found that bringing a little color into the lives of these infants born and reared for four months in the bland surroundings of a state hospital had a remarkable effect. Instead of being listless and dull, as such babies usually are, these infants were more alert and showed normal progress. The dullness and flatness in institutionalized babies may come not only from the absence of a mother but from the infant's limited opportunity to explore how the world looks and feels.

Judaism has always advocated the importance of color and of variety. On *Shabbat* and festivals we change the menu so as literally to add spice to our meals. Our wedding ceremonies are colorful because they have many rituals that are not only meaningful but also very beautiful and very charming. There are so many things we can do to add color. Not only in our rituals but also in our daily lives we can try new menus, read new books, buy a new hat, change the style of a suit, add a new picture in the home, seek out new friends, substitute brightness for blandness and open ourselves to new experiences. By opening ourselves to what's out there, we also bring forth something deep within ourselves.

*A ceremony is not adequately discharged unless it is performed with beauty and dignity.*

MOSES HAYIM LUZZATTO

# Self-Consciousness

One of the great problems in our technological and complex society is that everybody else is doing everything for us while we do very little for ourselves and by ourselves. We leave justice to the government, which passes the laws for us; we abandon decision-making to the news media, which form public opinions for us; we let the basic values about sex, honesty and God be determined by the social agency, the school and the church or synagogue. But, in all these instances, it is we ourselves who must be personally involved in a concern for justice, we who must take an active interest in public policy and we who must accept our individual responsibility to teach our families what we ourselves believe. If we want a better society, it is not something we must leave to others; we had better do it ourselves.

Indeed, in some things, unless we do them ourselves they will be left undone. No one can eat for us, no one can sleep for us, no one can mourn for us, and no one can love for us. Each of us must do these things for himself or herself. This principle is thoroughly emphasized in Judaism, which says there are no proxies for prayer. The rabbi cannot worship for you, the cantor cannot sing for you, the choir cannot chant for you.

A young child who was asked by the Sunday School teacher, "Can you tell me who made you?" replied: "God made part of me." And the teacher then questioned, "What do you mean by that?" In childhood wisdom the youngster replied, "He made me real little, and I just growed the rest myself."

Each of us must grow ourselves, with increasing self-awareness, until we recognize that what is our responsibility to do must be done.

*If I am here, all are here; and if I am not here, who is here?*
SUKKAH 53a

28

# All People In Common

Many religious groups feel that their particular beliefs are the most supreme of all. While a religion may be the only way for its particular adherents, can it in all honesty claim that it has all wisdom, all knowledge and, furthermore, dare it force its doctrines on others? This applies to any of us—to all of us.

We in the western world tend to feel very smug about western religion and civilization. But has it occurred to us that more than half of the inhabitants of this planet belong to religions other than Judaism or Christianity? There are almost as many Muslims as Catholics, twice as many Hindus as Protestants and four times as many Taoists as Jews.

While we can be loyal to our faith and respect our own private religious tradition, it ill behooves any of us in the world to feel smugly superior to practitioners of any other of the faiths of the world. Each of us sees God in his or her own way, but this is not necessarily the way someone else sees Him.

There is a delightful story about a little girl who had just come home from Sunday School. She was busy with her crayons and her mother asked whose picture she was drawing. "God's," she answered. "But, my dear, nobody knows what He looks like," her mother admonished. And the child answered, "They will when I'm done."

None of us can make the finished portrait of God. Therefore, none ought to assume a stance of "holier than thou," because each of us is just a person trying to achieve the surest way to walk on the tightrope of life. The last truth is, as we are taught by Judaism, every person is a child of God; and, therefore, everyone is holy, but no one is holier than *thou*.

*The Lord of heaven made the earth to be possessed by all people in common.*     SIBYLLINE ORACLES 3:47

# The Price Of Peace

In the community of nations is it not finally time that we abandoned rigid positions and sat down and considered other points of view, other feelings? For unless we know how a problem came to be, we will never know how to solve it. World peace will not come about by virtue of a single great leader. Harmony among nations will not come through a miracle. Rather, the tabernacle of tolerance will be set up when all of us decide to do our share. It is so easy to condemn, it is so hard to be constructive. But the latter is the only way. For peace cannot come through power but only through proper understanding and purposeful living.

A fable entitled "The Animals' Disarmament Conference" makes the point. When the animals got together, the bear looked at the eagle and said, "We must abolish talons."

"Oh, no," said the eagle. "It is claws that must go."

Next, the tiger looked at the elephant and proposed an end to tusks.

"But how silly—everyone knows that sharp teeth are the real danger," replied the elephant.

Thus each animal in turn proposed to abolish the weapons that threatened it the most. The talks were getting nowhere until the nearly defenseless deer spoke up, and said, "Friends, let us abolish everything . . . but let us not abolish goodwill and understanding." With that the animals' disarmament talks began making progress.

We can set up a world society of peace, but to do so we all have to participate. For any cause worthy of its name is completed not by a man nor a miracle but rather by all people working together. This commitment is the price of peace.

*Civilization is a constant quest for non-violent means of solving conflicts. It is a common quest for peace.* MAX ASCOLI

# What's In A Bagel?

The word "bagel" comes from the German *beugel*, which means "a round loaf of bread." The roundness symbolizes the unending process of life itself. The circle has neither beginning nor end and is considered a perfect form. This symbolized the presence of God Who is considered to be perfect.

In the year 1610, according to the Jewish community regulations of Poland, a bagel was given as a gift to a woman upon the birth of a child. It expressed the thought that life continues to go on. Similarly, if we see life in its entirety, then during adversity we can realize that as the world turns, the brighter side will surely show itself again. If we wait for the turn of the circle, things usually turn out for the best.

We apply for a job and don't get it, and suddenly we find that a better job is available to us somewhere else. We have an illness and we resent having to stay in bed. But often that very illness makes us rethink our lives so that we become more understanding, more relaxed, and more helpful to others. Whatever happens in life, it is our attitude that really counts. And the bagel can give us the real clue as to what we should do. This was expressed in an old poem:

Between the optimist and pessimist
The difference is droll:
The optimist sees the bagel,
But the pessimist sees the hole.

*The men and women who are happy themselves and who have the gift of shedding gladness, sunshine, and cheer wherever they go are those who share with the great leaders of Israel a chronic optimism in their own and their people's destiny. They have learned to look for the bright and hopeful side of life; they reside on the sunny side of the street.*                    BERNARD L. BERZON

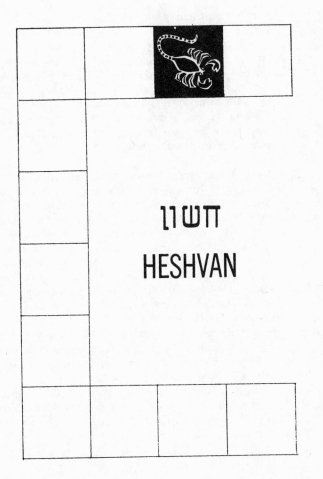

חשון

HESHVAN

# Hoarding A Moonbeam

It is an ancient Jewish tradition to greet the full moon with a special service that is known as *kiddush ha-levanah*, "the sanctification of the moon." It is a lovely ceremony in which, looking at the moon, one recites the prayers and at the end says, *shalom alaykhem*, "I greet you, oh, Moon."

With reference to this, there is a charming tale of a *shamash* (ritual director) who lived in the town of Chelm. Chelm is a mythical city in which everybody does something foolish, but it usually turns out to have a profound moral. It seems that this *shamash* took great pleasure in watching the people gather to participate in this special ceremony of blessing when the full moon appeared. One day, however, he began to worry about what would happen if the sky was overcast so that the moon could not be seen. He thought and thought and finally discovered a solution. He waited until the next full moon appeared, and then he filled a barrel full of water and left it in the open courtyard. The moment he noticed the moon's reflection in the water, he clamped on the lid and happily exclaimed, "Now we need worry no longer, for should the sky be overcast I will merely remove the lid and the congregation can look at the captured moon and say their prayers."

A delightfully foolish tale but what a wonderful moral is hidden within it! Some of us, like the *shamash* think that when we have an experience of meaning or particular beauty we can capture it forever. But, really, all we can do is to have the memory of that experience. Life changes, life moves, life grows. It is only our memories that can remain. And living intensely and joyously is the best way to insure that these memories will be rich ones.

*Memories are all we really own.*          ELIAS LIEBERMAN

# The Ideal Of Individuality

A recently-composed poem reflects the mood of modern man.

> I found out only yesterday,
> (My ego was somewhat jarred;)
> I'm just a lot of oblong holes
> On an IBM punch card.

Overcoming this impersonal quality is precisely the challenge that faces all of us. We can submit and become a part of the herd or we can develop our own consciences, thus becoming individuals who can truly affect the world.

The impact of one person on our thinking and our lives is demonstrated again and again. A Freud, an Einstein, a Florence Nightingale, a Margaret Sanger—how greatly these individuals shaped the lives of others.

But even though we are not Freuds or Florence Nightingales, we must realize that what each of us does in his or her life really matters.

Hans Habe wrote a fascinating book entitled *The Mission*, which is essentially the story of how nations could have saved a number of Jews at the Evian Conference (held in France during July 1938) but ultimately did not because a few statesmen refused to take action. Realizing how narrowly this effort failed, Habe made this statement: "The world is 1% good, 1% bad, 98% neutral. It can go one way or the other, depending on which side is pushing." This is why what each individual does is so important.

*Respect is accorded only to a personality which respects itself, to character, and not to a servile creature which surrenders its all and permits the effacement of its own individuality.*                                   SIMON DUBNOW

# The Wealth Of Health

From the Bible onward, Jewish thought has always emphasized health as an important aspect of religion. So, for example, it was forbidden to fast extensively lest it harm the human body. Piety could never be gained at the expense of a person's health. Religious Jews wash before every meal, and the dietary laws have as one of their fundamental purposes the extension of hygiene and cleanliness. The Talmud teaches that any time human health is endangered by Jewish observance, health clearly comes first. The Rabbis permitted even the violation of the Sabbath if it were necessary in preserving a life.

In the Middle Ages it was noted that the Hebrew people regularly took baths on Friday afternoon. Remember, this was during the period when a queen of England boasted she had taken only two baths in her lifetime: on the day she was born and on the day before she was married.

Page after page of Jewish literature has shown not only a concern for illness and healing but also the preservation of the human body as a gift of God. Indeed, Judaism sees in the balanced satisfaction of bodily appetites a fulfillment of the divine purpose.

The founder of the Hasidic movement, the Baal Shem Tov, always tried to apply his ideals. He urged the Hasidim to remember the importance of good health, and taught them: "Do not consider the time you spend eating and sleeping wasted. The soul within you is rested during these intervals and is enabled to renew its holy work with fresh enthusiasm." Physical fitness, from the Jewish point of view, is an authentic *mitzvah*.

*There is no wealth like health.*                    BEN SIRA 30:16

# A Sacrifice

Well over 2,500 years ago, Jewish tradition replaced the cult of human sacrifice with the teachings of the Torah. The real sacrifice that God wants from us is the sacrifice each of us must make in following the Torah, and living an upright life.

A man may be tempted in business to gain an advantage by doing something that is not quite correct. A woman may be tempted to deny some of her family responsibilities in order to satisfy some more personal needs. A young person may be tempted to do something that is immoral in order to keep up with the crowd. In so many ways each of us is daily tempted to follow the impulse, take the shortcut, seek the easy gratification of our baser motives. But the Torah asks that we sacrifice those to live an honorable life in keeping with its commandments. This is the ultimate form of worship, and this is the real meaning of the word "sacrifice." We must be willing to give up things to live according to the law of God. This is a task we have set for ourselves, and it requires tremendous discipline.

One is reminded of a story about General Robert E. Lee, who became the symbol of great character to the South. One day, a woman came to him seeking advice on how best to raise her son. What could she do, she asked, to help her son develop a good character? "Madam," General Lee responded, "teach him to deny himself." He was saying that sacrifice of personal interest is a sure path to character growth. God does not need our burnt offerings, nor can we even be sure He needs our prayers, but we can be very certain that we honor Him most when we keep His commandments—particularly at the cost of personal sacrifice.

*Offer the sacrifices of righteousness.*     PSALMS 4:6

# The Hope Of America

There is in America a sense of national unease, of things not working, of wrong turns taken and right turns missed. While the fever may vary, the virus of doubt is generally the same all the way from the Boston longshoreman and the Nebraska farmer to the Miami Beach businessman and the California rancher. And we should be concerned about this mood, because 19 out of 21 civilizations have died from internal decay rather than from conquest from without.

But the corrective to this despair lies within as well. It is the open searching, the questioning of our system, and the outspoken recognition of our common problems. Our salvation is to be found in the realization that democracy will work only if everyone participates.

Several years ago in the Midwest, a proposal for a charter amendment was to be voted on. A civic committee put up a number of signs around town urging the citizens to participate and they used the slogan: "Vote Yes or No—But Vote!" When the ballots were counted, election officials were astounded to find that a significant number of them were marked: "Yes or No."

We can no longer afford this kind of attitude. None of us dares remain indifferent, none of us has a right to refrain from decision-making. If enough of us care about participating, then we can save ourselves and our society. If we want democracy, we will have to pay the price. And those payments will take the form of being reasonable, being reliable and being responsible.

*We perceive a community enjoying life, liberty, and the pursuit of happiness: real happiness, not that of pasture beasts; actively participating in the civic, social and economic progress of the country.*     ISRAEL FRIEDLANDER

38

# The Price Of Stubbornness

Often, we become so stubborn and so set in our feelings that it is absolutely impossible to grow in our most vital relationships. The Talmud has a very interesting illustration of this in connection with the destruction of the Temple in Jerusalem. The rabbis in the Talmud explain the downfall of the sacred edifice in the following manner.

During the first century of the Common Era, when the Romans were the political rulers of Israel, a very wealthy person gave a lavish party. He had one friend whose name was Kamtza, and an enemy whose name was Bar Kamtza. On the day of the party he asked his servant to go and bring Kamtza. Through an error, the servant brought Bar Kamtza, the enemy. The man who came to the party immediately said, "Since I am already here, do not insult me. Permit me to stay and I will leave later." The host absolutely refused. Bar Kamtza offered to pay the price of the whole party if he could stay without offense, but the host refused and drove him out. In raging anger, Bar Kamtza then went to the Roman authorities and gave them information which brought on the full oppression of Jerusalem and its final destruction.

The ancient rabbis used this incident to show how ironclad anger can force the destruction of much that is good in the world. And, indeed, this is so.

We are, indeed, doomed into a stubborn mold of our own forging if we cannot break through our rigidity, our anger, and our inability to compromise.

*He who stiffens his neck in stubbornness will suddenly be broken beyond repair.*     PROVERBS 29:1

# The Bedrock

Religion is an important and established institution. While organized religion has changed and will have to change even further to keep up with new insights into the nature of man and the meaning of God, we must still hold fast to the basic traditions that strengthen us, and guide us in our search for the good life. If the roots of religion are torn out, then the tree of faith will shrivel and die, and with it will perish the great moral and ethical teachings which have evolved over the centuries. If this happens, what will take its place?

The basic function of traditional religion is to keep society ethical and stable. That is why religion as an institution must be kept intact while at the same time we try to breathe into it new direction, energy and relevance.

An analogy can be seen in the graceful Harkness Tower, the most commanding structure on the campus of Yale University. All the stones for this tower were brought in specially except for the bedrock foundation, which was part of the earth itself. That bedrock is clearly visible, for the first layer of the new stone begins several feet above the old stone which is embedded in the earth. The Harkness Tower is so heavy that without the bedrock it could not stand.

So it is that we need the bedrock of basic institutions upon which to build new ideas and new resources to help ourselves. In this process we must be careful not to erode or destroy anything that would continue to support us and give us the benefit of centuries of accumulated wisdom. Oliver Wendell Holmes, Jr., said it well in one sentence: "The continuity with the past is not a duty; it is rather a necessity."

*Blessed is he who keeps the foundation of his fathers.*
                                                    *II ENOCH 52:9*

# The Power Of Kindness

Eugene Debs, the great American social philosopher and leader, was sent to prison during the First World War because he was a conscientious objector. Out of spite, the prison staff gave him as a cellmate a most difficult prisoner, who had spent more time in solitary confinement than in his cell and had beaten up every one of his cellmates. Debs knew this and he began a campaign of kindness. He would leave an orange on the bed, he would refuse to be provoked into a fight, and when the difficult prisoner was sick he quietly nursed him. Every day he sought to do something helpful. Debs left after he had served his term; but the prisoner remained, because he was serving a life sentence. Years later when the news of Debs's death was received by the prisoner, he said, tearfully, "He broke me with his kindness."

What a wonderful phrase, "He broke me with his kindness."

What would the world think of Americans if instead of bayonets they brought bread? What would happen to Jewish life if instead of raising our voices we raised our standard of learning? What would happen to family life if instead of a clash of wills we had cooperation for everyone's welfare?

One of the major tasks of our time is precisely to learn how to make kindness explicit through small daily acts— serving a warm drink on a cold day, pushing a stranger's stalled car, helping the neighbor who has someone in the hospital, working in the synagogue or church kitchen . . . all the things that we do not because we have to, but because we want to.

*Charity is limited to the living, the poor, and money; kindness applies also to the dead, the rich, and personal service.*    TOSEFTA, PEAH 4:19

# A Meeting Place

In order to achieve something significant in life, we must be willing to meet halfway. We have to be willing to meet people halfway in order to bring a sense of achievement and happiness into our lives. In a family the husband and wife have to be willing to meet each other halfway, in a balance of give-and-take, in order to create the enduring and happy family.

The uniqueness of the American constitutional system was likewise based on the concept of the balance of power. The Founding Fathers of the Constitution wisely tried to balance the Executive, the Legislative and the Judicial forces in government.

Similarly, in order to acquire knowledge we have to meet it halfway. Education requires taking books home, going to lectures in good weather and bad, poring over texts and grappling with problems. Learning is an active process.

So, too, in order to discover God, we cannot sit still and wait until He taps us on the shoulder. We must spend time thinking about Him, we must be willing to go out and find Him by working for good causes, we must urgently, diligently read the books that invoke His presence.

Marion Anderson, the great American contralto, always used "we" to speak of herself. When she announced a song, she said, "We will sing it." If someone did her a favor she said, "We thank you." Miss Anderson used "we" because she believed that she did nothing alone: in everything, God was with her. She said she included Him in everything because if she met Him halfway she was certain He would travel the rest of the distance to meet her. Therefore, she was never alone in the world.

*And going out to meet You I find You coming toward me.*
                                                    JUDAH HALEVI

# The Difference A Day Makes

Every day is a new challenge. Every day is a time to turn over a new leaf. Every day we can start to learn, begin to live and commence to love. Days are the opportunities that God gives us to reopen our lives to the possibilities of what we may become.

Ralph Waldo Emerson, the great American essayist and poet, wrote, "It is one of the illusions that the present hour is not the critical, decisive hour. Write it on your heart that every day is the best day of the year. No man has learned anything rightly until he knows that every day is the most important day of his life."

What great words of wisdom, and how wise we would be to follow them. Do you have to wait for Mother's Day to send roses? If you see a nice tie, do you have to wait until Father's Day to present it? And if you can help someone of another color or another creed, do you have to wait until Brotherhood Week? Do you have to wait for a holiday to invite your family to dinner? Do you need a birthday as an excuse to go out with friends? Do you have to wait for a wedding anniversary to tell your mate how happy you are?

This was all expressed in the words of Bahya Ibn Pakudah, the medieval author who wrote in his splendid book *Hovot Halevavot (The Duties of the Heart):*
"Days are scrolls: write on them what you want to be remembered."

Or to say it in a contemporary way: Yesterday is a cancelled check. Tomorrow is a promissory note. Today is the only cash you have—spend it wisely.

*What is a day in a person's life? Isn't it the most precious treasure that can be given us?*     MORRIS GOLDSTEIN

# Deals And Ideals

Because of our rapid advances in technology, we are able to multiply vastly the world of things. As a result, we become preoccupied with deals rather than ideals. Somehow or other, our children get the notion that acquiring goods is more important than being virtuous. There is plenty in our society to mislead our young and even beguile ourselves into believing that the whole goal of life is a comfortable living. While creature comforts, security, material things make life a little easier, yet life requires more than just these material benefits.

Ideas are more profound than things. Ideas are the means by which we achieve anything worthwhile and lasting. The essence of life is how we think and not how we take. Life depends on the creative use of the mind.

The power of ideas as vastly more important than the force of material possessions is concisely portrayed by the quotation of Robert Galvin, once president of the Motorola Corporation: "If you were to take away all of Motorola's factories, all of our inventories, and leave me with ten scientists and engineers of ideas, we could rebuild our corporation in a few short years. But if you were to leave me all of our physical assets and take away all of our ideas, you leave me virtually nothing."

We must understand that ideas and ideals are the basis of life. All else is secondary. Not how much we have but what we do with what we have, not what talent we possess but what we do with our talent, not how much knowledge we acquire but what we do with our thoughts is the heart of the matter.

*Every dogma has its day, but ideals are eternal.*

ISRAEL ZANGWILL

# A Calculated Risk

Two farmers happened to meet at the fence which divided their fields. One was asked by his neighbor, "John, what are you going to plant this year? Corn?"

Said John, "Nope, scared of corn borers."

Said the neighbor, "What about potatoes?"

Said John, "Nope, too much danger of potato bugs."

Said the neighbor, "What *are* you going to plant?"

Answered John, "Nothing. I'm going to play it safe."

If we won't plant, then we won't have any crop failures, but neither will we have any harvest. If we don't try new ventures in business, we will not have any losses; but, then, neither will we have any profits. If we don't paint any pictures, write any poems, sing any songs, we will not get criticism, but neither will we earn applause. Unless you try and risk, you will never achieve anything. Unless you take a stand, you will never succeed.

Unlike Farmer John is the spirit of President John F. Kennedy, as described in Theodore H. White's book *The Making of the President 1960*. It is told that when Kennedy was a boy he and his friends would make their way across the countryside. When they came to an orchard wall that barred their way but seemed too high to climb, they took off their hats and tossed them over the wall—and then they had no choice but to follow them.

We have to be willing to throw our hats over the wall and make a commitment if we would overcome the hurdles of life. The only way to achieve anything is to risk. The only way to progress is to be willing to take a position and then to follow through, no matter what.

*In critical times people can save their lives only by risking them.*
                                                    LEON BLUM

# We See As We Are

There is a tale told of a beggar who called upon a fellow Jew and asked for alms. The man asked him where he was from and the beggar told him he was from Vilna. The man exclaimed: "Vilna! I was born in Vilna and I studied there. How are things in Vilna?"

"Very good," replied the beggar. "The synagogues and schools of learning are flourishing."

The man, overjoyed at hearing this, gave the beggar ten rubles. The beggar thanked him and left.

Outside the house, he met another beggar who asked him how the man treated him.

"Generously. When he heard I was from Vilna, his native city, he gave me ten rubles."

The second beggar then went in and told the man that he was a native of Vilna.

"I, too, come from Vilna," said the man. "How are things there?"

"Not so good," replied the beggar. "There are many taverns, gambling houses, cabarets, and much immorality."

"Is that so?" remarked the man. And he gave the second beggar half-a-ruble.

Crestfallen, the second beggar said: "The other fellow and I are both from Vilna. How is it that you gave him ten rubles, and me only half-a-ruble?"

"Ah!" said the man. "The other one spoke of synagogues and schools of learning. Evidently he had been in those places. You tell me about taverns, cabarets and gambling houses; evidently you must have spent much time there. So all you deserve is half-a-ruble."

The world is before us. Let us look on the beautiful side.

*See how the land is that they dwell in, whether it is good or bad.*
                                                    NUMBERS 13:19

46

# Community Responsibility

The fundamental truth about community responsibility is that it must be continuous. Participation in improving society is not a one-time venture, fulfilled in one program or one cause. For poverty, as stated by Scripture, will always be with us. Social problems will shift with human needs and conditions, but they will always exist. There will always be a need to serve our community.

We must, therefore, think clearly about the anatomy of responsibility. Do we really believe that one government administration will have all the answers? The same is true of our naivete about civil rights. Will the struggle be over in one generation? Even our concern for world Jewry—will it ever be over? In particular, our involvement and our concern for Jewry is something that must not be seen in terms of one protest meeting, one social action statement, or even one lifetime. It is a continuing responsibility and only when we see it as such will we have some measure of success.

A Quaker, once hearing a person tell of how deeply he felt for another who was in distress and in need of assistance, dryly asked: "Friend, has thee felt in thy pocket for him?"

If we would be compassionate, we must feel it in our pockets, in our hearts, in our minds and on our tongues.

Those of us who have the ability and the means must involve ourselves in community affairs. Through continuing commitment, we can fulfill our historic responsibility to community life.

*For there will never cease to be needy ones in your land, which is why I command you: open your hand to your poor and needy brother.*　DEUTERONOMY 15:11

# A Matter Of Degree

The whole world is a university, and we are all enrolled in the course of living. In our daily vocabulary, we recognize that experience is the greatest teacher. We often refer to daily encounters as the school of hard knocks. And in professional lives and business careers, graduation from the university only gives us a diploma and a license to practice. It does not guarantee that we have the full measure of skill or applied ability that require time and experience. And we all know in truth that it takes years of learning before we can begin to deal with business and professional problems. There are no easy ways to learn the wisdom of life.

George Gallup once said in jest, "Let colleges wait twenty-five years after graduation before awarding degrees." This idea has merit because it takes years before we can develop a degree of proficiency in our chosen fields. Perhaps we should all be given licenses to practice when we complete our studies but, then, we should be given degrees only after we have proven our worth.

One might then consider giving specially-designated degrees to people who took the time and effort to earn them. The degree of D.M., Devoted Mother, to one who raised a family. The degree of D.F., Dedicated Father, to one who gives his energy and concern to his family. The degree H.B. for the honest businessman who struggles all his working life to do what is right and proper. The degree M.C., Master of Citizenship, for one who voted regularly, who volunteered for community work, who gave a full measure of devotion to his or her fellows.

Then we might truly say we advance in life by degrees.

*Wisdom is not to be obtained from text books, but must be coined out of human experience in the flame of life.*

MORRIS RAPHAEL COHEN

# The Purpose Of Judaism

The ethnologist Konrad Lorenz has written a basic work called *On Aggression,* which examines the possibility that man has a self-destructive instinct which threatens to annihilate humanity. Professor Lorenz has studied the animal kingdom and the nature of man for more than a half-century. He comes to the conclusion that aggression and drive in man is not necessarily destructive, and often it is good. But man's aggressive forces must be correctly recognized and identified and then channeled through systems and ritual which at worst are harmless discharges of energy and at best are constructive programs to help man survive.

It is interesting to note that this thesis may be illustrated by the thrust of Jewish tradition. Judaism has created a system of rituals, of habit patterns, of conduct in order to give man a method to control aggression, a sense of identity, a feeling of being at home in the universe and a way to consistently raise his or her ethical behavior. All of which combined to insure the survival of Jews and Judaism. It also survived because thoughtful Jews understood that one of the purposes of the Jewish way of life was to civilize human beings.

Classic Judaism, however, did not contend that its religious culture was the *only* way to achieve this task. It was enough to say simply it was the *Jewish* way. The work of Konrad Lorenz supports the conviction that the most effective ritual systems are those which have been formed by ancestral instincts that are yet hidden deep within our psyches and souls and serve us in the moments when we need them.

*The only purpose of the mitzvot, the commandments, is to refine people.*    MIDRASH SHMUEL, CHAPTER 4

# Second Acts

The most important factor in change is our attitude. It is not enough to desire change. One must have the determination to work to preserve that change.

An essay in *Time* magazine entitled "Second Acts in American Lives" deals with the recurring theme of the American male who, in his 40's, feels fat and futile. He feels he is trapped by his way of life. He has achieved his top level of promotion, he is bound to the economic grindstone, and he wonders where he is going. The essay points out that there is a way to change. A wealthy and popular pediatrician in Boston gave up a comfortable income to work among poor people and he has found his life profoundly enriched by this change. Other men have stayed in their occupations, but learned to find a new outlook through art, music and community service. Women, too, are discovering in middle age a chance to begin again—study for new careers, go back to school for learning for its own sake, now that their "nests" are empty. These thing happen because people are facing change, not with fear but with hopeful determination to improve their lives.

When Emily Bronte was about eight years old, her clergyman father took her for a walk out across the moors from their little village of Haworth. He tried to tell her of the wonders of creation and growth and asked, "What is here which was not here a hundred years ago?" And Emily answered, "Me." It was a good answer. God is always bringing new forces into His world, upsetting the old and changing for the better, and it is always the individual who makes the difference.

*Time is change, transformation, evolution. Time is eternal sprouting, blossoming, the eternal tomorrow.*

ISAAC LEIB PERETZ

# The Radiance Of God

Thanksgiving Day is the only holiday created by a nation of the West on the basis of its own historic experience that has a distinctive religious character. This is not due to an accident of history because the fact is that the early settlers of America, specifically the Puritans, were a pious community. Thanksgiving, then, is a religious response to the harvest which in turn represents a relationship with God.

It is important to remember good times when times are hard and the pressures mount around us and in us. It is precisely then that we ought to stop and take stock of ourselves. America is never as great as one might hope, but yet not as bad as some would think. Thanksgiving is a time to remind us not only of our problems but also of our blessings. That we have much that burdens us is true, but it is equally true that we have many blessings that make life not only bearable but also worthwhile.

There is an old Jewish legend about two angels who were sent to earth to gather up the prayers of men. One was to fill his basket with the petitions of mankind. The other was to gather our prayers of thanksgiving. Some time later they went back to God. One had a basket heaped high and running over with the innumerable petitions of men. The other returned with a sad and heavy heart for his basket of thanksgiving prayers was almost empty. We are too concerned with asking for our needs to remember to be thankful for what we already have.

*For though there is ice underfoot, the climate of the heart may be warm and welcoming. It is a time to care. It is a time to share. Though deep snow lies at the door, the soul may be warm in the radiance of God.*                RUTH F. BRIN

# And Nothing But The Truth

The most essential ingredient of a good society is a healthy regard for the truth. Truth must be at the core of all of our relationships or else no one's word will be worth anything and we will surely disintegrate. The value of truth was so important in the Jewish way of life that another name we use for God is *emet*, truth. The question we must constantly ask ourselves is: How much do we really regard the truth about ourselves, our families, and the society in which we live? If we do not train ourselves to do this, we will settle for illusion rather than tasting the reality of life itself—whether this reality be pleasurable or painful.

The ability to deal in truth must begin in childhood and continue throughout an entire lifetime, as the following story shows:

A small boy was on the witness stand in an important lawsuit. The prosecuting attorney cross-examined him, then delivered, he thought, a crushing blow to the testimony. "Your father has been telling you how to testify, hasn't he?"

'Yes," the lad did not hestitate to answer.

"Now," said the lawyer triumphantly, "just tell us how your father told you to testify."

"Well," the boy said modestly, "Father told me the lawyer would try to tangle me in my testimony, but if I would just be careful to tell the truth, I could repeat the same thing every time."

By telling the truth, he confounded the prosecutor. Similarly, if we are careful always to tell the truth, then life will never ensnare or entrap us.

*Truth is the seal of God.*                    SHABBAT 55a

# Human Beings Are Different

It is always the individual difference that accounts for the advances in human achievement. It is for this reason that the Jewish tradition created the following blessing: "Praised are You, O Lord our God, King of the universe, Who has created each person different."

In the Jewish view, every human being is unique. Locked up in each person is a storehouse of opportunity, of ability, of achievement, but only the individual can make the ultimate decision about how he will use his potential.

There is the illustrative incident of the Detroit executive whose secretary burst into his office on May 21, 1927, and cried: "Mr. Murphy, a man has just flown from New York to Paris!" He continued to work calmly, and again she cried: "You don't understand! A man has flown the Atlantic *all by himself!*" Now Murphy looked up. "All by himself, a man can do anything," he said quietly. "When a committee flies the Atlantic, let me know."

Beethoven wrote his magnificent symphonies alone because a board of directors never composes music. Shakespeare wrote his great plays alone because a committee cannot create literature. Freud made his momentous discoveries in psychiatry alone because a consensus never achieves breakthroughs in creative thinking. These are just a few obvious examples of the way individual differences help to make our lives more meaningful and more profoundly human.

*If one sees a great crowd, one should thank God for not having made them all of one mind. For just as each person's face is different from another, so is each person's mind different from any other mind.*    BERAKHOT 58a

# Passing Through Customs

It is recorded that after Abraham conducted a business arrangement with the Hittites, "Then Abraham bowed low before the people of the land" (Genesis 23:7).

Now, this would appear to be a very strange thing for Abraham to have done. Why give such respect to these primitive peoples? After all, he was so much superior in culture, in knowledge, in religion and in affluence.

Yet Abraham taught us a great lesson: No matter who you are, or where you are, respect the customs and the traditions of the people with whom you live. It was the custom of ancient Hittites to bow low as a sign of gratitude, and so that is what Abraham did.

This is an important lesson for us all to learn. We must respect the traditions and customs of other peoples. It is not for us to pass judgment on them or to decide whether they are superior or inferior. This is totally beside the point. What is crucial is to be aware that it is important to *them*.

Even in home life, we must learn to go along with the wishes of other members of the family. It is not always important whether we like it or not but if the rest of the family wants to do something then we should be willing to participate.

As a matter of fact, isn't this also true of friendship? Friendship means willingness to be a part of the group and accepting what the group wishes to do. Of course, this flexibility refers to customs and ceremonies rather than principles. Principles are fixed no matter where, no matter when; but culture and custom vary. And, we must be willing to accept this, even as did Father Abraham.

*It all depends on the custom of the land.*       SUKKAH 38a

# Who Speaks For Man?

A book by Edith Hamilton entitled *Spokesmen For God* gives a fascinating description of the lives of the prophets and the nature of their message. These men truly spoke for God, but let us reverse the question and ask: Who speaks for man? That is an interesting question, is it not?

Is it the President of the United States? Well, he only speaks for the American people, and at times even that is questionable. Is it the President of the General Assembly of the United Nations? No, because he does not represent the non-member nations. So who speaks for those people?

Could it be the leaders of the religious faiths? But each spiritual head speaks for his or her own religion and not necessarily for all people. Therefore, the question still remains: Who speaks for man?

After considerable thought and after research in Jewish sources, we can work out an answer to this question. It is simply that nobody speaks for all men, but rather every person speaks for himself or herself. This is really the Jewish approach. Thus, for example, in the Book of Exodus we are told: "Let them bring Me an offering, every man as his heart prompts him" (Exodus 25:2). Here the Bible teaches us that every person has something to offer in his or her own way. It implies that every human being, in the first and in the last analysis, speaks for himself or herself exactly as the heart prompts.

*Each of us has a job to do which will remain undone if we do not do it. Each of us has love to confer which only we can give. Each of us has compassion to show which the world will be denied if we suppress it. We are indispensable in our small parts, and each is gilded with a glory of its own.*

SIDNEY GREENBERG

# The Path Through The Forest

The Hebrew word for Jewish law is *halakhah* and it comes from the root *halokh,* meaning "to go." So *halakhah* means literally "a path." Faith, with all of its laws, rituals and ceremonies, provides a well-worn path to guide us through the maze of life. Our rules and observances are not arbitrary, but are the results of wisdom wrung out of the experience of thousands of years.

The Sabbath comes once a week and tells us not that we *can* rest but that we *must* rest. By placing the *mezuzah* on the door of the home, we do not nail a magic charm on the entrance of a house but rather do we say that a home is a sacred place and a family is a religious unit.

If we did not have rituals of faith, we would quickly descend into chaos. For example: In a wedding there is a certain way to march, a specific way to stand and a set way to perform the ceremony. Can you just imagine what would happen if we assembled both families together before every wedding and tried to begin each time anew to agree to the form of the marriage?

Consider the story of a father and his young son who were making their way through a dense forest at night. Their only light was a flashlight which was held by the boy. The young boy became anxious and said, "Father, let us turn back. The light shines for but a short distance." The father replied: "Do not fear, my son. Let us proceed as far as we can see and the light will continue to shine in front of us."

When properly understood, the light of religious law can continually guide us as we go through the dense forests of life.

*The halakhah does not deny any emotion, it guides it.*
                                    *HAYIM NAHMAN BIALIK*

# The Spirit Of Things

The willingness to be involved is illustrated in this incident from the Israeli "Six Day War." When it became apparent that the Arab armies were intent upon wiping out Israel, the government in Jerusalem decided to call for the mobilization if its civilian army. There were no parades, no hysterical appeals, no martial music. Instead, there was what is called the "quiet alarm," a note under a door and a code word inserted in a normal radio program. Incredible as it may sound, the response of the reservists was close to the maximum, and in several units it ran as high as 100 per cent. The explanation for this is that some men did not even wait for the second call-up and came immediately.

In one brigade, a 63-year-old Jew appeared and, although he was in the third call-up, he refused to leave, insisting that he go with the first unit. Finally in exasperation the brigadier in command said, "O.K. If you find a jeep, I'll take you along" (knowing full well none was available). A few hours later the 63-year-old showed up smiling, sitting in a shining new jeep. The commander asked in complete surprise, "Where did you get that?" The aging civilian answered, "I went downtown and I got it at Rent-A-Car!"

A splendid passage in the Bible describes those who contributed to the building of the first sanctuary. "And they came, everyone whose heart stirred him up" (Exodus 35:31). As in all ages, those whose hearts are stirred, those whose hearts seek to be uplifted are those who come to serve and to help. Indeed, we must be wholehearted, personally involved, if religion and life are to be meaningful to us.

*The important thing is not how many separate command-ments we fulfilled but how and in what spirit we fulfill them.*                              BAAH SHEM TOV

# As A Seal Upon Your Heart

It is really not so difficult to train yourself to adopt the stance and the feeling of true love. Love and hate are very close to one another and in the extremes they seem to meet. For this reason we can often change hate into love. There is an extraordinary example in this story, very real, though humorous.

Two small boys were playing together when a very pretty little girl walked by. One of the boys said fervently to his pal, "Boy, when I stop hating girls, she's the one I'll stop hating first!"

In love we are all somewhat like children. We can stop hating and start loving if we truly wish to. We do not necessarily love people because they deserve it, but because they need it. Love, to be right, must be unconditional and constant and not related to what happened yesterday. Hatred and the wrongs and ills of the past belong to the past and should be consigned there for history. But new history is made by how we live and how we act today.

There are many passages in Rabbinic literature which express the affirmative power of love. If we are determined to accept these Rabbinic teachings, we can perhaps change the world; but, more important, we can certainly change ourselves. John Masefield, the English poet, said, "Love is a flame to set the will on fire." Touched by flames of love we can will a better world, a better America, a better family and, most basic of all, a better self.

*Set me as a seal upon your heart, as a seal upon your arm;*
*For love is strong as death, jealousy is cruel as the grave. The*
*flashes thereof are flashes of fire, a very flame of the Lord.*
*Many waters cannot quench love, neither can the floods*
*drown it.*                    SONG OF SONGS 8:6-7

58

# Equal In The Presence Of God

The Torah applies to everyone. There are not two sets of laws, one for the native and one for the stranger; the law is the same for both. The Torah applies equally to the High Priest and to the water-carrier, to the king and to the woodchopper. As a matter of fact, it is written in the Bible that the king must have his own copy of the Torah and it must be regularly read before him. This is so he shall understand that he is not the final law.

It is recorded that Frederick the Great had some ambitions as a poet. On one occasion he published a book of his poems. The entire court and all the critics praised him for his great writing. Only Moses Mendelssohn, the Jewish philosopher, honestly criticized his efforts. He was summoned before the King and asked how he dared to critcize the poetry of an emperor. Mendelssohn replied, "When emperors write poetry, they have to take the same chances as poets." Frederick asked, "And how do you know that?" And Mendelssohn replied: "That is what I studied in the Bible which told me: 'One Law for every person.' "

Civil rights laws are very good and very important in our generation. But it is interesting to note that in all the years following the Bible, the rabbis of the Talmudic era never passed a human rights law. The reason was simple. It was already contained in the Torah. In a real sense this means that Western civilization is finally reaching the stage of Biblical teaching. And that stage is a democracy of all human beings, each of whom is created in the image of God and all equal in the presence of God.

*The Jewish belief in democracy is based simply on the faith that God created man in His image, that all men are His equal children, and that each possesses within him a spark of the divine which may not be violated.*  SIMON H. RIFKIND

# A Call To Action

According to Jewish thought the assessment of any human being is not what he says but what he does. Consider: Is it better to promise and not deliver, or to deliver and not promise? Is it better to say, "I will give" and not follow through, or is it better to share and say nothing?

Judaism is centered upon the deed. Proclamations of faith are essentially meaningless. It is rather how we *live* that faith that truly matters. This is the meaning of a *mitzvah*. A *mitzvah* means participating in the community, helping a friend, volunteering for needed activities and doing good deeds. The emphasis is on the doing and not the speaking. It is for this reason that we find no real formulation of Jewish creeds, but we do have great emphasis on Jewish deeds. The importance of this Jewish emphasis on actions can be well illustrated in the following story.

A woman was watching a potter at his work. One foot, with never-slackening speed, turned the wheel, while the other foot rested patiently on the ground. The woman said to him sympathetically, "How tired your foot must be!"

Raising his eyes, the man said, "No, ma'am, it's not the foot that works that's tired; it's the foot that's idle."

There is a good deal of truth in that statement. If you want a job done, ask a busy person. The chronically idle are always tired. But active, alive, involved people are never tired—never too tired to do just one more thing for someone else. Active people are happy people. Active people are deeply religious people.

*Goodness is not theory or pious aspiration. It is action made practical.*
                                                    LEON ROTH

# What A Pleasure!

Often, we unconsciously foster a misconception that Judaism is a tragic religion. It is just not so. We may have had painful and cruel experiences in history but these were visited upon us by others, not by any precepts of our religion. Judaism stands for optimism, joy and pleasant memories.

As mature people we know we cannot have everything forever, and therefore we should treasure our best memories. We know also that now we should create the kind of experiences in our lives, and particularly in the lives of our dear ones, that will bring them inspiration and comfort when they come to think of us.

The one thing we can do for those dearest to us is to teach them the truth of Judaism, which is to enjoy in moderation and good spirits the pleasures of the world.

An old Jewish legend teaches us a great wisdom about this approach to life. Four men once stood watching the Almighty spin the globe. The first approached and asked, "How do You do that?" The second asked God, "Why are You turning the world?" The third said, "Give it to me." The fourth silently contemplated the Lord's actions for a long time and then he suddenly remarked, "God, it is a pleasure to watch You work."

Let us look at God's world and take great pleasure in watching it turn. What a beautiful thing it is to see spring turn into summer! What joy it is to see one's children turn into adults and become mature in their own right! How glorous it is to get up in the morning, turn back the covers, jump out of bed and say, "I am alive!" All of these pleasures are genuine expressions of Judaism.

*Pleasures are manifestations of God's love.*
                                    *SOLOMON SCHECHTER*

# The Inner Meaning

It is not necessarily the words that are spoken that often make the difference, but the context that expresses their real inner meaning.

So, for example, strong words may be used understandably in a time of argument, but the cold, calculated use of curses and vulgarities is indecent and destructive and provokes conflict and the general debasement of language.

On the other hand, "good" words can be misused, too. "Law" and "order" are hallowed and important words. But some people use them as code words for racism. It depends on who says them and how they are said that makes all the difference in the world. We have to sensitize ourselves to their context so that we may grasp their implicit meaning. Words like "dissent" and "freedom" denote precious ideals that have been hard won in the history of human progress. But some people use dissent as a tool for destruction and when they speak of freedom they mean freedom from all restraints and responsibilities. In this sense they are advocating upheaval and the release of antidemocratic impulses. Here, again, we must listen to the words and even more closely to the meaning behind the words.

Mark Twain, the famous American author, had a habit of using swear words constantly. This was undoubtedly picked up from his days among the dockworkers. His wife tried to cure him of this habit but she had very little success. One day she pretended to catch her finger in the drawer of a dresser as she closed it. She turned to her husband and hoping to shock him, she unleashed a string of profanity. He looked at her, smiled, and said: "Dear, the words are correct, but the music just isn't there."

*O Lord, guard my tongue from evil and my lips from speaking guile.*                    DAILY PRAYER BOOK

# Good Courage

A young artist invited a friend to view a group of his paintings. After the friend looked at the art he was assembling and noticed that they were so unlike any others he had ever seen, he asked, "Aren't you concerned with what the critics will say? Aren't you afraid they'll have trouble understanding what you're doing?" After a thoughtful pause the artist said, "I don't paint to please the crticis; I am only interested in pleasing myself." This is an example of someone who has the courage of his own convictions.

An even more telling and intense example of personal courage is the following true incident: A while back in a Chicago ghetto, five boys jumped a stranger and pushed him down. Then the boys turned to another young boy who happened to be walking by and said, "Now, kick him and prove that you're not a coward!" The boy replied, "Why should I? He never did anything to hurt me." With quiet dignity and courage he made his point; the boys were suddenly ashamed, and turned to help the stranger to his feet with apologies.

These incidents are examples of courage—the ability to stand firmly on the platform of one's personal conviction, no matter how hard the majority presses. Moreover, this kind of courage can be found in all classes, in all creeds and among all colors. Courage is more common than we think . And we can find it in ourselves when we are tested, sometimes when we least expect it:

> Heroes are common clay,
> Victors are but men;
> Courage has blazed their way,
> Courage will win again!

*Be strong and of good courage.*                    JOSHUA 1:9

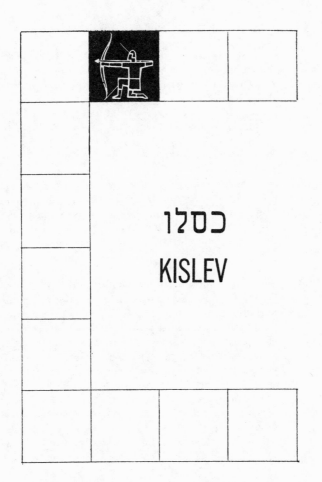

כסלו

KISLEV

# To Begin Again

A verse in Exodus tells that Moses was to set up the first tabernacle or portable sanctuary, but the very next line says, "And the tabernacle was set up by itself" (Exodus 40:17). This apparent contradiction seems to imply that the tabernacle was set up by a miracle. But the verb form of the Hebrew really means, "And it was gradually set up." The ancient rabbis indicate further that although Moses did start the building, "everybody helped him" (Shemot Rabbah 52:1).

From this passage we may learn that sometimes our responsibility is only to start something, and ultimately events, the life process and other people will come to help us. When we begin a program, we need not feel that we will do it all by ourselves but rather, in time, it will naturally find its own fulfillment. Indeed, a commitment to begin without being sure how it will turn out is probably the most fundamental act of faith that a human being can make.

For example, when young people marry is there any guarantee that the husband will succeed in life or that the wife will turn out to be a good mother or that a family will be properly raised? Yet, most people do begin a married life with a commitment and most marriages turn out all right.

In 1948, was there any assurance upon the proclamation of the State of Israel that such a state would ever really exist or that it would grow to its present stature? Certainly not! But a few people had faith, and soon the rest of the world's Jews joined to make modern Israel one of the greatest achievements in history.

When we begin any career, any business, any social program, any human project, there are no guarantees that it will turn out favorably. But people who have faith and start something good usually end up with something great.

*A daring beginning is halfway to winning.*  HEINRICH HEINE

# The Children Of Revolution

Ability and the desire for service can be found in all people. While the color of our skin may differ a shade, the shape of our nose may vary a degree, the pattern of our speech may change somewhat, our brain cells are composed of the same biological matter with the same chemical ingredients and are of the same color. Therefore, unless we promote the concept of excellence, regardless of any human difference, we will short-change ourselves.

How do we know that the secret for solving the cancer problem is not locked in the brain of a black child in a back county of Alabama? And if we deny him or her the opportunity for education, then whom are we harming except ourselves? How do we know that a new style of art is not now lying dormant in the hands of a child on an Indian reservation? If we do not allow and encourage that child to have art training, then whose feeling for beauty will be diminished except ours? How do we know if the formula for world peace is not now being puzzled out in the conscience of a youngster in a Puerto Rican tenement in New York City? Unless we make it possible for this young person to study political science, then we may have materially weakened our chances for peace.

Is is not time that we learn that if America's potential for greatness is to be realized, she must help all her citizens develop to their fullest? What Americans really want is not to win the arms race, or even the race to space; what we want to win is the human race. We want to be victorious in establishing democracy, creativity and possibility for all of mankind. Nothing short of this is worthy of us, the children of the American Revolution.

*It is the special blessing of this land that each generation of Americans has called its own cadence and written its own music—and our greatest songs are still unsung.*

WILLIAM HABER

67

# The Unique Gift

Everybody has a special ability and a certain uniqueness, and everybody has a contribution to make in the world. This idea should be simple and obvious, but just because it is so obvious we tend to overlook it. All too often we think there is not too much for us to do in this world, and we tend to berate ourselves. But in doing so, we actually deny a religious truth which is that every person in this world has something to give in a very special way and, therefore, is indispensable.

Do not underestimate what you can do, no matter how small. Who can measure the value of a little birthday card? What is the worth of a short hospital visit? What is the true measurement of a cake brought in to a new neighbor? Who can estimate what the offer of a new job can mean? All of these things are small but so important. All of us in our own way, by offering ourselves and being in the right place at the right time, have something very special and very precious to give.

The following story makes the point: It was a rainy afternoon, and a kindly old gentleman noticed a newsboy shivering in a doorway, trying to protect his papers from the rain. As he bought a paper, the old gentleman said, "My boy, aren't you terribly cold standing here?" The boy looked up with a smile and replied, "I was, sir, before you came."

Who knows when on a rainy afternoon your presence can warm the heart of someone else? For to give yourself is the best present of all.

*Every man shall give as he is able, according to the blessing of the Lord our God which He has given you.*

DEUTERONOMY 16:17

# To Do Is To Be

The things that we possess in life are the things that we use. God gave us the world and all that is in it. It cannot be ours if we abuse it; we can claim it only if we use it. He gave us brains and we must think or they are not ours. He gave us talents and we must develop them or we cannot claim they belong to us. All living things atrophy and decay if they are not used to their fullest.

Thus in the pools in Mammoth Cave, Kentucky, fish have lived for generations in the dark. The optic nerves of these fish have atrophied so greatly that they have become blind. Patients who are bedridden even for a few weeks find that their legs buckle when they first try to walk again.

We know of many athletes who have lost the tone in their muscles because they do not exercise them sufficiently. And, on a more abstract level, talents and interests can atrophy too. Charles Darwin tells us that he lost his love of poetry and music, which once was very strong in him, because he ceased to develop it.

These are the real clues to the art of living. Life must be felt and enjoyed in order to be personally fulfilling and of service to others. All of our senses must be employed constantly if they in turn are to give us true messages about the universe. An old Irish proverb says, "A thought, a spade, and a machine must be used or else they will rust." If we rest too much we begin to rust, but if we continue to keep on moving, to use all of our senses, to stretch ourselves to our fullest capacity . . . then we function at our highest, live to our fullest and find pleasure in a well-coordinated life.

*Act while you can: while you have the chance, the means and the strength.*    SHABBAT 151b

# Patches On Our Souls

At Midfield College there was a Professor of Romance Languages named Dr. Myron Garfinkle who was beloved by townsfolk and students alike, a familiar figure in his baggy jackets with the patches on the elbows.

Some appreciative students decided one year to make him a present of a beautifully tailored jacket. He expressed his gratitude graciously, but somehow seemed less enthusiastic about the gift than they had hoped. The next day, he appeared as usual before his class still wearing his old, patched jacket, explaining that the new jacket was too nice to wear around blackboards. When the students visited the professor's daughter, thinking they might exchange it for another more to the professor's taste, they found the lady neatly sewing patches to the new jacket. She told them, "My father taught at Leipzig before the war. All the professors wore old jackets with darning and patches to show they were above the material concerns of this world. The higher the professor in rank, the more patches."

In a sense, religion endeavors to teach us to wear patches on our souls in order to rise above the material cares of this world and be concerned instead with the meaning of our lives. We are constantly being asked in our prayer books to reconsider who we are, what we are, and why we are. We ask to be forgiven, even as we pledge ourselves to forgive others. We ask to be loved, even as we commit ourselves here and now to love others. We ask to return in faith perfect and true, even as we are sure that understanding and mercy await us.

One of the great purposes of religion is to train us to think in terms of values and people rather than in terms of possessions and things.

*Return unto Me, and I will return unto you.*    MALACHI 3:7

# The Proof Of America

A preacher once served a large congregation which had to have two services in order to accommodate everyone. He used to give long, rambling sermons that lasted an hour or more. One day, a visitor came up and asked him why the pulpit bore a flag with stars on it. The minister explained that the stars were for the men who were lost in service.

"Lost," the visitor questioned, "at the first service or the second service?"

Joking aside, many of us are "lost in service." That is, we have lost the concept of service in our lives. We need to revitalize our desire to serve the ideals upon which society was founded. There is a need to serve with common sense a common cause. There is a need to renounce self-hate and pessimism and replace them with hope and commitment. For what society needs today is not heroics but healing; not revolution but responsibility; not selfishness but service; not rage but reason; not the suffering of oppression but the spirit of opportunity; not jeopardy but justice; and, above all, not plundering but planting.

The ways were set for us by men like Madison, Franklin and Jefferson. They were not perfect, but they did create a Constitution that began with the words: "We, the people of the United States, in order to form a more perfect union...." The emphasis is on "We, the people." We, the people, must do it, for no one else will do it for us. There are no messiahs down here—only human beings.

*We pray that not by the rocket's red glare and the bombs bursting in air, may we have proof that the flag is still there—but by the tranquility of men's souls, the decency of their actions, and unspoiled quiet of nature's dawn will we have proof that the stars and stripes are forever.*

NORMAN LAMM

# God Is In Us

In the Book of Genesis we read, "And God appeared to Abraham." The questions we might ask are, did God appear only to Abraham and to no one else? Where does God appear? How does God appear? And, indeed, where is God in our time?

This age-old question was raised in the class of a well-known rabbi. A student asked, "Rabbi, where does God dwell?" The rabbi thought for a moment and then replied, "God dwells wherever people let Him in."

God is all about us, and He is with us whenever we choose to let Him in. If we do not act as though there were a God in the world, then there is no God in the world. But if we act as if God were real, then He really is here. The validity of this approach can be proved not from books or writings, but only from life itself. Consider the following story.

A group of worshippers was gathered near a syngagogue window just prior to the daily evening service. One of them looked out the window and saw a magnificient sunset of red, amber, gold, yellow, laced with dark blue at the onset of the evening. He asked the others to look at it. One of the group suddenly said, "My God, that's beautiful!" the first person said, "Wait, repeat what you just said." And the observer began, "My God. . . ." the first person interrupted and commented, "Isn't it interesting, you saw the magnificence of nature and you said, 'My God!' You looked at the sunset and you knew this was not the making of humans; it had to be the work of God. God was real, for you recognized His presence. For that moment, He dwelt in our souls."

*The Lord is with you while you are with Him.*
                                                    II CHRONICLES 15:2

# An Exercise For The Heart

There was a child who had to walk home each evening past a supposedly haunted house. Because it terrified him to walk past the house, his elders sought to give him courage. One gave him a good luck charm to ward off the ghosts. Another sought to influence the city council to install a street light on the dreaded corner. Another said earnestly, "It is sinful to be afraid. Trust in God and be brave!" Each one said something to the child but did not involve his or her own feelings and, therefore, was of limited help. But one person with compassion said, "I know what it is to be afraid. I will walk with you past the house." He did nothing to dismiss the fear—except to lift it from the child's shoulders and place it on his own.

Just think how you might use this approach to improve the lives of others. You could come to someone who has difficulties in business and say: "I had these problems once too, but I lived through them." Or when visiting someone who is ill one can say, "I know what it means to lie on a bed of pain, it's really rough and I understand what you are experiencing." We see an injustice in society and we say, "I know what injustice is personally and, therefore, I wish to give you my moral support." These are the things that really matter. This is the way we might live and so become fully human.

"Sympathy" means "feeling with." "Empathy" means "feeling into." By really projecting ourselves into the feelings of our fellow men we can truly help them.

*When a person does something and his heart is in the doing, then both the deed and the doer are blessed.*

BABA BATRA 9b

# Dare To Dream

The first book of the Bible records the dreams of Jacob, Joseph and Pharaoh. Why does the Bible place so much emphasis on dreams? It is because dreams play a very important role in the life of each person. They express our inner feelings, our fears and hopes, our visions for a better life.

And the work of Sigmund Freud demonstrated that dreams constitute not something peripheral in human experience but the essence of the dynamics of human personality.

No wonder, then, that one of the first things to occur during the debriefing of the astronauts was a thorough examination of their dream life. Perhaps, some day, someone will write a book based on the dreams of these men. And who knows from their perspective what visions they see on the expanding horizons of space?

A little story illustrates the sense of loss we feel when cut off from dreaming. A child was once suddenly awakened out of a deep sleep. The child began to cry and was very distressed and the mother asked, "What is the matter?" The child replied, "Oh, I have lost my place in my dream."

It is important never to lose our place in the dreams of our lives and the lives of all mankind. We must continually dare to dream of a time when war will cease. We need constantly to keep in sight the American dream of true equality for all Americans. We must believe in that day when our character can control whatever our mind can create.

We must never lose our place in our dreams.

*All the cultural, economic, social progress of man had its origin in the visions and dreams of some who were laughed at, scoffed at, scorned by those who lacked understanding, who were devoid of imagination, who were wanting in vision.*
                                        ABRAHAM J. FELDMAN

# Admiration For The Aged

The summons to rise to the challenge of aging is found in the words of the Biblical text below. Life expectancy is now in the seventies and soon will rise even higher as diseases are conquered. What will we do with the later years of maturity? Whether they be five or ten, or twenty-five, by using them wisely and creatively, we can be truly alive all our lives.

We must begin by radically changing our thinking about old age, and stop acting as if old age were second childhood for everybody. Surely, when people are restricted by illness they need special care at any age, but why assume that this restriction is the lot of every aged person? Most of the programs we devise for older people help them become children. Our preoccupation with games and hobbies and the over-emphasis on recreation, while they may eliminate boredom temporarily, do not give real inner satisfaction. The solution to making old age meaningful is to fill it with something significant. There must be work, love, study, growth and continued fulfillment all along the line.

There was an Israeli joke in which a tourist approaches a soldier in Tel Aviv and asks why the army has such a fine reputation. The solder replies that the average age of the top commanders is thirty-five. The tourist counters with, "But you forget that your commander-in-chief is over seventy!" And the soldier answers, "Ben-Gurion? Oh, you are mistaken. He just happens to be two young men of thirty-five."

Perhaps there are two maturities in the life of man. In middle age it is called achievement and in older age it is called fulfillment.

*You shall rise before the aged and show respect to the old.*
LEVITICUS 13:32

# Measure For Measure

"You shall not have in your pouch alternate weights, larger and smaller. You shall not have in your house alternate measures, a larger and a smaller. You must have completely honest weights and completely honest measures, if you are to endure long on the soil that the Lord your God is giving you" (Deuteronomy 25:13-15).

What do these verses mean? In ancient days products were brought and sold based on their weights on a balance scale. The weight was placed on one side and the product on the other. The text here tells that if you have a pound weight, it must be exactly that. And if the customer happens to turn his head, or happens to be foolish, or happens to be a child, it is not right to surreptitiously switch the weight with one that is less than a pound.

These verses also have a larger meaning. In everything we do we must have the same measure.

In dealing with nations we should not change our moral judgments because one nation has more power and the other nation has less power.

It is not right to have one set of standards for the white man and one set of standards for the black man, the red man, or the yellow man. Rights belong to everybody in the same way.

In our families as well, children must be loved by the same standard. We may naturally favor one child or the other. But fairness demands that we judge each child by the same standard, even while recognizing differences in their temperaments and personalities. All children in our families should be treated with equal love and firmness. A single standard and an honest measure—this is what we must provide.

*Before the Eternal One, the highest and the lowest are equal.*
MENAHEM MENDEL OF VITEBSK

# Lift Up Your Head And Shout

Near Caesarea in Israel are the ruins of one of the most interesting Roman amphitheaters in history. It was here that the Romans arranged the so-called games in which they pitted man against beast; and, in the gladiatorial contests, man against man. The ultimate charge was: Fight unto the death!

To the ancient rabbis, who taught that each person was fashioned in God's image, that saving or destroying one human life was like the salvation or the destruction of the entire world, these sports arenas became the embodiment of evil. It was unthinkable that a Jew should ever voluntarily attend any of these games and find even the slightest pleasure in seeing one human being kill another human being. But Rabbi Nathan disagreed with the prevailing opinion, saying, "A Jew goes and he shouts!" What this means is that when the victorious gladiator was about to strike the death blow he asked the audience for advice. If they shouted, "Thumbs up!" the loser's life would be saved. Therefore, if a Jew attended and shouted, "Thumbs up!" it was just possible a life would be saved.

We see and we read that all about us there are forms of destruction, community disintegration and social illness. Some counsel us to "drop out," but others advise us to move in even more strongly and help society survive. It seems to me this is a time to follow the advice of Rabbi Nathan, a time for those who believe much can yet be saved to go forth and shout their hope, their compassion, their belief.

*I shall not die but I shall live and declare the works of the Lord.*　　　　　　　　　　　　　　　　PSALMS 118:17

# Our Foolish Fancies

The first Hebrew sentence written in America has an interesting history. It is found in the diary of William Bradford, the learned second governor of the Plymouth Colony. In his journal he records that this new land was filled with uncleared forest, wild beasts and suspicious Indians. The winters were bitter cold, and the conditions were fearful. Because Bradford was a pious Puritan, the book also contains his Hebrew exercises. One year after he wrote about his early fears, he was seated in his comfortable home amidst plenty on Thanksgiving day. On that occasion he paused and wrote the first Hebrew sentence to be drafted in America. And it was, *"sham pahadu pahad, lo hayah pahad,*—There we feared a great fear, where there was no fear." It is a magnificent sentence: "there we feared a great fear, where there was no fear."

If we really made the effort to understand the Chinese, or the Africans, or the Russians, perhaps we could learn that they are just like us. Then we would drop our fears and with them our prejudices.

If we analyze our business worries or family conflicts with strict honesty, we may find that we have largely overestimated their intensity and have been fooled by our fears.

If we have specific fears—a terror of heights, of storms, of animals, of illness, of death, or of a hundred other shocks the flesh is heir to—and if we faced them head on (sometimes with professional help), we could find their origins and thus eliminate their harmful influence on our lives.

If only we could learn the folly of fearing where there is no fear, and the even greater folly of not doing something about it.

*The end of wisdom is the fear of fear.*    STUART E. ROSENBERG

# The Rest

The movie, *The Shop on Main Street*, which won a well-deserved Oscar for the best foreign film and other international film festival awards, is a sensitive study of the relationship between an elderly Jewish woman and a villager in Nazi-dominated Czechoslovakia. In the high point of the movie, the Nazis have rounded up the Jews in front of her little shop on Main Street. The officials point with pride at their great tower which proclaims pagan slogans of might and cruelty. The old Jewish lady, bewildered by all these happenings which are beyond her understanding but fully aware that it is Friday night, goes about her ritual of lighting the candles. The next day, her Czechoslovakian protector shows her through the window shutters what the Nazis are doing and urges her to flee for her life. And all she can do is say softly, *"Shabbas, Shabbas,"* and she refuses to move. It is deeply touching.

This *Shabbat* ritual is the high point not only of the film but also of Jewish thought. For *Shabbat* is the real answer to paganism. Paganism proclaims that days must be spent in drive for power and that men are animals. *Shabbat* presumes time is holy and man is sacred. Paganism admonishes that might makes right. *Shabbat* advises that strife is the enemy of life and that the peace of the Sabbath—*Shabbat shalom*—is life's greatest boon.

The entire system of rituals of the *Shabbat* is designed as help to control our lives so that its false and pagan values do not get out of hand to overwhelm us. To prevent our reversion into a modern paganism, we must hold fast to those forms and values that help us to remain civilized and sensitive human beings.

*The law of the Sabbath is the essence of the doctrine of ethical monotheism. It is the epitome of the love of God.*
HERMANN COHEN

# We Are What We Give

Money only represents frozen energy. It is a neutral force that must be released for the things one holds dear. In fact, it is a real *mitzvah* to ask people to give of their substance because by doing this, we help the institutions and we help the giver as well. An old proverb tells us that flowers leave part of their fragrance in the hands that give them.

And we really don't have to be rich to be generous. Have you ever thought as you live your life day by day how much you could give if you were truly moved?

Have you ever thought as you enter your place of employment of giving a smile of hello? Have you considered sending a note expressing a tender feeling for a friend? These are things that money cannot buy—they are gifts of the spirit.

A true gift is giving as God gives—unreservedly and with no thought of return. Giving must be wholehearted and unconditional—the giving of a part of one's self moved only by the promptings of the heart.

An old miser once kept a chest of money buried in his back yard. One night, a thief who had discovered the treasure dug it up and carried it away. When the old man discovered the loss he was frantic and aroused the neighborhood with his commotion. One of the neighbors finally asked, "What did you plan to do with the money?" "I wasn't going to do anything with it," wailed the unhappy miser, "but I like to come and look at the place where it was buried." "Then there is no loss," said the wise neighbor, "for the place it was buried is still there, and the gold is out in the world where it should be, instead of in a hole in the ground."

*God prefers your deeds to your ancestors' virtues.*

GENESIS RABBAH 74:10

80

# Let Truth Be The Prejudice

A man was once on a flight overseas. Suddenly, one of his seatmates began to berate him. The traveler's anger began to rise, but, somehow or other, he held his tongue. When the man finally stopped berating him and walked away, his seatmate on the other side said: "Forgive him. He has suffered much. He lost his entire family in the concentration camps and crematoria of Germany, and what you are wearing reminded him of his tragedy."

The traveler was wearing a washable cotton jacket with white and blue stripes similar to the sort worn by concentration camp victims. This triggered the man's memories and brought back painful reminders of the camps. The man was reacting to an image, not to an individual.

We might ponder how many times we, too, react to stereotypes instead of being sensitive to individuals. We will prejudge a policeman simply because we are angry at a uniform and we do not see him as a person. We will look upon a certain form of dress and think, "She is strange," instead of saying, "She, too, is a human being." Many of us are irrational toward authority and will oppose what someone in authority says, not out of principle but rather out of prejudice. On the other hand, people in power often tend to ignore human differences and demand that all rules fit everyone and every situation mechanically. We ought to see the uniqueness, the special truth of every person, every situation, every human activity. Someone wisely observed that if we knew the chronology—the life history—of a human being we judged harshly, we would have to concede that, under those life circumstances, we might act that way, too.

*Knowledge is not enough, unless it leads you to under-standing and, in turn, to wisdom.*                    DAVID SARNOFF

# A Cup Of Compassion

The Book of Genesis tells us in a very moving passage that when Abraham was growing old, he sought for his son, Isaac, a wife who would be of his own faith. He summoned his trusted servant, Eliezer, and sent him to his homeland to find such a woman. When Eliezer arrived at his destination, he was puzzled about how he could find the right person for his master's son. He offered a prayer to God. He had scarcely finished speaking, the Bible says, when Rebekah, who was a relative of Abraham's, came out to the well with a jar on her shoulder. The maiden was very beautiful. She went down to the well and filled her jar and came up. The servant Eliezer ran toward her and said, "Please, let me sip a little water from your jar." "Drink, my lord," she said, and she quickly lowered her jar upon her hand and let him drink. She also, unbidden, brought water for his animals.

Eliezer thereupon selected Rebekah for Isaac's bride. What made him do this? It was not so much her willingness to give him the water he had requested, but her compassion in offering water for the thirsty animals. Truly, it was a cup of kindness that distinguished the personality of Rebekah.

What is the compassion that we can learn from this story? It is simply the willingness to do a little more than we are asked. Being compassionate means extending oneself in passionate concern for the needs of others. Compassion means going beyond the letter of the law to produce a labor of love. And what our troubled world really needs is not so much treaties, or laws, or pronouncements, but rather people—ordinary people like ourselves—willing to give a little more, willing to offer to the thirsty a cup of compassion.

*The Torah begins and ends with compassion: God clothes Adam and Eve, and buries Moses.*                    SOTAH 14a

# Sail On, O Ship of State

Norman Cousins, the well-known editor, once wrote: "Human progress inevitably depends on enough men defining the values they want to live by and then backing up those standards by wise and appropriate means."

This approach, coupled with fortitude and faith, is necessary to bring forth programs to help people, to create the atmosphere and ideals necessary to strengthen Judaism, and, at the same time, live in a modern world. We must learn to appreciate the deeper purposes of Judaism and the very depth of the meaning of life itself.

One of the great American authors, Samuel L. Clemens, took as his pen name, Mark Twain. He borrowed it from the cry he would utter as a riverboat pilot on the Mississippi River. In order to steer the old boats properly to avoid rocks and sand banks, the pilot had to stand on the prow of the boat and watch the waterline, and when he was in the right channel for the boat to move he would shout: "Mark twain!" the second mark, which indicates a safe depth of the water. The safety of the ship depended on his wisdom, judgment and experience. One day, one of the passengers said to him, "Mr. Clemens, I suppose you know where all the rocks and banks are." And he replied, "No, but I know where the deep water is."

He enabled these boats to sail on safely and securely.

So, too, does the welfare of the Jewish community depend on pilots to guide the ship of the communal state into safe waters. Even if we don't know all the problems and the pitfalls, yet if we have sounded our convictions and know them to be deep enough, we will guide our ship safely.

*A man should ever be at the helm, like the captain on the ship, on the lookout how good may best be achieved and accomplished.*   LEVITICUS RABBAH 21:4

# Have You Heard?

"Hear" is the very first word in the *Shema* (Hear O Israel, the Lord our God, the Lord is One). It is possible that the most important word in the entire Jewish system of values is the little word asking us to listen. We can never learn unless we listen, and learning, after all, is the very heart of the Jewish way of life.

Indeed, one of the main problems in our society is that we have forgotten how to listen. In the home, conversation has been supplanted by television, and in the world, communication has been eliminated by shouting. To put it another way, everybody seems to be broadcasting, but no one is receiving. If no one is receiving, then who is learning? This breakdown of communications threatens our society at every level. In our hurry and our rush we have tended to cut short our listening, because that appears to be more efficient. But this is a costly shortcut that ultimately leads to misunderstanding and injustice.

In his autobiography, the noted psychiatrist who helped found the Menninger Clinic related his feeling about listening. He said that when he first began the practice of psychiatry he felt a little guilty about accepting fees for mostly just listening to a person talk out his troubles for fifty minutes out of an hour. After a few months in psychiatry, he learned that it is one of the most difficult jobs in the world to keep relatively quiet for fifty minutes and listen to another person. He said that when someone succeeds in doing this, one truly earns his or her fee. Indeed, anyone taking the time to listen makes a real contribution to society.

*It requires greater strength to listen than to speak.*

ZALMAN SHNEOUR

# Training Ourselves To Love

True love, like real maturity, begins to grow when your concern for someone else outweighs your concern for yourself. If you love others, you want to give presents, to express affection, even to dedicate yourself to the other. Instead of taking, love means really giving—giving money, time and emotional commitment. Think for a moment: what does a parent do for the love of a child, and what does a child do for the love of a parent? And the love between mates, how much do they strain to pay the price of their love? And what do we sometimes have to do in our love for America and for Israel, and for humanity at large? Finally, we may ask ourselves, are we really prepared to accept the efforts and the struggles involved in expressing our love for God?

Several years ago, Paddy Chayefsky wrote *Gideon*, an extraordinary play based on a Biblical theme. The play was resoundingly successful on Broadway. In the climax of the last scene, the voice of God pleads with the hero and says, "Will you not embrace me?" And Gideon sighs and replies, "It is not an easy thing to love you, God."

This is the real insight into love. It is not really easy to love God or even to love another person. It takes tenacity, it takes faith, it takes responsibility.

But the more we offer of ourselves in love, the happier and richer we find ourselves. This is the paradox: the more we give up in love, the more we ultimately take back in love. It is so easy to understand. When you use one hand to wash the other, then both hands become clean in the process. When you try to make someone else happy, you become happier. When you share something with another human being, then your own well-being is enhanced.

*Training through love breeds love.*  WILHELM STEKEL

85

# Good Or Bad

The fundamental premise of Judaism is that a person has a choice in the way he or she lives. A person must have the opportunity to choose if life is to be meaningful, if one is to develop his or her own individuality, to distinguish oneself from other human beings.

This question of choice calls to mind an anecdote about Henry Ford, whose early Model-T Ford always came in black. Once, somebody asked Ford why he made his cars in this color only and did not give his customers a choice. His answer was, "The public can choose any color for their Model-T's, provided it is black."

Clearly, where there is no choice things are black. A person who lives in prison is confined and, therefore, so often his life becomes a mass of frustrations. A person living in a police state, a totalitarian society, has little choice; his destiny is meaningless.

That is why Judaism believes that man is given a choice, so that he can endow his life with meaning. The choices present themselves daily on a simple or a complex level.

We can choose in minor things and in great things. We can choose to shout or speak softly. We can choose to smoke or not to smoke. We can choose to use abusive drugs or not to use them. We can choose to hurt people or to help them. And even when we are faced with illness or experience the death of a loved one, we can choose to be forever angry or else learn to accept it. True, we cannot always choose what happens to us but we *can* choose our attitude toward what happens to us. And it is our attitude that makes all the difference. The choice is ours.

*We are free agents insofar as our choice between good and evil is concerned. In the moral universe people remain their own masters.*    JOSEPH HERMAN HERTZ

# The Instant Saint

A novel entitled *The Instant Saint* by John Sherlock is a thinly disguised story of the life of Dr. Thomas Dooley, the man who established a hospital in Laos. The novel raises the question of whether the doctor was really interested in helping the poor downtrodden natives or whether he was expressing his own neurotic personality. Was the medical missionary trying to play God or was he a self-effacing humble man? Was he a humanitarian or a fraud?

The answer in the novel is that there is no answer. All we know is that he built a hospital and no one else did. Where before there was no medical treatment, no help, no food, no clothing, a man came and began to provide these things. That is all we know and perhaps that is all we need to know.

Such experiences occur not only in novels or in faraway places—they also happen right in our own communities. A person will give to a home for the aged and some sophisticated observer will remark, "He is doing it because he wants to buy off his guilt against his parents." Perhaps yes, perhaps no. At least he *did* something. Someone gives a great deal of money for education and someone else is sure to remark, "It is because he never finished high school—he just wants to prove something." Well, what is wrong with that kind of motivation? All that really matters is the act, the gift, the positive result. All else is mere conjecture.

Only God knows the heart; all we can really judge is the outward action. Every person has the right to the privacy of one's own reasons, one's own thoughts and one's own motivations. That is why in the Jewish tradition a thought is never judged, only an act; a motivation has no meaning, only a *mitzvah* counts.

*Man's deeds are the measure of his days.*   JOSHUA STEINBERG

# One Alone

In our mass society we must be careful that we do not lose the meaning of every person. All too often in contemporary society, people are reduced to IBM cards. We are told that we must not fold, mutilate, or spindle these cards. How much more important that we not mutilate our fellow humans by treating them as though they were all alike. Perhaps the most meaningful way to guard the uniqueness of others is to become fully aware of one's own uniqueness.

We must know who we are, whence we have come, and whither we are going. We must know our heritage and we must carry our commitment in our hearts. We must understand that which makes us precious and be prepared to defend those unique qualities.

The following story interestingly illustrates this thought:

When Zalman Shazar was inaugurated as President of the State of Israel, he raised his right hand as he read the oath of office in the Knesset (the Israeli Parliament). The opening sentence was: "I, Shneour Zalman, the son of Sarah and Yehuda Leib Shazar, undertake to keep faith with the State of Israel and its laws, and to fulfill my duties loyally as President of the State."

The very beginning was interesting. He gave his full name, the name of his mother, the name of his father, and he established his family heritage. He told who he was and he honored his family. He was a full person in every way.

In the same way, each of us must be able to stand up and proclaim: I am not a number. I am a person. I had a father and I had a mother. They bore me and gave me uniqueness. I pledge to cherish and preserve that uniqueness, so help me God.

*If I am like someone else, who will be like me?*

JEWISH FOLK SAYING

# The Unfilled Portion

In any diary if we turn to the first section, chances are that we will find it already filled. But if we flip through the latter pages, we will find them as yet unfilled or filled only with promise. No matter what we read in the past section, no one can be completely certain what will be written in the future pages. Therefore, it is not fair to judge a person only by his or her past and to assess one's potential solely by what occurred in days gone by.

A Chicago banking house once asked a Boston investment firm for a letter of recommendation about a young Bostonian they were considering employing. The investment concern could not say enough for the young man. His father, they wrote, was a Cabot, his mother a Lowell; further back his background was a happy blend of Saltonstalls, Appletons, Peabodys, and others of Boston's First Families. The recommendation was given without hesitation.

Several days later came a curt acknowledgment from Chicago stating that the material supplied was inadequate. "We were not," the letter declared, "contemplating using the young man for breeding purposes."

Regardless of the names with which a person was associated in the past, regardless of the causes with which he identified or did not identify, a person deserves a chance to make it on his or her own. No one must be chained to the past. Every person has the right to freedom of job opportunity, creative endeavor and hope for the future.

We would do well to keep this in mind as we interview for jobs, as we vote for candidates, as we choose friends, and as we relate to others in every human situation.

*Condemn no person and consider nothing impossible, for there is no person who does not have his or her potential.*
AVOT 4:3

# Struggle And Blessing

Nothing worthwhile in life ever emerges without a certain tension and even pain. The birth of a baby, the building of a business, the creation of a career, the development of a happy family life all are the products of people who are determined to wrestle with a challenging situation until it yields a blessing. The remarkable thing is that we really never obtain anything in life except by facing stress; as it challenges us, it tempers our iron and makes it steel.

This theme of tempering through stress is illustrated in the following true story. America has produced only one great form of the violin. The original maker searched all his life for wood which would enable the violin to have a certain haunting and beautiful resonance. He finally found the wood in the timberline, the last stand of trees above the Rockies, 12,000 feet above sea level. Up there where the wind blows so fiercely and steadily, the bark to the windward has no chance to grow. All the trees lean in one direction. But they stand firm and they do not fall to the ground. That wood, after facing years of challenge of the elements, is so resonant and beautiful that it sings to the touch of the bow.

All of us all our lives will have to face stressful elements. Like our ancestors the Maccabees, we must have the courage to think, we must have the tenacity that love demands, we must have the desire to be and become everything that we might be in time. We must hold life firm and in everything that we face we must be prepared to struggle and to hold fast until we have found our satisfaction.

*And Jacob struggled with a stranger all night. . . . Then the stranger said, "Let me go, for dawn is breaking." But Jacob answered, "I will not let you go, unless you bless me."*
GENESIS 32:25-27

# The Guiding Light

The Biblical instruction to create an Eternal Light can find meaning in our time in the words of the classic Rabbinic exposition on this commandment, "Anyone who performs a *mitzvah*, a good deed, has kindled a candle before God and by doing so one revives one's own soul" (Exodus Rabbah 36:3). What this beautiful and sensitive passage tells us is that the Eternal Light is not to be taken literally but symbolically, as an inspiration to do what is right, proper and good. When we do these things, our acts are as sacred as if we had lighted a candle in the Sanctuary and presence of God.

The Rabbinic commentary does not stop at this point, but wisely goes on to add that the *mitzvah* also revives the soul. This is the mystique of the process. When we do good for others, we are actually doing good for ourselves.

There is the story of a woman who was calling her friend. She complained that she was having the boss for dinner but she was encountering many problems: the cleaning woman was late, the baby sitter didn't show up, the garbage disposal needed repair, and other such minor disruptions, which obviously on this occasion one could consider major. The friend replied, "Don't worry, I'll drop what I am doing and I will come right over." She then spent the whole day helping to clean the house, taking care of the children, and running errands. Just before dinner, she returned to her own home to prepare dinner for her husband. At dinner her husband remarked, "You look very tired but radiant." And she replied, "I made somebody happy and so I am happy too."

The rule of a *mitzvah* is that when you do good you feel good.

*You shall further instruct the Israelites to bring you clear oil of beaten olives to maintain an Eternal light.*   EXODUS 27:20

# Jewishness Is Beautiful

Our heritage and our continuity is to be found in the traditions of Judaism. We do not claim that Judaism is the best of all possible traditions, but it is enough to say that, for us, Jewishness is the framework for building a home, for creating a life style, for fashioning an identity.

The following true story illustrates the persistence of our tradition. The Jewish Theological Seminary of America owns the first printed Hebrew book—a code of Jewish law edited by Jacob ben Asher, printed in Italy in 1475. As was the practice at that time, the book had to be submitted to the Church censor, and he carefully inked out all the complimentary references to Judaism. Recently, when the librarians at the Seminary went into the rare book room to check the books, they found that a remarkable thing had happened to this volume of the Jewish code of laws. The ink used by the censor had almost faded away, but the original Hebrew text of Jacob ben Asher is still clear as ever!

We all have a book of life which is our very own. As we go through life and turn the days of our years, occasionally we find lines that are glossed over, censored, or perhaps inadvertently smudged. However, if we go back after a period of time and reconsider and reevaluate and reshape our lives, we will find that what we were originally meant to be as human beings, as Jews, will become as clear as ever.

And you know what is the most fascinating thing of all? One of the phrases that the censor tried to blot out unsuccessfully was: "How fortunate we are, how goodly our portion, how pleasant our lot, how beautiful our heritage!" These words were destined eventually to stand forth with clarity for, after all, Jewishness is beautiful.

*The Greeks stressed the holiness of beauty; the Jews emphasized the beauty of holiness.*
                                                    EMIL G. HIRSCH

# Jews Stand For Justice

The pressures and prejudices against the Jew in the modern world have caused him to adopt a variety of postures. Some crouch before the power structure hoping for a crumb of approval here and admission to a club there. But isn't it time we stopped dancing to the tune of others and stood up erect, doing what is right not to please anyone else except ourselves and our own set of values?

Therefore, it is improper to engage in general community work simply because it will improve our image. But it is right to accept community responsibility and work for the rights of others because it is our moral obligation.

It is a distortion to see in every issue a Jewish problem or to consider every personal setback an anti-Semitic event. We must examine the issues honestly and objectively and make our way in life through the development of our own natural abilities, hard work and sustained excellence.

It is foolish—in the hope of being in fashion—to swallow whole, conservatism or liberalism or any "ism" that slavishly follows the line of national leaders or public relations handouts. Instead, Jews should look to Jewish tradition for a set of values and a standard by which to make independent judgments. The Jewish tradition, which has been shaped by the greatest minds of all time and subjected to every stress and strain, has developed the sense of social justice and the feeling of compassion, and joined them through the wisdom of Jewish thought and life. The only real security, then, for Jews, is security in the knowledge of doing what is right and being true to ourselves.

*There must be no surrender whatever by either Jew or Christian of the fullness of his inheritance. God still needs Jews as Jews.* JAMES W. PARKES

93

# The Third Temple

Israel is now on an archeology binge in which the Israelis, with terrifying devotion, are trying to restore the past great monuments of our people. Near one *kibbutz* a group of Israelis found the site of an ancient synagogue that had to be excavated and restored. It was amazing to see Israelis from all walks of life coming in to contribute their money, their time and their energy for this project. One kibbutznik worked hard all day in the fields and after he had eaten supper went right into the dig and continued to sift the earth by hand to help reveal the mosaics of the synagogue. A tourist came up to him and said, "Tell me, why do you do this and continue to drive yourself after a day's hard labor in the fields?" The reply was, "Mister, what I give is only a little energy. But in giving, I become a part of something beautiful."

This really is the modern expression of a long Jewish tradition. There was a time when someone who found himself in difficulty could always turn to a member of his extended family for help. This was, and is, the real beauty of Jewish life.

We are not very different from our ancestors. Our clothes may be of a different cut, our hairdos may be a little fancier, our homes might be more affluent, but basically we are still our parents' children. We can be moved if we are open to Jewish experience and values; if we choose to extend ourselves to reclaim the beauty of ritual objects and observances and the spiritual beauty of compassion and mercy.

*We shall not be deterred in our purpose, nor weakened in our resolve. For there is no power on earth which can invalidate the sacred bond that unites the Jewish people.*

PAUL ZUCKERMAN

# Finders Keepers

The Talmud tells us, "There are occasions in our lives when we can grasp the meaning of our existence in a single moment" (Avodah Zarah 10B). These moments occur in the lives of persons, nations, religions, and even entire civilizations. Events like the trial and death of Socrates, the writing of the Magna Carta, the French Revolution, the Battle of Bunker Hill and the first human walk in space mark our lives forever.

There are similar moments in Judaism which stand out in startling clarity because they changed the face of Judaism and at the same time altered the course of history. Such moments were experienced during the exodus from Egypt when the Ten Commandments were given at Sinai, the destruction of the Temple, the Holocaust in Europe, the establishment of the State of Israel and now, we—and by "we" I mean all Jews alive in our time—can personally add to the list the recent wars and peace in Israel.

In these latter events we clearly saw our entire existence as a people threatened, and in the wake of the response of Israel and World Jewry to these threats, there came moments in which we all instantly grasped the meaning of our existence as a Jewish people. Howard Nemerov, the modern poet, has written a splendid poem which ends with the line: "Oh, moment where the lost is found." During the wars of June 1967 and October 1973 and peace in April 1979 we Jews found what we had apparently lost in modern times. In living through these historical events, we relived our history as Jews and rediscovered through our feelings the faith of our fathers. It was then that we *believed* again.

*And when Israel saw the wondrous power of what the Lord had done to the Egyptians, the people were in awe and they believed.*
EXODUS 14:31

95

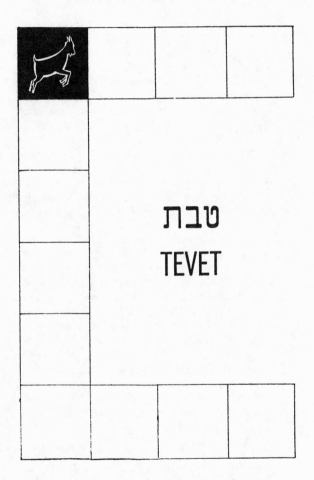

טבת

TEVET

# All Jews Are One

The Yom Kippur War taught us that Jews all over the world are one people, indivisible, with responsibility and commitment for all. To say that being Reform, Conservative, Orthodox, or Secular does not really matter in the long run as much as being Jewish, is not to utter a banality; it is to say something very basic. For each of us, regardless of his or her Jewish affiliation, knows in our heart of hearts that when put to the test, Jews in every corner of this earth will rise up as one and respond.

During the first bitter and black hours of the beginning of the Israeli war, when Jews all over the world were on the brink of sheer terror, we unconsciously revealed ourselves. There were many—both young and old—who distinguished themselves in spontaneous generosity and startling sharing. But there were always a few exceptions. One substantial Jewish family was called on with a request for help. The woman of the household replied, "I am afraid we cannot give anything." Because this was a family of considerable affluence, the caller persisted and asked, "But why not?" The answer was, "I don't want to get involved."

How completely naive and foolish was this response! For as a Jew, will it or not, this woman already was involved. Involvement is not something one can choose, because what happens to one Jew happens to all Jews. Therefore, all of us must recognize this involvement and respond to it by making sure that our moral, spiritual and economic strength will be shared not only with Israel, but with all the Jewish communities throughout the world.

*As God is one, though His name has seventy ramifications, so is Israel one, though settled among all the nations.*

ZOHAR, EXODUS 16b

# Act Of God

One windy day a snow-laden telephone pole crashed under its extra weight of ice and fell on the automobile of a Pennsylvania motorist. The automobile was damaged and its owner sustained personal injury. He promptly sued the Columbia Telephone Company. The County Court awarded him $10,830, holding that the telephone company was at fault because it had not inspected the pole in question for fifteen years. Of special interest is the fact that the court did not accept the company's claim that the pole fell because of an "act of God".

What is worthy of further thought is the reasoning by which the decision was reached. According to the judge, "There is something shocking in attributing every tragedy or holocaust to God. The ways of God so surpass the understanding of man that it is not in the province of man to pass judgment upon what may be beyond human comprehension. . . . In any event, no person called into court to answer for an act of negligence may find an excuse by asserting that it was not he but God who inflicted the damage on the injured party."

In cautioning us against using God as a scapegoat, the good judge gave us an excellent lesson in theology. Though much of our life is determined by factors beyond our control, including chance and Divine Providence, yet in the moral universe man remains his own master. We are free agents in determining how we shall use the elements of nature, how we shall deal with our fellow man, how we shall conduct our personal lives.

*What belongs to God is God's; what belongs to man is man's.*
                                            YIDDISH PROVERB

# The Light Of God

Within each of us an all-wise Creator has placed a marvelous reservoir of strength, creativity and wisdom for our use. The storehouse of memories and experience is called the subconscious or the unconscious mind. It is the essence of every person. In the words of the Bible it is termed the *tzelem elohim*, "the image of God" in us. In the theology of the last century we expressed it poetically as "the spark of the divine" in us. Now we might term it the "still, small voice" of the unconscious that stands ready to serve us. And it is a very powerful servant.

You are in the midst of a conversation. Suddenly, you wish to recall a name, a phrase, or a thought; and it escapes you. It is on the tip of your tongue and you just can't bring it forth. Then, later on when you are relaxed at dinner, or in the bathtub, or when you slowly awaken in the morning, the answer pops right into your head. The explanation is quite logical. Your relaxed unconscious mind, the gift of God, gave you the solution. You gave it a chance to work.

People who try too hard, people who are too eager to determine the outcome, people who fight desperately for control of every situation are not fair to themselves. They neglect that which is their greatest help in solving life's most difficult problems.

An ancient legend relates how God sought the safest place to hide the secret of a person's wisdom away from one's restless curiosity. He rejected in turn the highest mountain, the dark caverns of the earth and the depths of the seas. At last God decided to put it where one would be least likely to look—in his or her own heart. And the great sadness of history has been that people have gone on a far search for that which is the nearest of the near.

*The soul of man is the light of God.*    PROVERBS 20:27

# A Person Cannot Be Neutral

A minister once asked a congregant to come hear him preach at the next service when he would talk on Noah and the Flood. The man's reply was, "I'm sorry, Sir, I'm busy that day, but I'll send you a check for the survivors."

The concern for the victims of disaster and evil must go beyond the check-writing charity stage or the way we politely excuse our responsibilities with a shake of the head and an indifferent "Too bad." Responsibility demands our passionate involvement in helping to create a community life of worth and meaning. Ethics is substantially more than a series of traffic regulations for society. Equality is a great deal more than a set of platitudes or nicely-turned phrases. Freedom is vastly more than just being concerned about what clubs we can get into and what resorts are not restricted. Ethics, equality, freedom is everybody's daily business, for if one person is denied his or her rights we are all involved, for we soon learn:

How foolishly smug and complacent they be
Who say, "This never could happen to me."

Yes, it can happen to us unless we express our feelings and attitudes, unless we actively campaign for trustworthy candidates for public office, unless we lend our name and our energy to the cause we believe in.

In *The Fox and the Camellias*, a work by the Italian novelist Ignazio Silone, the most memorable line is uttered by Daniel, a man of firm political conditions. He is different from all his neighbors in his stubbornness and commitment, and when he is asked why he cannot remain preaceful and neutral, he replies, "I don't feel neutral. I am a man." Judaism says exactly that, "Don't be neutral, be a person!"

*Do not be indifferent to the blood of your neighbor.*
LEVITICUS 19:16

# The Ethics Of Prayer

The Prophets taught that prayer must be ethical, that the worth of a person's worship depends upon the character of his or her life. The core of prophetic teaching is that God is the essence of righteousness. He cannot be flattered, or deceived, or bribed. He responds only to sincerity, to honest dealing, to basic truth. Therefore, in praying a person ought to appear before the Almighty not as a greedy, selfish petitioner, but as someone who wants to make his life more ethical. One can readily imagine that God must look down on us and our selfish prayers and feel much like a politician being asked to distribute the spoils of office. The following story illustrates this impression.

When Woodrow Wilson was Governor of the state of New Jersey, he received a call at three o'clock one morning from a man who said that the State Highway Commissioner had just died. The caller then proceeded to ask, "I wonder whether I could take his place?" And Wilson replied, "It's all right with me if it's O.K. with the undertaker."

Like the inconsiderate, greedy caller, we, too, call upon God at all hours and make selfish demands on Him. Would it not be better if we were more thoughtful and even had the intelligence sometimes *not* to offer a prayer? A poor prayer is infinitely worse than no prayer.

But, when a prayer is uttered with a pure heart, with true concern for the welfare of others, then prayer fulfills its purpose and in the very act of praying we become ennobled.

*Any kind of injustice, corruption, cruelty, etc., desecrates the very essense of the prayer adventure, since it encases man in an ugly little world into which God is unwilling to enter. If man craves to meet God in prayer, then he must purge himself of all that separates him from God.*

JOSEPH B. SOLOVEITCHIK

# All Else Is Commentary

Look up the word "thanksgiving" in the *Jewish Encyclopedia*. On the page entitled "thanksgiving," no explanation for the term will be found, merely the statement: "Thanksgiving—See *benedictions*." This is a fundamental insight of Judaism on the method of teaching the concept of gratitude. It is simply that every time we enjoy a gift of God's wonderful world we say a *berakhah* (blessing) and we offer thanksgiving. Thanksgiving doesn't come just one day of the year for the Jew; rather every day of the year is an occasion for thanksgiving.

It is an old Jewish tradition that a pious Jew recites one hundred *berakhot* (blessings) every single day. This means that a hundred times a day we might find the opportunity for giving thanks to the Great Giver of all good things in life.

Judaism teaches us not to take the world for granted, but rather to pause and be sensitive to all the wonderful opportunities we have as human beings to enrich, ennoble and beautify our lives. It teaches us that a sensitive person—indeed, a religious person—knows how to offer thanks.

A writer on vacation was sitting with his family by a lakeside, watching a beautiful sunset. The family sat in reverent silence as the rays of the late afternoon sun shone across the lake and were reflected in the quiet waters. After a while, the four-year-old daughter touched her father's hand and whispered, "Father, let's return thanks." That is the Jewish point of view.

*We need the ability to thank God for the blessings of each day, for each sunset, for each new month, for each new year, for each new joy. And this, after all, is the essence of religion to which all else is tributary and commentary.*

STANLEY RABINOWITZ

# Five Minutes More

The concept of living life today—right now—is extremely important. Yesterday is behind us, tomorrow is before us, and what we do today is what really matters. Indeed, sometimes what we can do in just five minutes of any given day can change our life or someone else's life. There was a popular song several years ago entitled, "Only Five Minutes More—Give Me Five Minutes More." Think about it for a moment. What could happen in just this small segment of time?

Napoleon wrote that the reason he beat the Austrians was that they did not know the value of five minutes. It took Lincoln less than five minutes to deliver his immortal Gettysburg Address. William Jennings Bryan required less than five minutes to electrify a great political convention with but a single expression that gave him the nomination for the presidency of the United States.

On a personal level, in five minutes we can say an encouraging word to one discouraged or we can express appreciation to someone. It takes only five minutes to make a *shivah* call and to offer comfort. It takes only five minutes to select and mail a birthday card, a get-well card, an anniversary card. It takes only five minutes to call someone long distance just to say, "Hello. How are you?"

What these five minutes mean can only be understood if we are on the receiving end. If you have been comforted, inspired, made to feel a little happier by the efforts of others, then you know how important it is to do this for someone else. And you know you don't have to wait for any formal occasion or any specific time. You can do it in the next five minutes.

*Happy is he who performs a good deed; for he may tip the scales for himself and the world.*   KIDDUSHIN 40b

# Truth Is Where You Find It

A careful student of the Bible notes a significant difference between the Jewish story of Creation and the accounts given in other cultures. In the classic cultures, the beginning of the world and the origin of humanity is dominated by myths and legends, tales of gods and goddesses, stories of magic and animism. But the Hebrew Bible, by startling contrast, strives to suppress these primitive notions and instead focuses its attention on one supreme God, on ethical concerns and the nature of man. The founders of mankind, Adam and Eve, and the patriarchs and matriarchs of our people, Abraham, Isaac and Jacob and Sarah, Rebecca, Rachel and Leah, are not portrayed as superpersons or paper saints, but rather as real people who had real problems. They courted and they married, they quarreled and they reconciled, they worked hard and they raised families. All their concerns were anchored in reality. In a word, the greatest emphasis of the Torah is reality.

This has been the guiding light of Jewish thought down through the ages—the conscious striving to reject myth, prejudice and superstition; and to stress reality and truth.

The truth of the matter is that no particular philosophy has an absolute truth so that it can impose its idea of what is right on others. Indeed, when it comes to religion, why do we all have to be of one mind? If God wanted to make us that way, He would have created us as robots and not as persons. The fact is that there are many ways to view a given problem or experience and each view may be accurate and correct from its particular perspective. Only the sum total of these views may provide the ultimate reality.

*Both this view and that view are the words of the living God.*
ERUVIN 13b

# Days Of Our Years

It is interesting to contemplate some of the events that happened on January first in American history.

On January 1, 1502, Amerigo Vespucci first sighted the mainland of the Americas, and he wrote in his diary: *mundus novus*, "the new world." And America took its name from Amerigo Vespucci.

Contrary to popular opinion, it was not in July but on January first in the year 1776 that America first declared its independence. This was the day on which George Washington raised over his camp the first flag of the United States.

In the year 1863, on January first, Lincoln's Emancipation Proclamation abolishing slavery in this land became effective.

What do these events have in common? The answer is the courage to move out and discover new continents, new ideas and new commitments. The two land masses were always here, but it took Amerigo Vespucci's courage to find them. The colonies had the right to independence, but it took the courage of George Washington to make that right real. The abolition of slavery was a burning concern in the middle of the nineteenth century, but it took the courage of Abraham Lincoln to make it a public commitment. For these acts, these men will be remembered.

Indeed, when anyone—no matter how great or how lowly —is willing to search, to have courage, to make a commitment, whether it be on January first or any other day of the year, that act will be remembered. We must be willing to have the courage of our convictions, and to act on them if we would make our days memorable.

*Each day, in which good was done, weaves a garment for the human soul.*
HILLEL ZEITLIN

# True Leadership

When Moses was a shepherd tending the flocks of his father-in-law on Mount Sinai, it chanced that a lamb suddenly ran away. He pursued the lamb until it stopped at a water hole to drink. As the lamb was drinking, Moses said: "I did not know that you ran away because of thirst. Furthermore, you must be weary from running so far." And so he put the lamb on his shoulders and carried it back to the flock. The legend continues as God says to Moses, "You have shown kindness and compassion to the sheep. You shall, therefore, become shepherd to the flock of Israel."

He had the true marks of a leader, which are not oratorical flourishes and grandiose promises, but rather concern and compassion for the flock that one leads. A leader is judged by the daily work that he or she does sincerely and devotedly to help carry the flock and relieve their burdens.

Napoleon made himself master of France and most of Europe by the power of his marching legions, but Louis Pasteur made himself the servant of France and the world by fighting the germs of disease. Napoleon has only one monument in Paris, but the name of Louis Pasteur is found in every language under the word "pasteurization." Many generals of the European powers went into the Congo to dominate and devour, but Albert Schweitzer went to serve the natives. The names of the generals have now almost been forgotten, but the name of Schweitzer will be revered in Africa for centuries to come. When leaders serve their cause and their people sincerely, their names are revered for all time.

*When a shepherd is wise, his flocks follow him.*
PIRKE DE RABBI ELIEZER 42

107

# To Be Alive

The outstanding film of the last New York World's Fair was entitled, "To Be Alive." More than five million people stood in line to view it, waiting sometimes in the pouring rain and often as long as two hours. The film showed how people all over the world celebrate life.

In one scene a little boy looks at the world through a glass prism, turning it and watching the myriad colors and patterns dancing before his eyes.

In another scene a Japanese child looks lovingly at a leaf, as the following words are narrated:

> To pull the blinds of habit from the eyes,
> to see the world without names for the first bright
> time,
> to wander through its mystery, to wonder
> at every age and stage, at one with it—
> to be alive!

To be alive to all that the eye sees is truly to fulfill God's purpose and ourselves. The world is so packed with possibilities that we have only ourselves to blame if we do not experience them. There is always more to life than meets the eye. It is the difference between what we call sight and insight. One person can walk into the hospital and see nothing but pain and misery. Another person, walking the very same route, can see healing and hope. One child views the world as frustrating and frightening; another child looks at the whole world with openness and confidence.

"To be alive" can be a magical thing. It all depends on how we are trained to look and conditioned to see.

*The way we look at something determines what we shall say about it.*
                                                    MOSES IBN EZRA

# Duologue To Dialogue

We must feel what we say and speak honestly, and in this sincerity will we touch the hearts of others. And the reverse is also true. For we can only know others if we are willing to take the time in an atmosphere of love to listen to what they think, feel and believe.

Abraham Kaplan, a professor of philosophy at the University of Michigan, recently pointed out that we no longer have dialogues, in which people speak to one another but rather "duologues," in which everybody speaks but nobody listens. He said, "Duologue takes place in schools, churches, cocktail parties, the United States Congress, and almost everywhere we don't feel free to be wholly human." He added, "A near-perfect example of duologue would be two television sets tuned in and facing each other."

We might ask ourselves, hasn't the time come to express love by talking less and listening more? How will we understand the problems of conflicting minorities until we learn to sit down and listen to what each group has to say? Would not international talks proceed more positively if instead of shouting at one another, both sides would take turns really listening to one another? Would not many of the stresses of family life be lessened if the members of the family took the time to hear each other? In our private lives how important it is to have one friend who can listen to us as we confide our troubles, and thereby lighten our burdens. And if we want to have such a friend we must also *be* a friend who is willing to listen. There is a wonderful Yiddish phrase describing the meaning of love and friendship—having the opportunity *zich oysraydin dem hartz*, "to talk out your heart."

*Words that come from the heart enter the heart.*
ANCIENT HEBREW PROVERB

# Where God Is Revealed

Prayer is one activity that distinguishes human beings from animals. People can lift their voices in praise of God and creation, which animals can never do. The Psalms, in their sublime beauty, celebrate birth and marriage, suffering and death, the wonders of nature, the just society.

In a little chapel in the far south of Ireland, every window but one is of stained glass. Through that single clear window may be seen a breathtaking view: a lake of deepest blue, studded with green islets and backed by range after range of purple hills. Under the window is this inscription from the book of Psalms (19:2):

"The heavens declare the glory of God,
and the sky proclaims His handiwork."

So is it with miracles. Most of us think that a miracle is a one-time thing that occurs in a stupendous way. Actually, this is not so. There is so much to marvel at within us and about us that there is hardly a moment when we cannot see a miracle if we want to. The real miracle is what happens to us every day of our lives: The miracle of creation! The miracle of a healthy body that functions so normally and serves us so ably! The miracle of nature that brings forth through seeds and seasons all the glories of our universe!

Tennessee Ernie Ford, the singer and homespun philosopher, recalls that years ago there were two books that were always bestsellers. These books were the Bible and the Seed Catalogue. Ernie Ford commented on this and said, "The Bible tells us of the miracle of God, and the Seed Catalogue proves it."

*Revelation is the silent, imperceptible manifestation of God in history. It is the still, small voice; it is the inevitability, the regularity of nature.*    HERBERT LOEWE

# Only In America

In recalling the history of migration to America, we sometimes overlook the fact that most of the large-scale migrations took place following revolutions abroad. President Franklin D. Roosevelt once reminded a convention of the Daughters of the American Revolution of this fact in the following words: "Remember, remember always, that all of us, and you and I especially, are descended from immigrants and revolutionists."

The very recent migrations from oppressed countries to America only prove the point. And if we, the children of migrants, speak out passionately for freedom, we do it by historic right. We know what it means to be repressed and persecuted and tortured and denied freedom; and we are determined that it will not happen here. Sometimes this expression takes extreme forms. But, then, better to give vent to our feelings than to submit to the possibilities of repression here in America. And make no mistake about it, it is always a possibility and it can happen here.

We in this land must now go beyond the melting pot. We must not only help immigrants fit in, but we must also help them preserve their uniqueness. We must do this not only for them, but for ourselves. For as they are encouraged to foster their cultures, they will in turn enrich our arts, our sciences and our lives. We must teach people that every ethnic group has something special to say to us and an important contribution to make to our community.

*My folks were immigrants and they fell under the spell of the American legend that the streets of America were paved with gold. When Pop got here, though, he found out three things: The streets were not paved with gold. The streets were not even paved. He was supposed to do the paving.*

SAM LEVENSON

111

# What We Can Choose

We cannot really determine the course of some human events, for they are beyond us. Accidents of time and chance always have and always will happen to us. What we can determine is how we shall accept them, how we shall deal with them and what we shall make of them.

Shall we become angry and hostile, or shall we become thoughtful and wise? Shall we be resentful and hurt other people in the process of being hurt ourselves, or shall we become compassionate and thereby learn to help and to heal others?

This principle of choosing the positive can be applied to every circumstance: to business, to career, to family living, to our personal and private lives. We have a choice to make every single day of our lives, and the choice we make at the beginning of the day will determine our emotional and spiritual condition at the end of the day.

A wonderful old man appeared recently on a popular television program. In accepting a prize for having won a TV contest, he stole the whole show with his exuberant spirit and quick wit. "It's easy to see," remarked the admiring master of ceremonies, "that you are one very happy man. What's the secret of being as happy as you are? Let us in on it." "Why, son," the old man answered, "it's as plain as the nose on your face. When I wake up in the morning, I have two choices. One is to be unhappy; the other is to be happy. I'm smart enough to choose happiness. I just make up my mind to be happy . . . that's all there is to it."

*The road is predestined, but the way we walk it, the attitude with which we bear our fate, can be of great influence over events.*
                               RICHARD BEER-HOFMANN

# A Promise Must Be Fulfilled

In general, Judaism discourages the making of vows. But once someone has pledged his word, he or she must keep it. This belief is further emphasized in the Biblical words, "You must fulfill what your lips have spoken." A promise is a fuller and more public expression of a deep inner feeling, a guide to action, a spur to private goals and to the public good.

In the establishment and maintenance of charitable organizations, universities, hospitals and synagogues, a pledge is necessary. Without the advance commitment of support these institutions could not be continued, much less founded.

In professional life, commitments are significant. When the physician takes the oath of Hippocrates (or that of Maimonides), he sets the standards by which to conduct his or her practice.

When an individual is about to take a government position, he or she takes an oath to uphold the laws of the land.

A wedding ceremony contains within it an official expression not only of love but also of the responsibilities that love brings.

In all these instances, we see a clear relationship between a promise and its fulfillment. To make a pledge is only a beginning. The end is to be found in the fulfillment. But the promise is a means toward that end. For a responsible person always feels the tension that an unrealized promise creates—a tension expressed in the words of Robert Frost: "But I have promises to keep. And miles to go before I sleep." To keep the promise is to resolve the tension.

*When you make a vow to the Lord your God, do not put off fulfilling it.* DEUTERONOMY 23:22

# Plant Peace And Love

"The Lion In Winter" is a filmed account of Henry II, and of his fights with his sons and their fights with one another. At one point, Richard, one of the sons, says to his mother, Queen Eleanor: "The human parts of you are missing. You are as dead as you are deadly." Then in a moment of clarity after her son Richard nearly puts his knife through her son John's heart, Eleanor observes: "We all have knives. How clear we make it, O my children, we are the origins of war. Not history's forces nor time nor justice nor the lack of it nor religions nor ideas nor kinds of governments nor anything. We carry it, like illness, inside ourselves. Dead bodies rot in field and stream because the living ones are rotten. For the love of God, can't we love one another just a little? . . . We could change the world. We could change the world."

If we would change the world, then we must begin planting the seeds of peace in our personal lives.

If we would transform the Jewish people into a secure and safe people, we must continue planting mutuality and responsibility in our hearts and the hearts of our children.

If we would change America, we must continue planting understanding, proper values and commitment in our communities. In the words of the poet:

He who plants like a tree, plants love,
And has the approval of the One above.
Gifts that grow are best.
Hands that help are blest.
Just plant and life does the rest.
Heaven and earth help the one who plants like a tree,
And the work its own reward shall be.

*Blessed is the one who implants peace and love.* ENOCH 52:11

# The Mistake Of Moses

We all know that Moses was the greatest leader of the Jewish people and it was he who led the Hebrew slaves out of Egypt into freedom. But the great disappointment of his life was that he was permitted to reach the border of *Eretz Yisrael* but was not allowed to enter the Promised Land. The reason for this failure is that he disobeyed the will of God. At one point, the Jews in the wilderness were dying of thirst. God asked Moses to speak to the rock in order to perform the miracle of flowing water. Instead of speaking to the rock, Moses struck it with his rod. For this one mistake, he was not granted the privilege of entering the Promised Land. This punishment for a simple error points up an important lesson. The lesson is that everybody makes mistakes and nobody is perfect. Even the greatest of all Jews, the first of the prophets, was not without error. And as an object-lesson for all the generations to come, it is through him that we must all learn that making mistakes is part of being human, and that the mistakes we make have consequences.

All of us tend to try to alibi failure and rationalize our shortcomings. The one who alibis and runs away may live to alibi another day. But, this kind of person is not likely to grow morally and prevent further repetitions of the mistake. Mature people, people who want to grow, are never afraid to admit an error whether it be large or small.

All humans will make.mistakes. Humans who wish to progress will learn from their mistakes. Humans who wish to achieve will determine to go beyond their mistakes. And this is the way to learn. There is no better way. There is no other way.

*Moses did not enter the Promised Land, not because his life was too short, but because it was a human life.*

MARTIN BUBER

# The Long And The Short

In the Bible it is written, "And it came to pass, when Pharaoh let the people go, that God did not lead them by the way of the land of the Philistines, although it was very near" (Exodus 13:17). God deliberately chose to have the Israelites take a roundabout way through the desert to reach *Eretz Yisrael*, instead of going straight up the coast. The trip through the desert took forty years, whereas the coastal route would have taken less than a month. But the long way turned out to be the shortest way.

In fact, the ancient Rabbis observed that it *had* to take forty years to convert the people from a slave mentality to that of a free nation. There are no shortcuts in teaching freedom. It is a painful process. As in any form of character education, the long, hard way is the only lasting way.

It is very interesting to observe that the Eastern European Jewish term for synagogue is *shul*. The word *shul* means school. It was a way of saying that in order to acquire moral attitudes we must go to school all of our lives. Jews gave real meaning to this process by using the synagogue as a means for creating study groups which studied the Bible, Talmud and Jewish literature every day in the synagogue, between the late afternoon and evening services. Our present adult education system is a contemporary Jewish expression of the concept that learning for life lasts a lifetime.

All of these are by-products of the appreciation that when it comes to learning, to understanding and to wisdom there is no shortcut. Perhaps being reminded of the four-decade trek in the desert required to provide character education, we might be moved to observe the same truth in contemporary words: Education is not a destination. . . . It is a journey.

*Learning—learning—learning: that is the secret of Jewish survival.*                                                                AHAD HAAM

116

# People Power

There is a commonly-held myth that the individual is powerless against the masses and the machines and, indeed, the machinery of government. Often we feel deeply about an issue, but we lose our will when we consider the massive forces arrayed against us and our remoteness from the centers of political and social power. But the reality is that we do not count *only* if we choose to accept this attitude.

The fact is that one man, Martin Luther King, Jr., moved a whole nation to consider the plight of the Blacks. What was he before that? Just another Black preacher.

The fact is one woman, Margaret Sanger, moved a whole world, even an entire church, to consider the importance of family planning. What was she before that? Just another wife and mother.

The fact is just one small segment of Jews created a new state of Israel out of an atmosphere of hopelessness and a world of indifference. And what were they before that? Just another insignificant group of idealists committed to a vision.

The fact is that in a democratic society, in which we are fortunate to live, the will of the citizen and voter is respected. The government does listen to the grass roots and is perpetually searching for a consensus. Protests are heeded if they represent the real and true feelings of people. But we have to learn a sense of socially responsible criticism. We have to learn how to dissent without creating dissension. In the last analysis, world opinion is effective. And, who creates world opinion? People. And, who are the people? You and I. *We* are world opinion.

*We must remember that people do not belong to the government but that governments belong to the people.*

BERNARD M. BARUCH

117

# As Old As The Hills

There is a delightful story that came out of the last census. A census taker chanced to come to a Jewish section in a large metropolitan city. He started to interview one woman and began with the obvious question, "What is your name?" She replied, "Sarah Cohen." The next was the inevitable, "Your age?" Being Jewish, Mrs. Cohen naturally answered the question with a question, as she inquired, "Have the Hill sisters next door given their age yet?" "No," the census taker replied. "Well, then," the woman said, "I'm the same age as they are." The interviewer then remarked, "O.K., I'll put down, 'Sarah Cohen—old as the Hills.' "

The Jewish experience is as old as the hills. This implies, just as hills suggest, stability and strength, knowledge and wisdom, faith and reassurance. Psalm 121 is one of the oldest Psalms and was probably written by a Jewish pilgrim thousands of years ago as he approached the Hills of Judea. He lifted up his eyes and looked forward to visiting the Temple in Jerusalem and he prayed: "I lift up my eyes to the hills [and I ask,] 'What is the source of my help?' " And the poet-pilgrim answers his own question in the next line: "My help comes from the Lord, Creator of heaven and earth."

It behooves us to remember the grandeur of the universe and the possibilities the Creator has bestowed upon man. We ought to recall the rhythms of nature and the fact that there are ebbs and flows in the affairs of men as well. Anxiety, as in every age, is inevitable. We must not deceive ourselves and act as if we were immune to all the fear and trembling that is a natural part of the human condition. God does not ask us not to feel anxious, but to trust in Him no matter how we feel. And this faith is as old as the hills.

*Faith is devotion to God.*                    JACOB JOSEPH KATZ

# Be Reasonable

A unity of purpose must be a stabilizing factor in everything we do. A unified approach has been very helpful in solving many problems in science and in education. We used to think that each department in the university was sovereign unto itself. But since when could we ever isolate one body of knowledge from another? Therefore, we have now many interdisciplinary study programs. It is no longer biology and chemistry but biochemistry. It is no longer religion and psychiatry but mental health. It is no longer American history and American literature but rather American studies.

A person, too, must have a sense of unity within himself or herself to achieve anything of enduring value. By drawing all of our emotions together and binding them toward a common goal, we are able to focus our strength at the maximum point.

A boy recently asked his father, "Dad, what keeps people together?" The father assumed the boy had overheard some family quarrel. He explained how people love each other even if they have a few harsh words occasionally. Differences of opinion, he pointed out, did not destroy mutual respect and so on.

The child became impatient at not having his question answered and interrupted with, "When I asked you what keeps people together, all I wanted to know is what keeps people's heads on."

We have to learn how to keep our heads on our shoulders and let coolness of reason, calmness of thought and unity of purpose control our emotions.

*Whatever knowledge I may receive, I shall always brighten it with the light of reason. My religion enjoins me to think the truth and practice goodness.*    SOLOMON MAIMON

# The Human Touch

One reason that when we meet someone we offer our open hand to shake goes back to the ancient custom of demonstrating that we have no weapons in our hands. This, then, is the supreme gesture of peace.

The openhanded person is the one who is prepared to offer help, to lift, to share. Who really helps in any situation? The talker or the doer? How do we bring to light the very best in any situation? By ignoring it or by *handling* it? We must be involved in thoughtful, intelligent and wise ways if we wish to be of service.

One might think of the way children hold hands for mutual security as they cross the streets. One might meditate a moment on young lovers whose clasped hands communicate something much deeper than a word can ever say. One might give a moment of thought to the hand that pats an elderly head and says: "It's all right. We'll take care of you." Sometimes, the hand can say so much more than the mouth—and really mean it.

All of this is summarized aptly in a wonderful poem by Spencer Michael Free entitled "The Human Touch."

'Tis the human touch in this world that counts,
The touch of your hand and mine,
Which means far more to the fainting heart
Than shelter and bread and wine;
For shelter is gone when the night is over,
And bread lasts only days,
But the touch of the hand and the sound of the voice
Sing on in the soul always.

*Aaron lifted his hands toward the people and blessed them.*
LEVITICUS 9:22

# Dial M For Meditation

In our haste, in our noise, we have often forgotten how to be calm, how to be quiet and how to use our inner resources. Moderns seem to be afraid of silence. We are conditioned by radio, television and all the noise media. The theme is: America is on the move and we have to keep busy, busy, busy.

But authentic learning and growth happen quietly. Learning through lecturing is imparting information but the real learning that is done in the brain is accomplished quietly. Where have people made the momentous discoveries? Newton was sitting under an apple tree and discovered gravity; Archimedes was in a bathtub and he learned about density; and Socrates was walking in a garden when he developed the Socratic method of thought and investigation.

This calls to mind a wonderful passage by William Saroyan: "Walking alone . . . I began to think of the swift and bright truth of being, the truth that I had earned for myself by walking alone through the silence of the earth; and walking, thinking of it, I could feel myself whole again. . . ."

We have to create consciously situations in which we can walk and meditate; we need to walk through musuems and think, to stroll down the streets in solitude. But, why go so far? In your very own home you can recite the daily prayer, the *amidah,* which is also entitled, "The Silent Devotion," and silently stand before God and find in His world and in Him a sense of wholeness and peace. For what the people of this world really need is a time to think alone: a periodic spell of equanimity, a regular time to take not tranquilizing pills but tranquil periods of meditation.

*Each person was given two ears and one tongue so that one may listen more than speak.*　　HASDAI IBN CRESCAS

# Jewishness

We modern Jews have an identity problem. We are not exactly sure who we are, so we are not entirely certain how we must act in order to do our own thing. Often we see ourselves as weak, powerless, misbegotten accidents of history. This poor self-image denies our reason for being and our essential meaning as Jews in this last quarter of the twentieth century.

There is an interesting illustration of this problem. The Jewish bestseller of a recent year was *The Joys of Yiddish*. Following its publication, we suddenly heard on the lips of suburbanites of Idaho and Montana words like *shlemiel*, *shlep* and *kvetch*. Now, these are words that too often ridicule and distort. Words like *schlemazel*, *yente* and *fonfer* are, of course, part of the Yiddish vocabulary, but they become a travesty and a distortion if they become so popular. Certainly, we Jews had these types, but they were only minor characters in the great drama of Judaism.

*Shlemiels* don't survive two thousand years of fierce batterings. *Shleps* don't achieve the rebirth of an ancient homeland. *Kvetches* don't produce a Bible and make it a living book for millenia. These monumental achievements were made by men and women who had the courage of their convictions and the stamina to see them through. The authentic Jew is one whose image and purpose is expressed by the value-concepts found in terms like *torah*, *mitzvah* and *tzedakah*. Once we have understood this tradition, we will be better able to understand the meaning of being Jewish in modern times.

*Tradition is the life-giving soul in Judaism. When properly understood, tradition will ever enrich time.*

ABRAHAM GEIGER

# Quality And Equality

It is told in the Talmud that when two persons, one rich and one poor, appeared before the court of Rabbi Ishmael ben Elisha, he would order them to dress alike so that the judges would pass over external differences and concentrate on dispensing equal justice.

This practice calls to mind the story of the president of a small railroad who once sent a complimentary pass to the president of a large railroad and asked him to reciprocate. The recipient immediately returned the pass with the following note, "How dare a president of an eleven-mile-long railroad compare himself to the president of a railroad empire whose tracks stretch for thousands of miles?" The president of the little railroad answered back, "It is true that the tracks of your railroad are much longer than my railroad but my tracks are just as wide as yours."

These stories teach us that we should overlook the outward differences of people and see their true inner equality.

Isn't it about time that we understood that the color of a person's skin has nothing to do with the quality of his or her brains?

Isn't it about time that we understood that the shape of a person's nose has nothing to do with the condition of his or her soul?

Indeed, isn't it time that we treat people not according to our prejudices, but rather according to their merits and abilities?

Isn't it time we remember that despite our differences we are all equal in the sight of God?

*The Lord does not see as man sees: Man judges by appearances but the Lord judges by the heart.*

I SAMUEL 16:7

# Moral Motion

In our contemporary culture we have adopted a form of reserve about our feelings. Often we look askance at people who join protest groups and who express feelings of indignation. Actually, as long as protest meetings do not court violence, are not manipulated and are the free spontaneous expressions of people, there is nothing wrong with them. In fact, they are a healthy experience. Is it not one of the glories of America that a person should have the right to let go and speak his or her own mind so long as one does not hurt anyone else in the process?

There is a great wisdom in these simple lines of William Blake, a truth that is deeply personal even as it has social implications:

I was angry with my friend:
I told my wrath, my wrath did end.
I was angry with my foe:
I told it not, my wrath did grow.

Often we bottle up not only our anger but also our tears. Somehow or other, Americans seem to feel it is unmanly to cry. This is a misunderstanding of the human body. If God did not mean us to cry, then why did He give us tear ducts?

On the other side of the coin, it is equally important to give full expression to our happiness. If somebody does something nice, why not drop a note and tell him or her so? If a person has a birthday, why not help make it the happiest day of the year? If you are proud of someone in your family, if he or she brings you genuine *nahas*, real spiritual satisfaction, why not hold and hug the person and freely express your deep personal pleasure? If you are pleased, say so.

*It is the emotion which drives the intelligence forward in spite of obstacles.*
HENRI BERGSON

124

# God Does

One finds in society today a deep desire to celebrate life in the observance of births, marriages, birthdays, graduations and anniversaries. It seems to be an expression of the desire to make each moment count.

One of the most thoughtful books in the Bible is entitled *Kohelet*, and in this philosophical treatise (9:9) the author says: *"rehay hayim,"* which means "enjoy life." The enjoyment of life is the greatest command of all, because in cherishing life we are expressing our gratitude to God, the giver of life. This is a profound, deeply religious and Jewish idea.

It is a concept that is well conveyed in the following true story that was told recently by an elementary school teacher. The pupils in her class were listening to a lecture on plant life. "All living organisms," said the teacher, "are developed from a substance called protoplasm, which is made of oxygen, hydrogen, carbon, and nitrogen. This we know. But from where does the protoplasm derive its power of life and growth? Does anybody know that?"

"I know," said a boy at the back.

"If you know what makes protoplasm grow, then you are wiser than all the biologists. Tell us."

And the boy replied, "God does."

The child was intuitively wise, for growth is a condition of healthy life, and life is a gift of God. Thus, the one who cherishes life cherishes God, and the one who loves life loves God, and the one who continually celebrates life in all things is not only deeply religious but also profoundly Jewish.

*The whole world is nothing more than a singing and a dancing before the Holy One, blessed be He.*

NAPHTALI HERZ

# The Courage Of Conscience

An issue of *The Jerusalem Post* tells the story of an Arab judge by the name of Nihad Jarallah who is serving under the Israeli government as a member of the West Bank's Supreme Court and who continues to administer justice to his fellow Arabs. This man has received anonymous threatening letters by the score, many of them from Arab terrorists, asking him to resign from the bench. But he refuses. His exact words are: "People need justice as much as medicine. Violence will lead nowhere."

It is an act of conscience and courage for Nihad Jarallah to be a judge in an area where he is threatened personally. A man like this, continuing to dispense justice, will help to bring peace to the land.

A commitment to an idea that continues to endure, despite differences and irritants, is reaffirmation that if we hold fast to the laws or just human relationships there will be peace. In fact, anyone who sets a goal for himself, whether personal or communal, which is in keeping with the laws of humanity and keeps steadily on that course is to be commended and honored, and his or her ultimate reward shall be a more peaceful personal and communal life.

Many years ago, a British writer summed up this thought. "When moral courage feels that it is in the right, there is no personal daring of which it is incapable." This is something we should keep in mind. Once we have made a moral decision and then we have added to it the dimension of courage, we can achieve almost anything, including the greatest of all blessings which is peace.

*If you follow My laws and faithfully observe My commandments, . . . I will grant you peace in the land, and you shall rest untroubled by anyone.*    LEVITICUS 26:3, 6

# On The Town

Life is a mixed bag, and we can choose to see it as we wish.

Once an old philosopher was sitting under the shade of a tree. A man approached and asked, "What type of people live in yonder town? I want to move into it."

The old philosoher looked at the man and asked, "What type of people live in the town you are planning to leave?"

"Ah," answered the man, "in the town I wish to leave the people are cold, dishonest, unfriendly, and selfish."

"Do not move into this town," replied the philosopher. "The same people live here as well."

No sooner had the stranger left, when a second man appeared from the same town and made the same inquiry: "What type of people live in yonder town?"

Again the old philosopher asked, "What type of people live in the town you plan to leave?"

"I have to leave my town because of business reasons," answered the second man. "But I hate to go because it is filled with warm, friendly hospitable people."

The philosopher replied, "The same kind of people live here. So it does not really matter—where *you* choose to live, you will find friendship, warmth and hospitality."

Somehow we always find what we are looking for, whether with our families or with our friends or in facing the future. If we have faith in God and man we will find, despite all adversity and hardship, that our lives are enriched by ever-present feelings of friendship, warmth and hospitality. For life is as we choose to see it, and as we see it, so shall we live it.

*True vision requires far more than the eye. It takes the whole man. For what we see is no more and no less than what we are.*
RICHARD H. GUGGENHEIMER

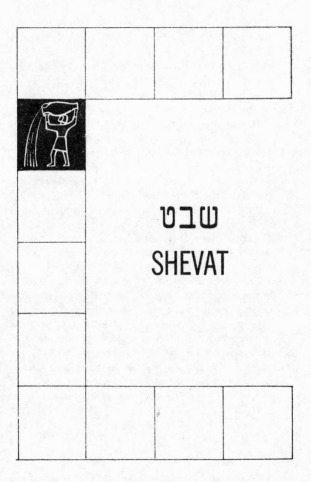

שבט

SHEVAT

# The Act Of Recovery

A king's son was at a distance of a hundred days journey from his father. His friends said to him, "It is time to return to your father."

He said to them, "I cannot. The way is too far."

His father learned of this and sent him the following message: "Go as far as you are able and I shall come the rest of the way to you."

It is possible to restore relationships that once existed. In every situation there is always a possibility of reconciliation, restoration, renewal, and recovery—that is, provided we want to.

Those who lived through the Great Depression of the thirties in the United States wondered if they would ever get out of it. But because they wanted to, they did. Through their own efforts and through the government-sponsored National Recovery Administration, people were able to recover because they had a deep commitment to restore the American economy.

Consider the meaning of the following story: One night a house caught on fire, and the fire spread rapidly to other houses. Each family ran frantically about, attempting to save its own individual possesions. A wise bystander noticing this remarked: "We are foolish, selfish people. Instead of each trying to save our own possessions, why don't we all get together and put out the fire so that it will not spread any further and we will all save ourselves."

The healing of the shattered elements in our society and our personal lives is up to us. We must all be involved if we want to help save ourselves.

*The pleasure of recovery has in it a touch of the joy of resurrection.*
                                                    DAVID OF TOLNA

# The Total And Its Parts

The Jewish community is the sum total of all of its parts. The Orthodox Jew has every right to his convictions and to assert them even though he does not agree with some of our thinking. The Reform Jew may carry on certain rituals which might not be within our taste or liking, but that is no reason to read him out of the bounds of Judaism. The Conservative Jew, who is sometimes branded as a great compromiser, has a right to his interpretation of Judaism. The secular Jew, who sees Judaism without any religious overtones, also is a full-fledged member of the Jewish people.

It was exactly this philosophy of inclusion rather than exclusion that enabled the emerging State of Israel to survive and grow daily in strength. It has been estimated that Jews from a hundred separate cultural units have come to settle in the land of Israel. Racially they were all colors of the rainbow, intellectually they ranged from the lowest to the highest I.Q., culturally from the most primitve to the most sophisticated, and the dress of some was strange beyond anyone's anticipation. And, yet, because the founders of modern Israel were committed to the concept of Jewish peoplehood, everyone was admitted, and everyone was made to feel at home. This is the true glory of Jewish tradition.

Leon Blum, the former Socialist Premier of France, once met Ben-Gurion. He introduced himself this way: "I had better tell you right away, Mr. Ben-Gurion, that I am a humanist first, a Socialist second, and only then a Jew. Whenever I write my name, that is what I believe." Ben-Gurion replied with a smile, "Never mind, we Jews read from right to left anyway."

*Ah yid bleibt ah yid, a Jew is always a Jew.* YIDDISH PROVERB

# The Pursuit Of Happiness

When Barbra Streisand once announced in London that she was an expectant mother, her business associates were stunned at the news. The startled agents estimated that this would mean the cancellation of a million dollar show tour. Her answer was classic as stated in the modern idiom: "Why is everybody else so hopped on money? They call it the 'million dollar baby.' Is that important? What's a baby got to do with it? I'll tell you what's important. Having a healthy baby, that's important. For that matter, what's success? A million dollars doesn't automatically give you happiness. I used to live well and was happy on $20 a week."

Happiness doesn't have a price tag. Its value is determined by the feelings of people. The Hebrew word for happiness is *osher*. There are many verses, particularly in the Psalms, that one could use to illustrate the Biblical concept of happiness, for example the one that says, "Happy are they who revere the Lord, who try to walk in His ways" (Psalms 128:1). In other words, we have to walk toward happiness.

It was well said by Bernard L. Berzon in a passage entitled "Chronic Optimism": The men and women who are happy themselves, and who have the gift of shedding gladness, sunshine, and cheer wherever they go, are those who share with great leaders a chronic optimism in their own and their people's destiny. They have learned to look for the bright and hopeful side of life; they reside on the sunny side of the street.

*A person's good deeds are used by the Lord as seeds for planting trees in the Garden of Eden; thus, each person creates his or her own Paradise.*   DOV BAER OF MEZERITCH

# The Stuff Inside

The Jew has rarely been a majority in any time or clime; but despite being a minority, Jews have been willing to accept the price of their position, and they have endured. As a matter of fact, a book by Max Dimont entitled *The Indestructible Jews,* points out how time and again the Jews have faced opposition. But, in the end, they not only endured but made a creative contribution to the world.

If this is true of Jewish history, it is equally true of recent American social history. We have had many problems with equal opportunity, with the struggles of minorities for their rights, for women to be recognized as persons and valued for their abilities as human beings. Yet there is emerging a clear sense of recognition for each person of what he or she can achieve despite religion, race, cultural background, or sex. Though progress has been very slow, the doors of opportunity in America *are* opening.

There is the story of a little black boy who stood fascinated before a display of toy balloons of every color. Suddenly, one of the red balloons broke way, rose rapidly, and disappeared. "Mister," the child asked, "would a yellow balloon go as high as the red one?"

The man grinned, "It sure would, son."

The lad asked further, "And would a white one go as high and as far?"

Receiving the same reply, the boy then proceeded to ask about the rising capacity of a black balloon. The man finally replied to the child, "It isn't color that makes it rise. It's the stuff inside."

Perhaps we should take that as a motto—to ignore the color and look at "the stuff inside."

*God decides what shall befall a man, but whether he shall be righteous or wicked is his own decision.*   NIDDAH 16b

# Change Is A Part Of Life

A friend of J. P. Morgan, the very famous financier, once asked him what the stock market was going to do. The friend obviously was thinking of a valuable tip for an investment. Mr. Morgan merely replied, "I am sure the stock market is going to change." And, of course, he was right. What the banker said about the stock market is also true about life. The only sure thing we know about life is that it is going to change. We begin in life by changing diapers, when we grow up we change friends and as we grow older we change ideas. Our body is always changing whether we know it or not. It is a medical fact that the human body actually changes its tissues every seven years. Chemically speaking, we are completely different persons every seven years.

The point of all this is not to be fearful, but rather to understand that it is change that makes life challenging, exciting, worthwhile. The Talmud speaks of the concept of *koneh be-shinui* (Baba Kamma 65b), of possessing something by interacting with it and changing it (and ourselves). Change can be very significant, depending on how we use it.

We can react to change by sticking our heads into the sand like ostriches, or else we can look at events from a new point of view, understand them, and make the most of them. The winds of change are constantly blowing about us, and it is important to chart their direction so that we may ride the currents to a better way of living. Once we do this we can control events rather than letting them control us.

*Each year in this age the world changes as rapidly as once it did in a century. The changes themselves are not always bad. It is only the way in which we meet many of these changes that can be bad or blessed.*                    DAVID POLISH

# Love Moves The World

Eric Fromm in *The Art of Loving* (which is not a sex manual but rather a more profound study of the meaning of love), makes this observation: "Most people see the problem of love primarily as that of being loved, rather than of loving, of one's capacity to love."

When we really love our fellow men we are willing to open up our hearts to sharing and caring, to giving and understanding. Love of mankind is an empty phrase unless we are willing to do something about it and make it practical and realistic. Dreams of a better world are useless unless we are willing to do something about them. And that something has to be measured in terms of personal sacrifices. Sacrifice is not a popular word. But unless we are willing to give up something significant for other people, we are not really expressing our true capacity to love them.

Once a father, while having dinner with his family, suggested to his ten-year-old son that he ought to give up something for a disaster—something that would really hurt, such as candy. The boy hesitated, and finally asked what his father was giving up.

"Both your mother and I are giving up liquor," the father replied.

"But before dinner you were drinking something," said the boy.

"Yes, acknowledged the father. "But that was wine. We have given up hard liquor."

The boy thought for a minute, then said, "Well, then, I think I'll give up hard candy."

If we feel we belong to the human race and are serious about it, then we will not make a half-hearted gesture but will be willing to give up something that matters.

*Love one another from the heart.*        PATRIARCHS, GAD 6:3

# A Mistake Is A Lesson

It is not sufficient just to acknowledge our errors; we must be persistent and go beyond them. It is well known that Babe Ruth was the home run king, but very few are aware that he also held the record for strike-outs. His persistence in the face of his failures paid off.

We must learn from our mistakes. That is the only way we can redeem them for our own benefit. Consider, for example, the tradition of the Oriental rugweavers: Many of the world's finest Oriental rugs come from little villages in the Middle East. Each rug is hand woven by a crew of men and women under the direction of a master weaver. Occasionally, one of the workers absent-mindedly makes a mistake, introducing a color that is not according to the pattern. At this point, the master weaver, instead of pulling out the work and ruining the rug, skillfully finds a way to incorporate the mistake into the overall pattern. With great care, he weaves the mistake into the whole structure so that it becomes unnoticeable and even a subtle improvement of the basic design.

The same thing is true of our lives. We have to learn to accept our mistakes and find a way to incorporate them into the patterns of our living. We have to take each error and make it harmonious with our greater goals. If someone could photograph our lives for a day or a week and then at a later time these events would be shown to us again in slow motion, undoubtedly we could learn some of the errors of our ways. Through this process we might discover some of the mistakes that we continually repeat only because we are not aware of them. First, we must acknowledge our mistakes; then we must learn from them.

*Correct your ways and improve your doings.*

JEREMIAH 7:3

# The Divine Partnership

How does one plant a field? First, one clears the rocks and weeds, then one cultivates the soil, and after that one plants the seed. But, the work is still not over. One must water the land, one must chase away stray animals and birds. Even then the work is not complete until the final effort of gathering in the harvest.

Thus it is with a person and God. God gives us the opportunity but we have to make the most of it. God gives us the raw material, but we must process it. He gives us land, but we must till it and toil on it. He gives a mind, but we must develop it. Without the basic material nothing can be done; and without its proper shaping, it remains only a potential resource.

So, for example, the moon was always there, the forces of nature have always operated, yet it was only in this generation that we learned to use these forces for spectacular voyages to distant planets. "The poor you shall have with you always," says the Bible. But it was only in our time that we determined to use all of our moral and mental resources to wage war on poverty. The laws of healing have been operative throughout the ages. But only in our own day were these laws sought out so vigorously and applied to prolonging life and preventing the ancient illnesses which have plagued mankind.

It is all so simple really. Without God, there would be no world. But without people, there would be no civilization. As much as people need God to create a better future, God needs human beings to fulfill the purpose of creation. Judaism has always taught that God can as little do without us as we without Him.

*Man can become a partner with God in the act of creation.*
DOV BAER OF MEZERITCH

# A Toss-Up

A driver who came to a corner and could not decide which way to turn sat through three changes of traffic lights while thinking it through. A policeman watched him and finally came up to him and said, "What's wrong, Mister? Don't we have a color to suit you?"

Time and time again choices will be presented to us at emotional intersections where we are not sure how to proceed. We can see red and stop; look at green and go; or else watch the amber and proceed cautiously. But then, there comes a time when philosophy must come to an end and a new course of action must begin.

One need not fear to make a choice if one acts thoughtfully. We must deliberately choose what we wish to do so that our lives will become what we want them to be. Decision-making is not always easy, but a responsible person, a religious person, must choose as he sees fit, and be prepared to accept fully the consequences of his decision.

We must realize that life demands a system of priorities. Because we cannot do everything, we must use our heads in choosing where and how to commit our energies.

We can change our direction but the change can only come about through a willful conscious choice, thoughtfully considered and then acted upon.

All of this was expressed in a little poem that summarizes it well.

> The Lord gave us two ends to use,
> One to think with; one to sit on.
> It all depends on which you choose:
> Heads you win, tails you lose.

*What is freedom if not the possibility to change?*

JOHANAN TWERSKI

138

# Who Owns The Bible?

Thomas Merton, the renowned Trappist monk and one of the most sensitive voices in American literature, once said: "One has either got to be a Jew or stop reading the Bible. The Bible cannot make sense to anyone who is not spiritually a Semite." What he was saying in effect was that the Jewish people are the authentic links to the Bible and the Biblical tradition.

Very few people realize that Judaism bears in its very name the name of God. The Hebrew word for "Judaism" is *yahadut* and the Hebrew word for "Jew" is *yehudi*. Both begin with the letters *yud* and *hay*, which spell *Yah,* one of the oldest known names for God. Every Jew thus personally attests to the divinity of his faith. This should be a source of pride and a cause for responsibility as well.

For if Jews were part of the dawn of the conscience of mankind, should they not now also continue to serve that purpose in our society and in our times? We must not merely glory in our ancestry; rather we must contribute greatly to the welfare of all men.

Once a child with nothing better to do saw a black book on a shelf. Since it caught his eye, he picked it up, brushed off the dust, and asked, "Whose book is this?" The father answered, "Why, son, that is God's book." The boy noticed that the book was not used and said, "Maybe we should give it back to Him. We haven't used it much lately."

The Bible is of no use unless we use it. Since we gave the Bible to the world, it is only fitting that we should live by it.

*Who reads a Biblical verse and its proper interpretation promotes the good of the world.*    SANHEDRIN  101a

# The Staff Of Life

A pediatrician had just completed a physical examination of a child. Because the young patient was so cooperative, the doctor gave him a lollipop, which he accepted without a word. The mother prompted the boy with, "What do you say, son?" And the child replied, "Put it on my bill." What this reveals to us is that we are a credit-oriented and materialistic society.

While it is important to have certain basic necessities, we must never forget that the basic satisfactions in life do not derive from bread alone. Unless we constantly restock our mental storehouses, we will find our lives insignificant.

It is interesting that in the current medical debate on precisely what constitutes death for the purpose of organ transplants, doctors now agree that clinical death has technically occurred when the brain waves cease. What this tells us is that when we cease to use our brains, we cease to exist. Thus, man is more than a breathing organism and more than a workhorse. Man is a creature who marvels at the wonders of the world and constantly seeks to express feelings about the universe. There are books to read, there are theaters and films and art shows to attend, there are politics and problems to study and work at, there are places to visit. All these can help us stretch our minds and our souls so that we continually experience a sense of growth. When we do not grow, we degenerate; but when we grow, we glow. We generate enthusiasm and we acquire a satisfaction that far exceeds the pleasure that comes from acquiring material things. While it is important to have a full stomach, it is just as important to have a full mind.

*For man does not live by bread alone.*   DEUTERONOMY 8:3

# Try It! You'll Like It!

The possibilities of enhancing, deepening and enjoying life are infinite—provided we are willing to try new experiences. When we are willing to consider new ideas, new alternatives and new life styles, we open up for ourselves whole new areas and opportunities for improvement.

The following story from Israel illustrates the point in a humorous but nonetheless instructive way.

A woman from Haifa shared this incident. All year round she and her husband enjoy eating "matzah brei," or "fried matzot," a Passover delicacy consisting of matzah dipped in beaten egg and fried. Her husband always sprinkled sugar on his, but she ate it without sugar, insisting that he was losing the naturally good taste of the crisp matzah. But he wouldn't change his ways, and she wouldn't change hers.

One day in sheer desperation at the pleasure he was missing, she made a bargain with him: if he would try her way once, she would try his. How else could the matter be decided? And now there is real peace and happiness in the family. He has discovered that fried matzah is also good without sugar, and she also enjoys it his way, with plenty of sugar on it.

We will never know anything that is better unless we are ready to experiment. We can never improve life unless we are prepared to entertain new ideas. Indeed, we should be willing at least to try new experiences; because, after all, if you try you might like it.

*To be intelligent is to be open-minded, active-memoried and persistently experimental.*   LEO STEIN

# A Memo

What we choose to remember tells a great deal about us. Often we tend to remember the ills of the past, but soon forget its benefits. We are constantly dredging up the injustices of our American past, but at the same time we neglect to remember the good things in American history. What about our Constitution and our Bill of Rights? What about our dedication to granting equality and freedom to people? While we should acknowledge our failings, we must not forget our achievements.

In our own lives as well, some of us tend to remember only our pains and our losses. However, a sense of balance would indicate that we should recall our pleasures and our achievements as well. It is not only a religious commandment but the wisdom of life itself to focus on the very best rather than concentrate on the worst, to keep faith with our best impulses instead of letting them slip away unheeded.

A story is told of two children who ran away from home. They took two cans of soup and set out, but by and by they got hungry and went home. Why not eat the soup and go on? They had forgotten to carry a can opener.

Have you forgotten something today?

It is important to remember not only our good intentions but the goodness that life itself has yielded to us. It is particularly important to draw on our memory as a resource when we are under pressure. For remembered beauty pleases us, remembered faith strengthens us, remembered achievements inspire us, and remembered acts of goodness ennoble us.

*Remember all the days of old.*          DEUTERONOMY 32:7

# Talk Is Expensive

The phrases and words we daily use are not merely utterances, but they can express our deepest feelings. During a scientific test of survival techniques which was conducted at Princeton University, a young couple and three children were confined to an eight by nine foot fallout shelter. Unknown to them, a hidden microphone was placed in the shelter, and every sound they made was recorded on 38 miles of electronic tape. When they left the shelter, they were told about the microphone and the tape recorder. The mother of the family was embarrassed and said, "Of course, if we had known we were being recorded we would have lived differently."

The question that we really ought to ask ourselves is, if we knew that every sound we made were being recorded, would we really live differently? Would we?

We spend so much time teaching our children to say "please" and "thank you." But how often do we remember to say it ourselves? As Jews, we resent phrases that demean our Jewishness, but how often do we disparage other ethnic and religious groups? It is not that we always do this consciously, but unconsciously and unthinkingly we hurt others.

And looking at the other side of the coin, how many people have been helped by the right words at the right time—a word of hope when someone is depressed, a word of encouragement when someone faces a new challenge, a new enterprise or a new career? The history of mankind is filled with illustrations of people who were renewed and restored to life itself by hearing the right word at the right time.

*Words are vehicles that can transport us from the drab sands to the dazzling stars.*     M. ROBERT SYME

# Beauties Of Nature

*Tu Be 'Shevat*, the fifteenth day of the month of Shevat, is the Jewish Arbor Day. This holiday, which had its origin back in the first century, is also called "New Year for Trees." In Israel, children celebrate the event by going out into the fields and planting seeds and saplings which are destined to grow into trees and forests. In America, this event is commemorated in the Hebrew Schools with special assemblies, readings and, most important, purchasing trees to be planted in Israel.

Although it is winter here in America, *Tu Be' Shevat* reminds us that in another part of the world and another time to come there will be renewal and growth. It reminds us that nature takes its own course and eventually winter will melt away and in its place will come spring. It emphasizes the importance of appreciating nature, of acting natural, of natural beauty which is still the greatest beauty. Cut an apple in two and you will discover a design and a sculpture that is truly magnificent. Observe a cobweb: it is more delicate than the finest lace. Study a bare tree when the foliage does not obstruct your view and ask yourself if this is not more striking than anything the greatest artist has created. All this natural beauty is ours if we but take the time to observe it.

A tourist who arrived in Taos, New Mexico, and found himself in a hotel room with a huge picture window overlooking a beautiful mountain, turned to his wife and said, "It would be a nice view but I can't see the scenery because that big mountain is in the way." Let us not be like that tourist, blind to the natural wonders around us.

*When you see the beauties of nature, pronounce the benediction: Praised be He Who created beautiful things.*

TOSEFTA BERAKHOT 6:4

# A Jewish Response

In Jewish life the time has come to remind ourselves that we had better stop looking for miracles and go back to our task of tending to the growth of our people. We Jews have had long and bitter experience with social and political movements: Hellenism, Egalitarianism, Socialism, Communism. While they all contained some elements of truth, yet in the supreme test when the welfare of the Jew was involved, they turned out to be gods that failed and we ended up disillusioned and disappointed. And so we learned the hard way that there is only one true "ism" for the Jew—and that is Judaism, or, to put it more exactly, the concept of Jewish peoplehood.

The concept of the Jewish people is unique and unparalleled; it cannot be defined—only experienced. It is not rooted in space but in time.

Thus when Moshe Dayan once was asked what he was, he replied with characteristic bluntness, "First, I am Moshe, and then I am General Dayan."

He was not trying to be cute or coy. He was simply saying, My first name is Hebrew and of historic origin and so first of all I belong to the Jewish people. Only then am I an Israeli, with a specific responsibility to Israel.

He has, as we all have, learned from the history and the experience of the last forty years that the only ones we can truly rely upon are ourselves. We can no longer place our faith in resounding causes and pretend to be the humanitarians of the world in the hope our self-righteousness will win us friends. We Jews have a right to be, just because we *are*. Let us accept this truth about ourselves and continue to develop in our lives and in the lives of our children a sense of responsibility to the Jewish people.

*All Jews are responsible for one another.*     SHEVUOT 39a

# Humility Is Hard

A Western film was being shown at a movie theater in New York. Two native Indians, dressed in all their Indian finery, were employed for advertising outside the theater. An inquisitive woman walked up to one of the red men and asked, "You are a real Indian, aren't you?" He courteously responded, "Yes, madam." The woman went on with a question. "How do you like our city?" And the Indian replied, "Fine, madam. How do you like our country?"

To whom does America really belong, to the conquerors or to the natives? Should the white men feel they are the proud possessors, or should they feel a little humility when they contemplate exactly how they took this land?

Indeed, in the entire order of the universe, it is important for a person to know his or her place. Often our technological achievements induce in us a false sense of importance. We forget that we are simply using the laws of nature and the universe; we do not own them, nor did we even make them. Human beings have reached the moon, but when we arrived there, we were only specks of dust in comparison to its surface. If we remember this, then, even with our fantastic accomplishments, we will have a sense of humility. We will know that what we are comes from the world about us and we will understand how dependent we are on the forces of nature and the labors of other men.

This was well summarized in a statement by Albert Einstein when he said: "A hundred times a day I remind myself that my inner and outer life depend on the labors of other men, living and dead; and that I must exert myself in order to give in the same measure as I have received and am receiving."

*Humility is a virtue which all men preach, none practice, and yet everybody is content to hear.*        JOHN SELDEN

# The Best Way To Serve

No human being or society can ever achieve anything worthwhile or build anything lasting except by concentrating on one problem or one project at a time. When we begin the process of education, do we start the child on higher calculus or do we go about it grade by grade? When we established this country did we develop it all at once or was the Union built section by section? The obvious answer to these questions—one step at a time—is surely something we ought to contemplate.

When we are faced with personal problems, we must learn not to be overwhelmed by them. If we will approach them step by step, quietly and patiently, we will find the right solutions.

In modern America, we face massive problems. Racial and cultural conflicts, the growth of the cities, increasing rates of crime, the devastation of our environment, the massive disaffection of the young—these trouble all of us. Here again there is no need to push the panic button. If we sit down and patiently apply our best talents and creative energies to each area of concern, we will eventually come up with programs and plans to develop and enrich American life.

In the world situation, and particularly there, we must learn how to concentrate our energies on one thing at a time. We must not allow fear to distort our capacity to think clearly. What is at stake is the very survival of our species and our planet. How can we guarantee this survival? Someone once put it very aptly: "We can best serve a desperate world by refusing to be desperate."

*The wise will remain serene in the face of trouble.*
                                      SOLOMON IBN GABIROL

# Faith Is Essential To Healing

Beginning with the earliest parts of the Bible, Jewish literature has taken a strong affirmative attitude toward medicine, physicians and healing. One reason is that Judaism recognizes the important role of faith in the healing process. Our attitudes toward ourselves and the world make a great difference in determining the health of our life patterns.

Sociologists are familiar with what they call a "self-fulfilling prophecy." An anxious student who is convinced he will fail an examination and does more worrying than studying often will fail. In 1932, a false rumor of a bank's failure caused a run of depositors making withdrawals, so that it did, in fact, collapse.

On the other hand, an affirmative view of life can heavily influence a patient's recovery. There are many cases on record of dramatic improvements occurring because the patient gets up one morning and announces, "I am well!" Going back to the '30s, one has only to remember the election campaign of President Franklin D. Roosevelt and his statement, "We have nothing to fear but fear itself," which reversed the whole nation's attitude toward depression and marked the beginning of the climb toward recovery.

Our physical well-being, our emotional health, the tone of our society, and much of the function of our personalities depend upon our outlook on life. This is the reason that the Torah in all of its wide literature emphasizes that faith is essential to healing, that healing springs from deepest commitments of faith.

*The Torah gave permission to the physician to heal; moreover, this is a religious precept and it is included in the category of saving life.*   YOREH DE'AH 336:1

# What's The Rush?

There are times when rushing forward is a proper response to certain demands in life. In some instances it may be proper to "cool it," but in other instances we must have the courage to act swiftly. There are moments in which we must strain ourselves to do certain things. Should not a young person be quick to accept the newcomer in the classroom? Should not a woman understand that she should be the first to bake a cake to welcome a new neighbor? Should not a man feel that he ought to be the one to extend greetings to a new employee and fellow worker?

We will always need courageous people to speak up for equal rights and opportunities. Certain problems should be stamped "urgent," and we must move toward solving them quickly. Poverty, degradation and illness are still rampant, and those who suffer need prompt attention. It is all too easy to abandon our responsibility for a sophisticated stance of thoughtfulness "that overwhelms the need for action."

A somewhat facetious version of this problem is seen in the story of the man who noticed something missing when he visited a friend's executive office. "What happened to all of those big 'Think' signs you used to have for all your empoyees?" he asked.

"I had to take them down," the businessman said. "The people in the office were sitting around thinking all day and none of them was doing any work."

There is a time to think and there is a time to do. There is a time to relax and there is a time to rush in with a compassionate response.

*The truly religious are quick to do the mitzvot (commandments).*  
PESAHIM 4a

# The Room For Self

When a person reflects only the opinions of others, when an individual goes about merely reproducing the words and the ideas of other human beings, he or she is adding nothing and is boring others. But when one is truly an individual and gives to the world, the community and the family the stamp of his or her own individual ideas, then that person really makes an important contribution to life. The person who is a "me too" drags along in existence. The person who says "this is what I believe" carves out new highways of experience.

In religion, there is a time to proclaim the faith of our ancestors, but there is also a time to speak up for what we believe. In fashion, there is a time to be in style but there is also a time to set our own style. In the family, there is a time for the whole family to cooperate on common ideas but there is also a time to become an individual. All of life depends on a very delicate balance between allegiance to the past and commitment to the future.

Perhaps one could best express this idea in the following simple analogy: Look into a mirror and what will you see? Only yourself. Nothing new, nothing different, nothing visionary. But look through a pane of glass and what will you see? Horizons, visions, a whole world beyond. It is the world beyond and the vision of a better future that should continually guide us. Reflect a moment and do not bounce off the ideas of others. Take time to think for yourself and then let your voice be heard.

*King Hezekiah's ancestors left something undone whereby he might distinguish himself; so in my case, my ancestors left room for me to distinguish myself.*    HULLIN 7a

# Mixed Sorrows

Everything in life that happens to us contains a mixture of good and bad. We open the morning newspaper and read of all the car crashes—and that is bad. But then perhaps we remember how many people drive safely to and from work each day—and that is good.

We suddenly learn from our accountant that our profits have gone up considerably—and that is good. But then we realize that because of this, we have to pay increased taxes—and that is bad.

Often our young people harshly criticize the system—and that is bad. But the fact that they are deeply concerned about it and want to change it for better—that is good.

If we take stock of every situation, and if we have some perspective, we discover that all of life is such a combination of good and bad.

As human beings we are always faced with the problems of challenge and adversity. The only question is whether or not we are willing to go forth and do something about them, and what we can learn from them. All of our lives we struggle: growing up, getting married, starting businesses and careers, facing the future. Whether it be in illness, in aging, in anything that befalls us, we must determine to keep on going and to face up to our challenges despite our fears. It would be wrong to deny that often our situations look grim and life is difficult. But if we are determined, we will find a way to triumph. No matter how grave the situation, we must never lose hope in finding the good. For the good is there with the bad, if we are willing to search it out.

*The Holy One created light out of darkness.*

LEVITICUS RABBAH 31:7

# Aid To Refugees

Since the earliest times, Jews have regarded the duty of *pidyon shevuyim*, ransoming captives and delivering our brothers and sisters in distress, as one of the most sacred obligations of the community. Many instances in Jewish history testify to personal sacrifices in keeping this commandment, including the moving story that follows:

The Talmud relates that when Rabbi Joshua ben Hananya, who lived in the first century, visited Rome, he was told that a young Jewish boy was put into prison by the Romans on a false charge. Rabbi Joshua went to the doorway of the prison and said, "I will not move from here until I secure his freedom" (Gittin 58a). After many months of hard work, he obtained the boy's release. In time, the young man became Rabbi Ishmael, a great teacher in Israel who helped to edit the early portion of the Talmud.

In our own time, too, we have witnessed the fulfillment of the *mitsvah* of *pidyon shevuyim*. Since 1939 the United Jewish Appeal has rescued and rehabilitated more than three million men, women and children who were the victims of war and persecution in many parts of the world. In recent times the Jews of the Soviet Union seeking freedom have been added to these numbers. It was the generous and determined efforts of their fellow Jews that made possible this unprecedented humanitarian achievement.

The responsibility for world Jewry has always been and will always be a prime commandment. As in every past generation and in every time of trouble, Jews will continue to ransom their captive brothers.

*The ransoming of captives is a religious duty of greatest importance.*   BAVA BATRA 8b

# Everyday Mysteries

One of the reasons God created the Sabbath was to teach that there is a time to sit and do nothing in the world. Actually, Shabbat is a truce between human beings and nature. According to the Talmudic rules as found in the volume entitled *Shabbat* it is forbidden to pluck a flower, to break a twig, to do anything to interfere with the natural world. This is a way of saying that we should let nature take its course, for it is a very wise course.

As a matter of fact, we Americans are so busy changing nature that we have no time really to appreciate it. A Japanese can spend hours rearranging a few simple flowers. A Norwegian can just stare at the snow and watch the changing patterns. The Frenchman can sit and savor slowly and easily many varieties of grape.

Have you ever picked up one leaf and watched the path of its veins? Have you ever cut an apple in half and spent time just staring at the core? Why even last night, did you notice the magnificence of the sunset?

Our inability to attend to the mysteries of the commonplace was expressed in a short couplet by W.H. Davies.

"A poor life this is, full of care,
We have not time to stand and stare."

*Shabbat* tells us, "stand and stare."

*The Sabbath signifies an abdication on that day of the right to be master of certain things enjoyed during the six other days. It means not only resting oneself, but letting all other things rest. A Sabbath so observed...is an essential affirmation of faith.* HAFETZ HAYYIM

# Yield And Merge

The Riverside Museum in New York City once put on a novel and fascinating Pop Art exhibit, featuring neon lights, traffic signs and common objects artistically re-arranged. Children walked about, touching the various pieces and having a wonderful time. The curator explained that it was an attempt to let children become familiar with the world around them, and he added, "We are trying to teach people that if you approach your environment in a friendly way it will respond in a friendly manner." He then picked up a sculpture made with common traffic signs entitled, "Yield and Merge." He went on to say that it people would only learn how to yield and merge they would be happier people.

The resistance of some people to the just rights and demands of others creates terrible hostility and confuses children, who become conflicted and disturbed at seeing how their parents treat other human beings. If only they would learn to yield to the rights of others and merge their interests with the entire nation how much happier they would be.

Even in our daily lives, how often do we stubbornly insist on our own point of view? How often do we collide with others because we won't give an inch?

We have to approach our relationship with God in exactly the same way. Many of us fight God and resist Him. Then we end up with misery and unhappiness. We cannot break any of His commandments without breaking ourselves in the process. We cannot ignore Him without personal suffering. But when we yield to His ultimate wisdom and judgment, we find an inner peace that passes all understanding. When we finally merge our own persons with His wishes, we are able to live with serenity and contentment.

*Make God's will as your will.*                    PIRKE AVOT 2:4

# Tinsel Vs. Truth

Often we lack the ability to know the fake from the real. Or, as a humorist said about Hollyood: "Scrape off the tinsel on top and you find the real tinsel beneath." The point is that we have to dig down deeper beyond all the tinsel to arrive at that which is truly important. We have to learn how to experience life directly. The failure to do so leaves us with a sense of frustration and lack of satisfaction.

Speaking of the artificial and the genuine, one might recall that a new plastic has just been developed to simulate a lawn. Some homeowners, remembering seasonal battles against crabgrass, drought and just plain growth, may welcome the idea of a false lawn that requires no more care than an annual scrubbing. Golf courses and parks may one day boast of only durable plastic under the trees. That is fine as far as it goes. But what about that indescribable sensation of walking barefoot on a newly-sprinkled lawn on a hot summer day? Where will the robins go? What does plastic grass smell like after the rain?

We must re-create a sense of the totality of life by learning how to distinguish between that which is enduring and that which is only fleeting. The truth is to be found not in distance from nature but in closeness to the world of growth; not in estrangement from reality but in ;the ability to touch, to feel the quality of the world about us; not in creating issues which divide us but in building relationships which will bring us closer to one another as real people. We must make every effort to come closer to our environment as well as to become a real part of the whole world.

*Only through intimacy with nature can human beings learn the meaninglessness of luxury and thus set themselves free.*
BORIS SCHATZ

# To Feel With And For Others

True sympathy can only be learned by living. We can talk a great deal about helping others, but it means little until we actually empathize with the needs of a person or a group

There is a school in England where sympathy is actually taught as part of the curriculum, and this is the way it is communicated: In the course of a term, every child has one blind day, one lame day, one deaf day, one day he cannot speak. The night before the blind day his eyes are bandaged. He awakes blind. He needs help, and other children lead him about.

Through this method he grasps what it is really like to be blind. His friends help him, and having had this experience themselves, they are able to direct and guide him through the day with real understanding.

There is something wonderful about this kind of instruction, for it is really learning from life itself. We say we want to help people, but do we really fully understand them?

Have you ever taken the time to visit a nursing home and spend an entire day or night there to appreciate the problems of the aging?

Have you ever worked in a factory or in an assembly line and felt the fatigue and boredom of repetitive work?

Have you ever really put yourself in the place of a college student who is seeking to find meaning for himself or herself in life, and who is faced with all the bewilderments of a confused society?

The fact is that we will never learn how to help people until we are willing to live with their problems in a very deep and participating manner. Problems are never solved from the top down, but rather from the inside out.

*True love of man is to know his pain and bear his sorrow.*
MOSHE LEIB OF SASOV

# Simplicity

The classic Jewish statement of ethics is most simple. The Ten Commandments, which the world recognizes as a religious masterpiece but so rarely follows, is composed of just seventy-two Hebrew words. There is no complicated theology here. It is all quite simple: "You shall" or "You shall not."

In this simplicity is to be seen the Jewish approach to God and man. One does not become involved in doctrinal disputes, dogmas or other philosophical complications. The approach to God and morality must be simple and direct. Whatever ultimately hurts a person is wrong; whatever finally helps a person is right. Whatever removes us from God and thereby makes us more hostile and irresponsible is wrong; whatever brings us closer to God and makes us more loving and compassionate is right. Whatever dehumanizes us is wrong; whatever makes us a part of humanity is right. It is as simple as that.

A student was once asked by a career counselor, "What do you want to make of yourself?" The student, rather than saying he wanted to be an engineer, or a businessman, answered instead, "A human being." This is what one should strive to become. In personal feelings we must bear in mind that the simple acceptance of our own humanity is a significant achievement. In religion we must ever be reminded that the way to God is not devious and subtle but direct and straightforward.

*God watches over those who are simple of faith.*

PSALMS 116:6

# A World Of Patience

All of us must learn that if we want to produce something of quality and achieve a worthwhile goal, we will have to go about it patiently. Step by step—all learning proceeds in this manner. This is what our youngsters are finding when they study "the new math." If a student misses one step, then the rest of his learning is hampered. All human development—physical, mental, moral, spiritual—is a goal toward which we climb one step at a time.

A child once attended his first concert. As he was listening to one of the numbers, he was deeply impressed that the ninety members of the orchestra were able to play the symphony so well. He mentioned this afterward to one of the performers and the reply was, "Young man, you must understand. Each performer rehearsed all of his life and patiently trained himself to be a skilled musician." It then occurred to the child that it took hours and days and years to prepare such a great symphony, and each performer had to begin by first learning the scales and then advancing gradually to the achievement of a finished musical performance.

In this vein, an admirer once asked the famous concert pianist Paderewski: "Is it true that you still practice every day?"

"Yes," said the pianist. "At least eight hours a day."

"You must have a world of patience," said the other.

"I have no more patience than the next fellow," said the renowned pianist. "I just use mine."

Everybody has aspirations, but only those who use their patience will reach their goals.

*The patient in spirit is greater than the proud in spirit.*
ECCLESIASTES 7:8

# The Natural Law

A story about George Washington illustrates that there is a relationship between naturalness and virtue. Once when he was riding with a party of friends, their horses leaped over a rock fence and one steed kicked off several stones. "Better replace those," suggested the General.

"Oh, let the farmer do that," was the careless reply. When the riding party was over, Washington turned his horse back the way they had come. Dismounting at the fence, he carefully replaced the stones.

"Oh, General," said the companion, "you are too big to be doing that."

"On the contrary," answered Washington, "I'm just the right size."

We must learn, like George Washington, to size up the situation and to fit in and literally lend a hand. In any human involvement, we must learn to do what comes naturally—acts of simple goodness.

In Judaism, naturalness and directness have always been dominant themes. The naming of a child at birth involves only a simple prayer. The Jewish marriage ceremony itself is modest in length. Even in death, Jewish practices and the burial service have always been simple and direct. Those who add to the length of the services do so on their own for their own needs, but that is not the way of traditional Judaism. In the Sefardic Jewish community it is the tradition to have a tombstone that lies flat on the ground so that no one can try to show superiority by boasting of a bigger and better monument. Naturalness, unpretentiousness and directness are the Jewish ways.

*The higher the truth, the more natural it is.*

ABRAHAM ISAAC KOOK

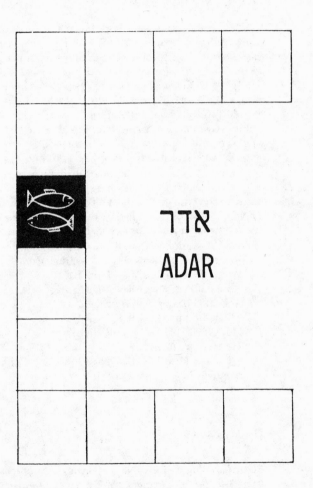

אדר

ADAR

# The King And I

A few years ago a New York bus driver made the front pages of the newspapers. All his working life he had taken the same bus route—down the avenue, crosstown, up the avenue, back crosstown, into the garage. One day he could not stand it any longer. On this trip he went down the avenue and kept on going. He drove the bus all the way to Florida before he was intercepted.

But even more interesting than this was the fact that the whole city of New York, from the citizen on the street to the editorial writer of a major newspaper, rose to his defense.

As a matter of fact, this desire to affirm life is the meaning behind the *Shaharit,* the Morning Service. It is an opportunity to shed the shell of the dead day and to begin to live in a new day. It is the time when we can look into ourselves and discover what it really means to be alive.

This observation was well put in a very simple peoem entitled, "What the King Has," by Ethel Romig Fuller.

> What the king has, that have I:
> Rose-gold of dawn, bejeweled sky,
> A wealth of days slipping by.
> What the king has, that have I!
> Hopes deferred, ambitions high,
> Hungerings to satisfy.
> What the king has, that have I:
> A crown of love naught can buy,
> Once to live, once to die.

*Blessed are You, O Lord our God, King of the universe, Who has given the mind understanding to distinguish between night and day.*                              DAILY PRAYER BOOK

# The Muscles Of Flexibility

As we read the history of Judaism, we find that it is an evolving tradition. The thoughtful leaders of every Jewish generation found ways and means to adapt Judaism so that it might survive. Those who preserved it were neither orthodox nor heterodox but rather those committed to understanding what had to remain and what had to be refashioned. It is the flexibility of Judaism which enabled it to survive the centuries in a creative manner.

Even in our own families, the principle of flexibility applies. We must learn to adapt ourselves to our children as they grow older and as we grow older. Our love for one another is constant. But our concern for one another should lead us to accept change in them and in us. This adjustability can help us not only to stay together but to appreciate and enjoy one another.

The Talmudic story of the willow and the oak illustrates this approach to life. The mighty oak stands straight and tall and powerful. It is truly a symbol of awesome strength. But one day a big wind comes and topples the oak with a great crash. And then there is the willow—soft and slender, bending and yielding. Yet, when the big wind comes, the willow just sways, gives a little here and there, and thus endures until the wind dies down. After the storm has passed, the oak is felled, but the willow remains as lovely and as graceful as ever.

So it is with life. Those who are rigid break under pressure, but those who are flexible adjust, survive and continue to flourish.

*He who resists the wave is swept away, but he who bends before it abides.*    GENESIS RABBAH 44:1

# The Outdoor Advertisement

Very often in our pursuit of canned beauty and contrived pleasures, we overlook the enormous pleasure that nature gives us—from its great vistas to the infinitely complex patterns in the smallest snowflake. Every plant and tree gives mute testimony to the order and design in the universe. And most of these grand scenes of nature are centered about the infinite.

This brings to mind the story of the city youngster who was more accustomed to man-made wonders than the marvels of nature. One summer, his family took him for a vacation in the country. As he came to the edge of the lake, he suddenly lifted his eyes and saw a grove of trees on a ridge. He gazed at this gorgeous landscape and he said after a moment of thought, "Mother, it is very beautiful, but what is it supposed to advertise?"

The answer to this child's question is simple. The natural world advertises the fact that there is a God, a God Who gives us all the loveliness of nature for our health and our enhancement, for our joy and our sustenance, for our pleasure and all our human purposes.

The traditional Hebrew blessing over fruit emphasizes this thought. The entire prayer reads: "Blessed are You, O Lord our God, King of the universe, Who creates the fruits of the tree." These are not mere words but rather the expression of the Jewish conviction that the natural world, like the moral world, was created by God for human use, welfare and pleasure. All of nature advertises this.

*My God, may there never be an end to the sand and the sea,*
*to the whispering of the water, to the glistening of the skies,*
*to the prayer of man.*                    HANNAH SENESH

# Today And Tomorrow

A woman telephoned a friend and asked how she was feeling. "Terrible," answered the friend. "My head is splitting and my back and legs are killing me, and the house is a mess and the children are simply driving me crazy."

"Listen," the caller said, "go and lie down. I'll come over right away and cook lunch for you, clean the house and take care of the children while you get some rest. By the way, how is John?"

"John?" the complaining housewife asked.

"Yes, your husband."

"I've got no husband named John."

"My heavens," gasped the first woman, "I must have dialed the wrong number."

There was a long pause. "Does that mean you're not coming over?" the other woman asked plaintively.

When hope is lessened, our will to achieve is loosened. But when there is faith in the future and hope for tomorrow, then we can face almost anything.

A doctor practices on the basis of faith and hope; faith in research and his medical training, hope for the patient's welfare.

A businessman runs his business on faith and hope; faith in himself and his ability, hope for a better market.

A teacher educates on the principles of faith and hope; faith in knowledge, hope that each student can improve.

In everything we do we know that despair destroys our morale, and hope lifts us beyond ourselves.

*Hopelessness is the true condition of hell. On the other hand, hope is not wishful thinking, nor fanciful imagination. Hope is the realism of the man of faith who knows that there is a line of meaningful development from the past, through the present, into the future.*    JOSHUA O. HABERMAN

# To Love Is To Live

Nobody really wants to be an enemy; everybody wants to be a friend.

Sholom Aleichem, the perceptive Yiddish author, once described a child in a short story in the following way. He said the boy's expression seemed to cry out, *hob mich lieb,* "Love me!" This boy is an expression of all of us. We all hunger to be loved and this is the root of all human understanding.

If we could just take the time and the patience to listen to everyone's life story, if we would make the effort to understand that most strange behavior is the product of difficult life experience, then surely we would be moved to love and to want to help. This is the deeper implication of the thirty-six admonitions in the Torah to be kind to the stranger. We do not love naturally; we must learn to love. And once we have learned this, we can bring so much to others and the world.

Rabbi Rafael, a spiritual leader of a century ago, was on a journey. In the middle of the trip the rabbi asked his disciple to sit next to him in the carriage. The disciple declined saying, "I am afraid it will be too crowded for you." Rabbi Rafael affectionately answered, "Let us love each other more, then there will be room enough for both of us."

All of us all our lives are in need of love. We are all a little lonely. Other people's attitudes and habits may appear odd to us. But as long as no one is hurt, does it matter that people look different and act uniquely? Is not uniqueness and difference the right of every person? And, ultimately, if we could teach ourselves how to love each other more then there would be room enough for all of us in this world.

*If not love, why live?*                               IMMANUEL HAROMI

# Make An Offer

An offering is not truly worthy unless it be accompanied by the passion of a willing heart. Religion teaches us that the main gift is the sincerity of the offering and the depth of the feeling that accompanies it. Unless we can give freely and openly, until we can share warmly and lovingly, the gift is as naught.

If one wants to offer a prayer in memory of a dear one, it should be given from the heart. Casting a prayer into the vast universe must be motivated through a personal involvement. Thus, it is offensive to a sensitive religious conscience to believe for one moment that we can buy a prayer or that we can get someone else to pray for us.

The logic is all too obvious. No one can eat for you. No one can sleep for you. No one can learn for you. So how can anyone pray for you?

The year 1561 saw the publication of a wonderful Hebrew book entitled *Marpay Lanefesh,* written by an Italian rabbi named Raphael Norzi. *Marpay Lanefesh* means "the healing of the soul," and on the sixth page of that book this medieval rabbi said: "Anything done in sincerity and reverence of God, though it have nothing to do with Torah, will ensure us eternal life."

Therefore, each of us must search in his or her own heart; and as we are so moved, whether our prayer be offered twice a day, once a day, once a week, or even once a month, it must be prayed with the whole heart. Nothing less is acceptable as an offering to God Almighty.

*The Lord spoke to Moses saying, "Speak to the children of Israel that they make offerings, and accept an offering from every person whose heart so moves him."*    EXODUS 25:2

# No Gain Without Pain

In the techniques that modern medicine uses to treat people, progress is made only at the price of persistent strain. In physical rehabilitation we have to stretch the muscles in order to gain full use of them. In dealing with mental illness, we often have to face painful emotions and insights in order to find the way toward healing relationships.

These examples show us that the path to proper living is not strewn with roses but filled with rocks that have to be lifted out of the way. And even when there are roses along our path, when we reach to pick them we may be stuck with thorns and have to pause to pull them out of the flesh.

A physician once prescribed some pills for a young patient. The pills were coated with sugar to make them palatable. When the youngster failed to show any improvement, the puzzled doctor asked the mother whether the child had taken the medicine regularly. The mother was determined to watch her son when he took the pill. She noticed that the lad licked off the sugar coating with his tongue and then threw the pill down the drain. Now she understood why her child was not getting better.

Accepting only the sugar-coated parts of life and avoiding its bitterness will not yield strength. But, if we are willing to accept the pressures and the struggles along with the joys, we will live a healthy and successful life. Life will be good if we determine that, no matter what, we will achieve our worthiest and most honorable goals. Given this commitment, we will learn that the real miracle of existence is not what God does for us but rather what God inspires us to do for ourselves and others in spite of the pain and strain.

*The more valuable the thing, the more effort is demands.*
SAADIAH GAON

# Number One

Ultimately, each of us must solve personal problems for himself and herself. No two of us are alike. The marvel and wonder of the Hebrew Prayer Book is that it contains so much wisdom that it gives us the opportunity to select from it what each of us needs to meet our own personal concerns. Only we can know what bothers us; and, therefore, we must seek the solutions ourselves.

A psychiatrist visiting a state hospital was particularly intrigued by one patient who constantly sat huddled in a corner scratching himself for hours at a time. Finally the doctor approached the unfortunate man and asked quietly, "Would you like to tell me why you sit here all day scratching yourself?"

"Because," replied the man heaving a great sigh, "I'm the only one in the whole world who knows where I itch."

Only you know where that certain problem itches, only you know where that certain insult was intended, only you know when you could have helped and did not.

On the other side, only you truly know of the times when you gave and did not have to, when you shared without being asked, when you offered hope, unsolicited.

Most of our prayers are spoken in the plural form, and we worship in community. Yet we must realize that it is the individual that really matters. Their consensus makes for the community. But as a poet put it, "The single secret will still be the individual"—each of us suffering, hoping, praying, and giving.

*Offer your prayers and meditations not as a commandment of men learned by rote, for only prayers that express your own heart and mind can bring you near to your Father in heaven.*
              JONATHAN EYBESCHUTZ

# Do It!

When the first steamboat was being assembled, many said: "It won't work!" When the first automobile drove down the village street, there were catcalls of "Get a horse!" When wireless telegraphy was proposed, the sceptics said: "It is not practical." When yellow fever was first encountered, some medical personnel said: "It cannot be stopped!" When the airplane was first being designed, one critic wrote: "If God wanted people to fly, He would have given them wings." When some sensitive souls said human slavery ought to be abolished, the retort was: "There have always been slaves."

However, today we see that we have not only created a steamboat but dishwashers and rockets and vast heating plants. The automobile has replaced the horse as a means of transportation. Not only do we have wireless telegraphy, but radio telescopes have wireless contact with our whole solar system. We have stopped not only yellow fever but also polio and a hundred other diseases. We have succeeded in reducing human slavery and, although we are far from the goal, we have improved human rights in the world.

From these experiences we learn that if we desire to do something very deeply, despite what critics may say, we still can do it. Edward A. Guest, the popular American folk poet, said it this way:

> Just buckle in with a bit of a grin,
> Just take off your coat and go to it;
> Just start to sing as you tackle the thing
> That "cannot be done," and you'll do it.

*Fifty productive people are better than two hundred who are not.*
                                    JERUSALEM TALMUD, PEAH 8:8

# Unclaimed Deposits

Occasionally, a savings bank will run a newspaper advertisement that is required by law. It is usually headed in bold letters, "Unclaimed Deposits," followed by a long list of names and addresses of people in whose names various sums of money are on deposit but who for years have made neither deposits nor withdrawals. One wonders how it is possible for a person or his or her heirs to forget that there are assets due them on demand. But apparently hundreds of people do forget or are too lazy to make the effort, so ultimately the unclaimed money reverts to the state.

This neglect has a direct analogy to our spiritual and our cultural life. Is it not possible that we have deposited in our religious or cultural banks of experience and thought enormous assets that are ours simply for the asking? Is it not probable that we have access to vast riches in the past accumulation of artistic treasures, great heritages, untold wealth of wisdom that we simply are too lazy to claim? And when we do not, is it not sad that all these treasures revert back to the state of indifference?

In all of Jewish history, literature and experience we can find a range of resources and vast holdings in the form of musical, artistic, religious, and literary achievements. The interest belongs to us. The only point is that we have to make the effort to claim it. We have to go to the bank of Jewish knowledge and make the withdrawal. We must fill out the slip, whether it be in the form of adult education, Jewish reading, or a concern for what is happening throughout the Jewish world. It is all there just for the asking—redeemable on demand.

*Torah iz de beste schorah, "Learning is the greatest asset."*
YIDDISH PROVERB

171

# When The Server Is Served

The command to love the stranger is not only deeply ethical but it also enriches us emotionally. We accept as natural the fact that we will help our family and friends, but when we go beyond that, we derive a unique and satisfying pleasure from it. To help those near to us is only right, but to help those who are more distant from us is righteous. When we help the needy, the homeless, those who lack food or shelter, we feel a sense of inner peace.

A successful businessman in New York City was bored. He had all the money that he needed, and his work was no longer challenging. He became irritable and acutely depressed. His physician, being a very wise and practical man, ordered him to go to Grand Central Station, sit down, look around, and find someone who needed help. The executive felt foolish doing this, but since his doctor had recommended it he proceeded to carry out the assignment. As he was waiting in the railroad station, he suddenly saw an elderly woman sitting on her suitcase, weeping. The man went over to her and asked what her problem was. She replied that someone had not shown up to meet her. He found out where she was going, took her in his car and delivered her to her daughter's home. As soon as he left her, he rushed to the corner telephone, called his physician, and said, "Doc, it works! I feel better already."

Whenever we help someone else, often not necessarily someone near and dear but just a stranger—we find our lives fulfilled because we have supplied them with meaning. To put it in the words of a philosopher, "To live well we must have a faith to live by, a self fit to live with, and a cause to live for."

*Religion should have not only the sacrament of prayer but also the sacrament of social service.*   ISRAEL I. MATTUCK

# Patience For Peace

We must feel a deep attachment to peace but, more important, we must be willing to carry it through. We don't obtain peace by signing treaties, or by creating Fourteen Points, or writing reams of propaganda releases. We do it by setting our specific projects of cooperation, ways of living together, programs to implement what we deeply believe.

Winston Churchill, who probably knew more about war and peace than anyone else in our century, once made this statement: "I am looking for peace. I am looking for a way to stop war, but you will not stop it by pious sentiments and appeals. You will only stop it by making practical arrangements."

It is for this reason that we must be patient as the details of peace are being hammered out. Our pain in waiting is as nothing compared to the pain of realizing how many lives have been lost in wars. Those who died need not have died in vain, and we can prove this if we remember their sacrifices and commit our consciences to a concentrated concern for peace all over the world. And we must believe in it deeply or it will never occur.

A story that makes exactly this point is told of two American Indians talking in a foxhole during World War II. "Why is there another war?" asked one. "Why didn't they establish lasting peace after World War I?"

The other replied, "When white men gathered around the conference table to smoke peace pipe, nobody inhaled."

If we want to bring peace in the world, then we must join creativity and commitment to patience and practicality.

*A little known folksong ends with an important truth: "Peace in the world or the world in pieces."*   AMIEL WOHL

# The Wonder Of Woman

A scientist rushed madly into the main control room of the missile center at Cape Canaveral and proudly announced a new discovery. "Men," he shouted, "there are women on the moon." Another scientist asked how he could be sure. Replied the first scientist, "We shot a communications missile up there and got a busy signal."

Women today are in a sense busier than ever before. Now that much of the drudgery has been removed from their lives through technology, we understand that part and parcel of their purpose is essential to the entire business of life itself.

In the Bible we are told that when God created woman she was created *ayzer k'negdo*, as "a helpmate." A woman, according to the philosophy of the early chapters of the Bible, is not just a sexual being or only a mother; she is someone who helps in every aspect of civilizing human beings. In truth, a woman is civilization. It is men who make the roads, but it is the women who teach the children to walk on them. It is the men who make the living, but it is the women who make living worthwhile. It is the men who write the prayers, but it is largely the women who say them. In a recent church census it was found that seventy-five per cent of the people who attend worship services are women.

It is revealing that in one of the most trying moments of Jewish history, the head of the nation should have been a woman, Golda Meir. It was not only a tribute to her but a tribute to the people of Israel who were willing to accept leadership and other abilities wherever found.

We should not wish to lessen the fact of the biological and psychological differences between the sexes—indeed, we rejoice in them. But, women have much more power to help and heal our society than we have understood until now.

*Woman has a thousand souls.*                    YIDDISH PROVERB

# Time To Stop

The ultimate defeat of fear comes about through faith: Faith in ourselves that we can solve our problems and faith in God that He has given us the resources and the hope to solve those problems. Faith is not a magical device, but rather a sure scale against which to measure our fears. If fears are to be resolved, they must be seen in the perspective of a good God, a helpful society and a friendly universe.

When the French tyrant, Napoleon, started to move his powerful armies, all of Europe was in a state of fear and trembling. In Spain an embattled army under the Duke of Wellington was trying to resist his advance. One day a young lieutenant came into the British general's tent with a map clutched in his trembling hands and declaimed in near hysteria, "Look, General, the enemy is upon us!" "Young man," the General replied, "get larger maps, the enemy won't seem so close."

If we possess the larger map of faith, the great enemy of mankind, called fear, will not appear so close. The world has existed for millions of years and will continue to do so. People have solved their problems and will continue to do so.

Four decades ago, a great American President said, "The only thing we have to fear is fear itself."

Three centuries ago, a great New England governor said, "Here we feared a fear where there was no fear."

Over two millennia ago, a great Hebrew prophet said: "Fear not, nor be anxious for I am with you, for I am Your God" (Isaiah 41:10).

*You shall not be afraid of the terror by night, nor of the arrow that flies by day.*                    PSALMS 91:5

# The Map Of Faith

Very often when people are tormented by a personal problem, they will go to a friend and tell him or her all about their trouble. When they have completed describing it in detail, they often end up saying, "I have exhausted every resource. Now I don't know what to do; I have tried everything." At this point, a good and wise friend might suggest, "Well, don't try any more."

It sounds ridiculous, doesn't it? But if you think for a moment, you may find it a very simple truth. Sometimes we just try too hard. We become so zealous and so driving in our attempt to find a solution that we overlook the fact that the answer is within us.

You wonder, "Why am I running everywhere, but seem to be getting nowhere?" Then sit down quietly for several evenings and look deeply into your own soul. You will find the answer.

You are concerned about what is the best way to approach a family matter. Spend a weekend honestly examining your own feelings and you may come up with the answer.

You are bothered about how much responsibility you have toward your community. Then take the time to sift values and to weigh thoughts. Then by trusting your own conclusions you will live with ease of conscience.

The truth is that most of us react to problems rather than thinking about them and using our inner strength and ability to solve them. A retreat into the self may be the best way towards wisdom. Trust yourself—you are wiser than you know.

*It is depth of understanding, profoundness of thought that constitutes the best form of living.*    AZARIAH FIGO

# Preserving Life

An important and central value in Jewish life is *bal tashchit* (you shall not destroy). This means it is forbidden to destroy natural beauty, among other things. Jewish law deems it a transgression to waste natural resources. It is part of our heritage to understand that God's world is a gift to us. When we use a gift wisely and well, we reflect honor on the giver. But when we abuse a gift, we bring discredit and insult to the one who was thoughtful enough to give it.

As we wander through God's world, and as we move into the glories of outer space, we must be fully aware of the nature of our gift. We must be very careful that we do not destroy natural beauty as we have in the past—with detergents glutting our rivers and industrial wastes polluting our air.

We must *all* rededicate ourselves to preserving God's natural world. To litter is not merely to break a civil law but a religious one. To break branches wantonly is not a civil offense but a moral one. To fill the air with smoke may not violate a city ordinance, but it does violate a natural one. Therefore, let us unite to make this world—God's world—beautiful.

Henry Thoreau, the naturalist and author who invented the lead pencil and refused to patent and cash in on it, knew all the birds and enjoyed watching them. He took pictures of them, but he refused to shoot them because he said, "A gun only gives you the body, not the bird."

*Just as one must be careful not to destroy or injure his own body, so must he be careful not to destroy or injure his own environment. Whoever spoils anything that is fit for human enjoyment breaks the commandment, "You shall not destroy."*
ZALMAN SHNEOUR

# The Still Small Voice

England has tried out a worthwhile experiment. In British jukeboxes there is one selection that is used for silence. For a coin one can buy a few minutes of quiet, during which one can drink a cup of tea in relaxation. At last report, silence is number one on the British Hit Parade.

This points out that in our increasingly noisy world there is an increasing need for quiet. We are beginning to resent the sounds that bombard our ears, the shock waves of noise that batter our bodies.

Even more than this, we must realize that great periods of development and growth usually come not with crushing intensity but rather with calm quiet. Consider the flowers. Do they push their way up from the earth noisily, or is their work done in silence? When a bird builds a nest, is it with clamor or with quiet? When we think, we say we hear the wheels turning. But that is really a figure of speech, because deep thought is usually done in deep silence.

Einstein once indicated that the heart of religion is "to wonder and stand rapt in thought." He used to look at the universe and meditate about mathematics and matters of the spirit. And Moses went up on the mountain and lived there for forty days and nights alone in meditation before he came down with the Ten Commandments. From these two men of genius we can learn that creative social thought requires quiet. One does not develop ideas about the universe and man's place in it without first examining one's inner conscience. It is in the quiet recesses of the soul that we make our important decisions. So, true religion is not noise but rather a silence and an inwardness that precedes the taking of public stands and the making of commitments.

*And God was in the still small voice.*    I KINGS 19:11-13

# A Spiritual Pacemaker

Why is it that when someone is lying on the road in obvious need of help, some people will pass by with indifference until finally someone stops to help the victim? Why do some people simply walk by and why do some stop to help?

Motivated by this curiosity, not long ago two psychologists at Princeton University set up an experiment in which a person playing the part of the victim was lying on the street. The scientists observed the following: Of forty people who passed by, twenty-four did not turn aside from their path and one of them even stepped over the victim to continue on his way. The remaining sixteen did pause to see if they could be of help. But, the fascinating fact was that all forty reacted as a function of the rate of speed they had been maintaining. Those who were in a tremendous rush continued to move on quickly. Those who were walking at a moderate pace tended to hesitate. Those who were simply ambling along inevitably stopped.

Think about how this observation applies to our lives in a wider sense: When we have many things on our mind, we are less concerned about others. When we are in a rush to get somewhere, we tend to become careless about driving. When we are pressing toward our goals, we often neglect the feelings of those about us.

One of the great truths we may have to face is that our accelerated speed may very well be our undoing. Perhaps, the time has come to slow down the pace of our daily lives. Maybe those of us with religious "heart" trouble need a spiritual pacemaker to regulate our lives and keep us going in the right rhythm.

*The wisdom of a learned man comes through leisure and he who goes at a slow pace shall become wise.*    BEN SIRA 38:24

# A Harvest Of Hope

A three-sentence story in *The New York Times* put it all very well: "The first world war—everybody's fault. The second world war—somebody's fault. The third world war—my fault."

Ultimately, each of us as an individual is responsible and holds in balance the fate of the future. As a part of humanity, as a citizen of our land, as a member of the Jewish community, as an integral part of the family circle, as a neighbor, we matter and whatever we do changes something in the universe in some way.

A *midrash*, an oft-told Rabbinic parable which bears repeating, tells that the Roman Emperor Hadrian was once riding through the countryside in the land of Israel. He found an old man planting a fruit tree. He stopped and asked, "Old man, what sense is there in your doing this? It will take years until fruit appears!" Whereupon the old man answered, "If I am found worthy, I shall eat of it. If not, just as my ancestors toiled for me, so I am laboring for my children." A few years later when Hadrian passed that way again he found the old man and his family sitting under the tree enjoying its fruit.

The ancient lesson is clear and obvious. Let us work for the peace of all mankind, let us cultivate the teachings of morality and let us plant the seeds of good deeds in our daily life. If we are found worthy, we will enjoy their fruit. If not, then our children will have a harvest of hope.

*All of you are pledges for one another, the world exists through the merit of a single righteous man among you, and if one man sins the whole generation suffers.*

YALKUT SHIMONI, NITZAVIM

# How Deep Are Your Roots?

In the Talmud it is recorded that the great Rabbis of old used to utilize the outdoors as a natural classroom. Rabbi Yohanan taught in a vineyard, Rabbi Eliezer used to sit on a rock with his students gathered about him, Rabbi Akiba liked to lecture in the shade of a broad-leaved fig tree.

Once a young student came to Rabbi Akiba and said, "Teach me about faith." Rabbi Akiba showed him a tiny sprout and he said, "Pull it up." The young man did so quite easily with his fingers. Then the sage showed him a young sapling and told the young man, "Pull that one up." The lad did it with just a little more effort. Then he showed him a small shrub and asked him to remove it from the earth. With both hands and a little more strength, the young man tore it out of the soil. Finally, the rabbi showed him a full-grown tree and he requested, "Uproot it!" The student put his hands around the tree and pulled with all his might but he could not even shake a leaf. And Rabbi Akiba said, "Just so, my son, is it with faith. If our roots are deep, if our religion is grown and mature, no one can uproot it. Remember this, your faith will always be as strong and as powerful as are your roots."

And what is it that roots require? Roots demand cultivation and nurturing. They must continually be refreshed and cared for. Faith, in a similar manner, requires constant concern and nourishment. It requires our constant tending through study, thought and periodic recommitment. Roots in trees and in faith must not be neglected. They connect us with the nourishing earth and keep us growing ever upward.

*The stronghold of the wicked crumbles like clay, But the root of the righteous bears fruit.*     PROVERBS 12:12

# A Matter Of Timing

Has it ever occurred to you that every twenty-four hours in the natural state of living you accomplish prodigious feats?

Your heart beats 103,689 times.

Your blood travels 163,000,000 miles.

You breathe 23,240 times.

You eat 3½ pounds of food.

You turn in your sleep 25-35 times.

You speak 4,800 words.

You exercise 7,000,000 brain cells.

If within each of us there is so much potential power, then each of us must ask: What am I doing with my physical and emotional energy? Am I letting it remain idle and unproductive? Am I discharging it wastefully or even harmfully? Or, am I channeling it to its greatest possible effect?

Now, consider this: it just takes one heartbeat to perform an act of compassion. It takes just one breath to say, "I love you." It takes less than one ounce of food to energize an act of courage. It just takes a few words to speak a commitment. It takes a fraction of our brain cell capacity to think purposefully about social problems. Any of these acts can convert this day into the greatest day of your life. For, after all, what is greater than love, what is stronger than hope, what is more powerful than an idea whose time has come? We can experience all of these any day of our life that we choose to. The important thing is to realize our potential and then to act upon it. All of it is really a matter of timing.

A great pianist was once questioned by a reporter about the difficulty of playing the piano. He replied: "It is quite simple. All you have to do is to put the right finger on the right note at the right time. That's all."

*This is the day that the Lord has made. Let us rejoice and be happy in it.*
                                                                    PSALMS 118:24

# Compassion As Excellence

Excellence is a many-splendored thing. We usually think of it in terms of scholarship, but intellectual achievement is only one aspect of human experience and need. John W. Gardner in his book *Excellence: Can We Be Equal and Excellent Too?* warns us that "we need excellent plumbers as well as excellent philosophers or else neither our pipes nor our theories will hold water." We need creative musicians and artists, dedicated social workers and teachers, talented businessmen and athletes, good citizens and good community workers and, above all, devoted mothers and fathers. We need a sense of excellence in *compassion*. For if we educate a person in the mind but not in morals, then we are creating a menace to society.

Someone recently observed that the way we describe people today is different from the way we would have spoken of them in olden times. She said: "Today, we say Eisenhower the General, Johnson the Politician, and McNamara the Computer. But in times gone by we described men in humane terms like these: Richard the Lion-Hearted, Eric the Good, John the Kind."

This touches upon the core of a great contemporary concern. That is the fact that our value system has lost the traditional American emphasis on humanitarian values. Would it not be a wonderful thing if we could say the name of a person and add with pride: the wise, the creative, the community servant, the kind. All of us potentially have ability, but the only meaningful use of ability is that which helps others. The only ability that really matters is responsibility.

*The highest task of education is training for duty.*

BERTHOLD AUERBACH

# Sharing The Teachings

While the Torah was essentially written in the Hebrew language and was the direct responsibility of the Jewish people, it also has worldwide implications. The great concepts of morality, justice and peace all find their origins in the Bible. Because of this, the Bible is now available in 1,232 languages and dialects. Yearly some seventy million copies of the Bible are sold or given away throughout the world.

These are most impressive figures. But there is an even more startling observation. Most of the events recorded in the Bible occurred in an area only 200 miles long and 80 miles wide. The tiny land of Israel has had a stunning impact on the manners and the morals of the whole world. All of Western civilization is based on the Ten Commandments, and the rest of the world has somehow or other been touched by the words of the holy Hebrew books.

The noted religious skeptic Voltaire once said in Geneva, "In one hundred years the Bible will be a forgotten book found only in museums." And ironically, at the end of those hundred years, his house was occupied by the Geneva Bible Society! It will always and forever be thus, for what was given at Sinai and what was created in the land of Israel is a part of the conscience of mankind. But it is not enough to take pride in this heritage; more important, we must share it with the rest of the world. For this reason, we must not only study the Bible regularly but make it available to all those who seek it.

*The Torah was given publicly in the wilderness, in no man's land, so that Jews may understand its teachings are to be shared with others. Anyone wishing to accept it is welcome to it.*          MEKHILTA TO EXODUS 19:2

# The Face Of Freedom

Daniel Defoe, the author of *Robinson Crusoe*, writing about society, said: "Though I don't like the crew, I won't sink the ship. I'll do my best to save the ship. I'll pump, and heave, and haul, and do anything I can though he that pulls with me were my enemy. The reason is plain. We are all in the ship and must sink or swim together."

This is a lesson for our time. If we are interested in the welfare of people, if we want to improve our society, then we must be willing to work within the system in order to improve it. We must be willing to reason. We must be willing to compromise in order to introduce needed change. For if we refuse to do this, we set up conditions for destruction and disaster.

This is extremely pertinent to the problems of America today. When organizations or people want democratic change we should listen in the expectation that true dialogue will be possible. But the moment we move into non-negotiable demands and either/or choices, then we are begging for trouble.

What can we do? We still can work for the truth as we see it. We can determine our future by the way we vote. We can protest through gatherings, marches and petitions. We can refuse our presence or our money for causes we think are wrong. We can express our feelings in letters to the newspapers or to officials or organizations.

For many people are willing to change if it is sought in an orderly way within the system, and if their own rights are recognized. What we must do we can do if we do it in a democratic way.

*Democracy can face and live with the truth about itself.*
SIDNEY HOOK

# Climb Every Mountain

One reason a mountain was selected for the site of the giving of the Commandments is that a mountain provides people with real physical uplift and vision that corresponds to their inner aspirations and dreams. As we must climb to get to the top of the mountain, so we must climb to reach our own peak development. As mountains have a summit, so we, too, must have a goal towards which we move.

Once four men decided to climb a mountain. The first man wore new and expensive shoes which did not fit, so all he did on the climb was complain constantly that his feet hurt. The second man kept looking for a restaurant or a bar because all he wanted was a drink. The third saw the gathering clouds and he worried for fear it might rain. The fourth man kept urging the others on, saying over and over, "Wait 'til we get to the top. Push on! Push on!" When they reached the top, the fourth man turned to his three friends and said, "Isn't the view magnificent! Wasn't it worth the effort!" The others reluctantly admitted he was right.

It is worth the continued effort for people to climb mountains, both physically and intellectually. We should never be content with the life we have before us but always seek to keep moving with new aspirations. True, there are some moments in human endeavor when one must rest. Yet we must never forget that mankind is involved in a constant climb out of the valley of despair unto the hill of hope. The peaks achieved by great creative geniuses should inspire us in our time to move onward—and upward—with courage and daring.

*All the commandments were spoken at Sinai.*

SIFRA TO LEVITICUS 27:34

# The Way To Worship

Hymns, music and words are all necessary to worship, but that which is truly indispensable is a certain frame of mind, an attitude of sincerity. We must understand that everything else is a form of embellishment; sincerity is the heart of the matter. For it is only the honest heart that can enter into a dialogue with God.

We cannot step on people's heads and hope to raise ourselves to God. We cannot be dishonest and think that He will look into our hearts with blessing. We cannot hope to win Him over with flattery and smooth words. God is beyond all this, for God is absolute truth. One need not go to outer space or even to the great outdoors to find God, for He is to be felt right in the sanctuary of our own hearts. But if we do not have the right attitude, the proper spirit, then He will never appear to us anywhere.

The late President Franklin Delano Roosevelt was a devout churchgoer. Except when he was sick, he attended the local church of which he was a vestryman whenever he visited his home in Hyde Park. It is told that one such Sunday morning, when Roosevelt was ill, the minister of the church was awakened early by a phone call from a congregant who only attended sporadically. The question the caller asked was, "Will President Roosevelt be at services today?" And the minister answered, "No, but God will."

God is present everywhere, no matter who else is there or who else is not there. And if we seek Him sincerely, we will find ourselves in His presence, and find Him in our presence.

*Sincerity is a prerequisite of worship.*     DAVID OF TOLNA

# The Cultural Climate

Walt Whitman said many years ago of America: "Here is not merely a nation, but a teeming nation of nations." Rather than regarding our differences as a source of threat and fear, we should think of them as a bottomless reservoir of enrichment through diversity. Consider for a minute the diverse ethnic backgrounds that inspired some of our most popular musicals: "Fiddler on the Roof," based on warm Jewish family feeling; "Finnegan's Rainbow," with the lovely and lilting melodies of the Irish; "The King and I," the charm of Oriental society; and "Illya Darling," the delight of Greek music and dancing. Here is but one simple illustration of how we enjoy a richer culture because of our differences.

Each of us has the potential of developing our cultural uniqueness and contributing something to American life, just as we can value the cultural contributions of others.

A professor in an Eastern college asked each of the 141 freshmen in his class on American civilization to tell him how many of their grandparents were born in America. Only one member of the class had all four grandparents born here. He happened to be the only American Indian in the class.

All of us have come from other ethnic backgrounds. Each has something special to contribute . . . not the least, as the story reminds us, American Indians, who have their own history and culture. In our growing awareness of this culture, we learn to feel a respect for others which, in turn, gives them the self-respect to choose responsibly.

*We are a nation of immigrants. It is immigrants who brought to this land the skills of their hands and brains to make of it a beacon of opportunity and hope for all men.*
HERBERT LEHMAN

# The Inner Guidance System

Why do we attend synagogues? Not because anyone makes us, but because we want to express reverence for God and dedication to Judaism. No law on earth could make us worship but the law of love.

Why do we give to charity? Because of the dictates of conscience, not because of outside force.

Why does one uphold sexual morality? Because of one's sense of decency and feeling of family loyalty.

In all these instances, we see that morality is always more demanding than law. It is the heart of each person that moves him or her to ever higher levels of morality, the ultimate controls that guide a person's life.

There once was a man who had a beautiful garden and particularly fancied roses. He learned that in a nearby public park there grew a strain of roses that he did not have in his garden. One morning, he awoke early and asked his son to accompany him to the park where he would fulfill his cherished dream. As they came closer to the plants, the boy suddenly understood the purpose of the trip. The father first looked to the left and then to the right, and then he bent down to remove the plant.

Suddenly, the boy said, "Father, you forgot something, didn't you?" "What?" asked the father. And the boy replied, "You forgot to look up."

This is the difference between the law of man and the law of God. One has us look from side to side; the other has us look up.

*And the wind, not the mast, drives the ship on the sea; not the rhyme makes the song, but the deep thought in me.*

ABRAHAM REISEN

# Curb Your Anger

We must try to exercise every caution and restraint so that others who are innocent do not become the targets for our terrible feelings. As we would not want to be wounded by angry words, so we must try our best not to inflict suffering on others.

It is for this reason that we must find safe ways to release our pent-up emotions. We must recognize negative feelings when they begin to stir within us and must consciously seek avenues to release our fears and our frustrations. There is a wonderful example of this principle in the life of Abraham Lincoln. Lincoln once read to a member of his Cabinet a harsh letter he had written in answer to an attack upon his integrity. When he finished reading it, the President tore the letter into shreds. "Why did you do that?" asked the astonished Cabinet official. "I never send such letters," Lincoln replied. "I just write them to blow off steam."

There are some obvious ways that we have in our society to blow off steam: sports, political campaigns, hammering together a bookcase, scrubbing the kitchen floor. One reason that spring cleaning comes at the end of winter is to give us the opportunity to find physical outlets for our pent-up feelings. We can also let out our anger on the handball court, new projects or campaigns in the business world and even politics and poker. And religion, too, with its regularized prayers and rituals, can help us channel our energies for constructive purposes.

We must all find ways to discharge harmlessly our angers and our frustrations. This is an important way to healthy and sane living.

*All Hell rules over the person who is angry.*     NEDARIM 22a

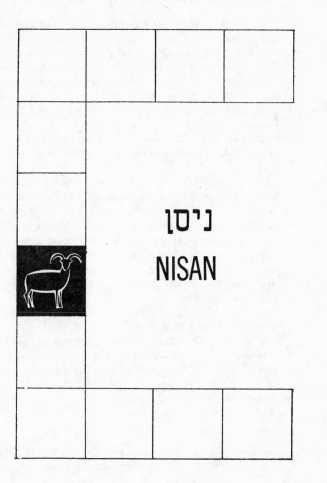

ניסן

NISAN

# Does God Believe In You?

An article in the *Jerusalem Post* demonstrates the courage of character based on God. Alfonso Boaron lost both legs when a guerrilla mine blew up the taxi he was driving. Instead of wallowing in self-pity, he determined to be self-sufficient. Fitted with artificial legs, he walks and drives again. He asks no special help. He said his faith in God gave him the will to carry on. This is a truly religious person.

We may well ask, where is God found today? The answer is that the God Who entered the huts of Pharaoh's slaves in Egypt is working for freedom and opportunity in the ghettos today. The God Who spoke at Sinai to Moses is the God Who is with the Israel of today. The God Who spoke to Adam and told him that all men are one is the same God working in the world councils through people who are willing to take every setback and every devious dealing and still persevere in their work for peace and harmony. God will always appear where people of good will, of good faith, and good hope will let Him in—or better still—let Him work through them.

On a classroom blackboard a theology professor was amused to find this message: "God is dead!" signed, "Nietzsche." The class watched him and waited for his response. So he picked up a piece of chalk and wrote underneath: "Nietzsche is dead!" and he signed the message, "God." And so the ultimate question is not, do you believe in God? But, does God believe in you?

*"You are My witnesses that I am God" (Isaiah 43:12) When you are My witnesses, I am God; when you are not My witnesses, I am—as it were—not God.*

MIDRASH TEHILLIM 123:2

# Fair Is Fair

Often we are disillusioned when we read of incidents in the lives of great and idealistic leaders which seem inconsistent with their moral pronouncements. But we must realize that all of us—no matter how great—must struggle all our lives against overwhelming impulses. Rather than judge others smugly, we should recall the Talmudic proverb that teaches: "Do not judge a person until you have stood in that person's place."

The point is that all of us must struggle with problems. Our truly great heroes had such problems but overcame them, finding ways through great idealism to help their people. Thus in Jewish history we find that Moses was not permitted to enter the Promised Land because of an incident in which he acted incorrectly. But Moses failed to realize his life's dream *not* because he was a bad person but simply because he was human. He made mistakes. With great pain, the Bible points out that he was neither a saint nor a sinner. And taking him as model, we are to understand that we, too, are neither saints nor sinners but simply human beings trying the best way we know to live our lives and meet our responsibilities.

Oliver Cromwell was once having his portrait painted and the artist asked, "How should I do you, Mr. Cromwell?" And he replied, "Paint me, warts and all." We all have our spiritual warts. We are, indeed, a mixture: good and bad, hateful and loving, malicious and kind, intransigent and compassionate. But, we must strive with all our might through idealism and through rationality to control our base impulses and emphasize our positive characteristics. And when we judge others, let us judge them as we would wish to be judged—with understanding.

*Judge your neighbor fairly.*　　　　　　LEVITICUS 19:15

# Five-Finger Exercise

We can take any human action, any human event, any physical property—in fact, anything on this earth—and make it holy or sacred. For example, drugs can be used to demean and destroy or they can be used to help and heal. A piece of cloth can be used to tie someone's hands in a robbery or to bind up a wound. Words can be used to crush or to console. A knife can be employed to hurt or, as a scalpel, to cure. Bricks can be fashioned into a prison or a school. Thus we, ourselves, determine what we want to make of ourselves and our world.

Several years ago, *Life* magazine ran an interesting article on Willie Sutton, the notorious bank robber. The article told how he spent many years exercising his fingers in order to train them to open locks of houses and banks. The writer then went on to observe that a man named Mischa Elman, who was born in the same year as Willie Sutton, spent years on finger exercises in order to get the finest and richest tones out of the strings of his violin. Both worked hard. Sutton ended up serving a jail sentence, while Elman delighted the ears of thousands of listeners. Sutton brought calamity to himself and others, while Elman enriched the lives of his fellows.

All of us will have such opportunities, though they may not be as dramatic. If we alert ourselves to watch for them, we can turn them to good purpose. We can do as we wish with our lives. Life can be a source of harm or a source of harmony, and hence of holiness.

*Holiness is every man's privilege. This democracy of holiness is one of the magnificent emotions of the Jewish religious genius.*                    DAVID DE SOLA POOL

# Our Own Bag

The present situation in Jewish life in America is to a great extent of our own making. If there is confusion about Jewishness in our children, it is to a high degree a reflection of our own ambivalence toward Jewishness. Can a child be required to attend services if his or her parents do not come fairly regularly? Should a young person be lectured on Jewish responsibilities by his elders who neglect or even reject their responsibilities toward strengthening the synagogue and the Jewish community? Can we preach the high ethical truths of Judaism if we do not practice these principles daily?

There is the story of a tall and husky movie actor who arrived in Kenya to play the title role in a jungle picture entitled, "Tarzan the Magnificent." A group of small African boys gathered about him, all asking to carry his luggage. He chose as a "porter" one skinny little fellow who stared up at him with awe. "You big!" the boy said. The movie star nodded. "You big like tree," the boy said. "You got arms like tree trunks." The actor smiled modestly. "You must be strong as lion," the boy observed. The star beamed proudly and admitted that he was quite strong. The boy then turned and walked away as he said over his shoulder, "You carry your own luggage."

Jews in America are strong and powerful. Some say American Jewry is the most powerful Jewish community in history. We ought to carry our own Jewish responsibilities. It is our own bag. Once we start to do this, our children will follow. We must, therefore, take our personal stake in Judaism seriously.

*Help and respect can come to a people only through self-help and self-respect.*　　　　STEPHEN S. WISE

# It Is Up To You

When Jan Paderewski, the great Polish pianist, tried in his younger years to play the piano, his instructor said, "You have stubby fingers. Try the cornet." He bought a cornet and went to a master who said, "You don't have the lip for it." In desperation, he went for advice to Anton Rubinstein who said, "Young man, you might be able to play the piano. In fact, I think you can, if you will practice seven hours a day." Following this word of hope and life, he began the step-by-step process of becoming one of the greatest performers in music.

All of us all day long, as we face ourselves and as we face the world, have the opportunity to increase our well-being. It is so simple. One word of praise can make, quite literally, all the difference in the world. As it is written in Proverbs 16:24, "Encouraging words are as honey, sweet to the soul, and health to the being." A teacher's word can make or break a student. A parent's praise can lift or drop a child. An employer's judgment can be given gently or caustically. A friend can bring hope or harm. These things are very real and very important. All of them come out of the heart of a choice and a faith. Faith in one's self and faith in others, choosing a way of being that celebrates life—these make happy and productive human beings.

Given this understanding, we must constantly emphasize the positive and eliminate the negative. Negative feelings frustrate, deny and destroy, not only opportunities for fulfillment, but the life-giving impulse itself. On the other hand, positive expressions, encouragement, hope, help the individual to realize himself and affirm the meaning of life.

*I call heaven and earth to witness this day: I have put before you life and death, blessing and curse. Choose life that you and your offspring may live.* DEUTERONOMY 30:19

# Creation Is Continuous

Creation is a part of everyday living. The daily wonders of God can be seen in the birth of a baby, the budding of the trees, the varieties of the birds and the infinite glory of the growing flowers. Creation may also be reflected in the endeavors of the artist who continually seeks to add beauty to life even as the creative person desires to deepen the experience and meaning of life itself. This thought was given fine expression by Rabbi Abraham J. Heschel in his book, *The Sabbath*. "Creation, we are taught, is not an act that happened once upon a time, once and for ever. The act of bringing the world into existence is a continuous process. God called the world into being, and that call goes on."

It is this call that should continually summon us to become more creative in our daily living. We should seek the newness to be found in every moment. To reject opportunities for exciting experiences and new possibilities for living with fulfillment is to deny the very essence of the meaning of creation. This does not mean a frenzied pursuit of novelty and stimulation. What it requires is trying to look at one's life in a new way, to be receptive to new ideas. The most creative adventures take place in *inner* space.

Upon some ancient excavated Assyrian tablets, a series of curses was found. The last curse was: "May nothing new happen to you." When we try only the banal we become bored, but with discovery we add to our lives the blessing of seeing God's lovely creations anew in the world. The world about us and the world inside us offer infinite opportunities for creating and living. So look alive.

*We must implant firmly in our hearts the understanding that creation is a continuous process.*

MENAHEM BEN MOSES HABAVLI

# Earned Interest

Two elderly people in a nursing home were having a conversation. One said, "I didn't sleep well last night. My head aches, my digestive system is upset and my ankles are swollen." The other replied, "Let's face it, aging is not for sissies."

Real illness deserves our full concern, the best of treatment and, if necessary, institutional care. But if it is only an imagined or exaggerated device for attention-getting, the person must face up to the fact that we get attention not because we demand it, but because we truly earn it. Moreover, creative aging should mean keeping active and involved. It means that to be loved, one must be lovable.

The need for developing outside interests in retirement can be a matter of life and death. Older citizens must resist the temptation to withdraw into themselves and grumble at the world. They must be literally outgoing. The world is filled with men and women who did their best work and began to enjoy life most fully in their older years.

Oliver Wendell Holmes started to learn Greek when he was eighty. When he was ninety and saw a pretty woman passing by he was heard to say, "Oh, to be seventy again." That is the spirit that keeps one alive to the end, for age is not measured by revolutions of the earth about the sun, but in challenges accepted and achieved, pleasures created and shared, love given and reciprocated. A person whose mind remains flexible and humorous, whose spirit keeps resourceful and alert, will not only live all his or her life but will also depart this world in grace and peace knowing that one's memory will be honored and extolled.

*There is nothing more enviable than to have an old head and a young heart.*
                                                    DANIEL SANDERS

# Person To Person

One of the great purposes of law is to protect people; to help the individual, and to preserve not only the sacredness but the welfare of each human life. The importance of every person is an unchanging eternal fact of life as well as of religion. People are the ultimate values in this world; everything else comes second.

No matter who we are or where we are or what we do, it is the person that should determine our thoughts and our actions. When a physician is about to operate, he is not merely cutting into flesh or dissecting a body, he is treating a living person. When a lawyer is involved in a legal matter, he should think of his client not as just a case, but as a human being. Almost every undertaking in this world could be improved if we would but be aware that we are dealing not with things or decisions or programs, but rather with persons.

We should struggle to maintain this awareness even more fully in our technological, computerized and automated society, which tends to obliterate the person. All of us tend to forget that the essential purpose of living is to make ourselves truly human.

A secretary at an airline office in Washington, D.C., recently was heard to answer the phone: "Our automatic answering device is away for repair; this is a person speaking." Let us resolve to speak as a person to other persons. And in the last analysis we must also listen carefully, because in every case "a person is speaking."

*The welfare, right, and honor of every individual, even the lowest, is the community's concern.*    FRIEDRICH J. STAHL

# The Ideal And The Real

There is a close relationship between the mind and the body, the emotions and the person. In the totality of life we cannot isolate one aspect of a human being and still understand him or her as a human being. Similarly, thought must not be isolated from action. Ideas are essentially meaningless unless we give them some concrete form of expression. Learning must be followed by doing or the learning has no practical meaning.

This is the essential philosophy of Judaism. And that philosophy can be summed up in the word *mitzvah*, which means "deed." Most of our rituals are involved with doing something. On the Sabbath we do not just pray but we gather as a family around the Sabbath table, we light candles, we recite the *Kiddush* over wine—we literally do things. The *Seder* is not just prayer but also participation in many activities, not the least of which is the eating of a festive meal. Judaism emphasizes *tzedakah*, which means "charity" or "community responsibility" in an active and realistic manner.

A stout man once took up tennis. He was explaining to a friend just how he went about the game. "My brain immediately barks out a command to my body. 'Run forward, but fast!' it says. 'Start right now! Drop the ball gracefully over the net and then walk back slowly.' "

"And then what happens?" he was asked.

"And then," replied the stout man, "my body says, 'Who—me?' "

Good intentions are not enough. Now is the time for us to follow our good intentions with suitable actions.

*Busy yourself as much as possible with study of divine things, not merely to know them but to do them.*

MOSES OF EVREUX

# God's Frozen People

*Shabbot Hagadol*, the Great Sabbath, is so named because we use this Sabbath to prepare for Passover. For example, on this Sabbath afternoon we are instructed to review the *Hagadah* in preparation for the *Seder* Service. In the Morning Service, there is also a special prophetic reading which heralds the advent of the Passover holydays.

This Sabbath is a signal that Pesah is only a few days away, and Pesah always comes at just the right time of the year. It always arrives as the symbol of spring. The winter is hard. We are landlocked and the freeze lasts a long period of time. In a sense, our emotions become hardened and our sense of pespective becomes blocked. We are frustrated as we look out at the world.

It is exactly at this time when we have this mood of frustration and frozen feelings that Pesah comes to remind us that winter is just about over. At the *Seder* the use of the green parsley is a symbol of the freshness of the coming of spring. During Passover we read from *The Song of Songs*: (2:11-12): "For, lo, the winter is past . . . the flowers appear on the earth and the time of singing is come."

With the rebirth of nature, faith is rekindled, joy returns to our lives and we feel like singing. The blooming of the flowers, the cheerful chirping of the birds, the gladness of the sunshine, is an irresistible message of hope and good cheer. It is as if God performed for us another act of the drama of creation. The spring is the easiest time of the year to believe in God as we witness the powers of recreation.

*In the winter the earth is pregnant. It bears within itself a great secret. In the spring the secret is disclosed.*

NAHMAN OF BRATZLAV

# To Be Content With One's Lot

Courage is one of society's most honored values. The British give their finest medal, the Victoria Cross, for "extraordinary bravery in the presence of the enemy." The French award, the coveted Croix de Guerre, is given for outstanding "acts of bravery." In the United States the highest decoration, the Congressional Medal of Honor, is presented for "gallantry above and beyond the call of duty." In civilian life, the Carnegie Medal is given for "heroism for voluntarily risking one's life in extreme danger." These great honors attest to the high value we place upon courage.

These awards have all been designed to recognize outstanding heroism in unusual situations that are dangerous and challenging, though rare. But there is also a different kind of courage, a courage we tend to neglect. Why not give an award to those who have the courage to be happy? happy?

National heroes deserve all sorts of recognition for their single dramatic acts of bravery. But we should also extol the sustained, consistent kind of courage that involves many small acts over a long period of time. Real courage is nothing less than the power to overcome danger, misfortune, fear, and injustice, while continuing to affirm inwardly that life with all its sorrows is good, and that experience is meaningful even if for the moment it is beyond our understanding. The courage to be happy, despite all the problems and pains of life, is a deeply religious virtue and should be honored among other values and achievements.

*Who is well-off? He who has the ability to be happy with his lot in life.*
                                                                    AVOT 4:1

# Wait A Minute

Before we do anything we first ought to stop and think about God. This is particularly so in terms of the good things in life. In trouble and in anguish we turn to God, but so often we forget about Him in pleasure and in plenty. The Bible tells us that upon good fortune, we should remember to pause and express our gratitude.

An old farmer, after taking care of some business at a neighboring estate, was asked to stay for lunch. Noting that his well-to-do companions began immediately to eat, the old man bowed his head and quietly said grace for himself. When he looked up the host asked, "Do many of the people around here follow such an oldfashioned custom?"

"Most do," replied the old farmer.

"This must be a more backward area than I thought when I bought this place," remarked the gentleman in a bantering tone. "Isn't there anyone nearby sufficiently enlightened not to parade their prayers at the table?"

The old man thought a moment and said, "Well, I reckon there are some over at my place who never pray over their food."

"College graduates, no doubt?"

"No, sir," said the farmer, "my pigs."

Prayer is one thing that distinguishes a human being from an animal. A human being takes a moment to say a prayer before he or she partakes of the goodness of God. Upon coming home and finding the family healthy and safe, one expresses thanks to the Almighty. A person who is blessed with material possessions does not take them all for granted but lets his or her gratitude speak for him or her.

*The first step of all wisdom is reverence for the Lord.*
PROVERBS 9:10

# More Beyond

Judaism is distinguished by a commitment to search and exploration. From the Jewish point of view, life is not necessarily a fixed map but rather a quest on an open road.

One finds this restless searching in many aspects of Judaism, but it is revealed in a most unusual custom which is observed on the night before Passover. The ceremony of *bedikat hametz* is the final search for leavened bread before the holiday begins. The ancient Rabbis interpreted this as the search for self-improvement. It is part of the human desire to explore the inner and outer world for ways to better life.

In the Middle Ages it was the custom for a city to adopt a motto. A city in Portugal chose as its theme: *Ne Plus Ultra*, "Nothing More Beyond." That is because they believed that Portugal was the end of the world. Then, one day, a man named Columbus questioned the validity of that motto. He sailed out and found a New World. When he returned, a conference of the city fathers was called and they changed the motto to read: *Plus Ultra*, "More Beyond."

This really is the story of all great adventurers of the mind: Of Copernicus who taught us that the sun and not the earth is the center of our solar system, of the Wright brothers who proved that people could fly, of Sigmund Freud who found new ways to understand the human psyche, and of others like them. The list of such explorers is endless. Everything in this world that has enlarged and ennobled us is the result of people who live by this motto: *"Plus Ultra!"* "There is yet more beyond!"

*If you're told: "I searched and didn't find," believe not; "I didn't search and I found," believe not; "I searched and found," believe.*                    MEGILLAH 6b

# Ask, Ask

The words of the *Haggadah* that stay with us most vividly are *mah nishtanah*, "Why is this night different?" It is interesting that this very important evening service in the Jewish year begins with a question. Usually, a statement of faith is couched as an assertion of positive conviction and belief. But here we begin with a question. This is because, as Socrates well knew, asking and answering questions is the best way to learn. When we say things that others have said before, we are only repeating and adding nothing to human knowledge. But when we ask questions, we begin to discover new facts, to awaken new thoughts, to plumb the depths of the human mind. As a matter of fact, one significant way that man differs from the animal is that he asks himself questions. An animal eats, drinks, carries on the rest of his actions, and simply exists. On the other hand, a man lives because he keeps asking himself about the *meaning* of things and events: Why is the sky blue? Why do I feel this way? What should I do?

So it follows that in dealing with people it helps to open up relationships by asking questions rather than stating opinions. Instead of saying emphatically, "You cannot stay out after midnight!" it is wiser to ask, "How late do you think a teenager like you should be able to stay out at night?" In hiring an employee, teaching a student, helping a person in distress, it is first necessary to find out where they are before deciding where you want them to go.

In human relationships, closeness and warmth only occur when we *ask* about one another, when we are concerned about one another, when we seek to know how we can help one another. Until we ask, we will never know.

*One who persists in inquiring will in the end be exalted.*

BERAKHOT 63b

205

# Exodus

It is interesting that every time we recite the evening *kiddush* we add the words *zaykher liyetziat mitzrayim,* "in remembrance of the exodus from Egypt." We say these words not only on Passover but on every Sabbath and festival. And because Jews have remembered, they were the only people in history to return after 2,000 years of exile to reclaim and rebuild a homeland.

In 1946 a special Anglo-American Commission of Inquiry was created by President Harry S. Truman and Prime Minister Clement Attlee to hold hearings on the possibility of creating a Jewish state. The first person to appear before the twelve commissioners was David Ben-Gurion, then Chairman of The Jewish Agency. The statement he made before them contains a profound observation about Jewish history. In effect he said this:

"Three hundred years ago, the *Mayflower* sailed for America. That was a great event for Americans. But other than historians, who remembers the sailing date, the number of passengers or the food served?" Then Ben-Gurion pointed out that more than 3,300 years ago the Jews left Egypt. He said, "Nearly every Jew knows that event occurred on the fifteenth day of Nisan. We know the Jews ate *matzah*. We know the very words spoken." He concluded, "Gentlemen, it is the nature of the Jew to remember the source of his being."

Jews have survived as a creative group because they take the time to remember and revere their history. Because they remember their past, they are prepared to carry their responsibilities in the present and the future.

*All those who dwell at length on the exodus from Egypt are indeed praiseworthy.*                                    HAGGADAH

# The Daily Count

During the period between Passover and Shavuot, we are instructed to number the days seven times, seven weeks: "And you shall count *every day* for seven full weeks and on the fiftieth day it shall be for you Shavuot." The Torah is telling us in effect that as we count every day, every day must be made to count; for every day that we live has a special purpose, and a special meaning.

Many of us think that to achieve anything worthwhile in our lives we must make special efforts at special times on special days. But this is not really so. Real fulfillment is achieved only by making *every* day count.

Consider the art of loving, for example. Most of us think of love on the day of our marriage, on an anniversary date, or on a birthday. But actually, those days are merely artificial times when we formally express our love. Love would not mean very much if we did not tend it and water it every single day.

Several years ago, a teenaged Canadian girl, Barbara Ann Scott, won the skating championship in the winter Olympics. Many a teenager must have read the story of her triumph and envied the acclaim she received. Barbara estimated that in preparation for the event she practiced daily until she had averaged 1,000 hours a year. Imagine— thousands of hours of daily preparation for this one event! Small wonder that she won. She had talent, but in addition she had made that talent count every single day of her life.

Those of us who wish to achieve anything worthwhile in our lives must pursue with intensity daily what we value and what we would achieve.

*An honest man keeps a strict account of his days so that he can spiritually balance his books.*     AZRIEL HILDESHEIMER

# Don't Let It Sour

Very often Rabbinic literature uses a play on words to make a telling point. A wonderful illustration is the advice: *mitzvah shebaah leyadekha al tahmitzenah.* "If an opportunity to do a *mitzvah*—a good deed—appears before you, do not postpone it." The Hebrew word for "postpone" is *tahmitzenah* which means "do not let it become *hametz.*" Or, to put it in our language, "don't let it sour."

This is something that we might well consider not only during the week of Pesah, but every day of our lives. So often when we have the chance to do or say something worthwhile, we let it pass and find ourselves saying regretfully later, "If only I had done it."

If you have something nice to say, say it now. If a child does something good, compliment him or her now and not later. If someone in the community achieves something, send a note now, not later. And how much better to say loving things to your friends and family now—while they can still hear them—rather than saving your praises for a eulogy. If you have time and money to give, give some of it now. As the *Sabbath and Festival Prayer Book* tells us:

"He who gives when well, his gift is gold;

He who gives only when ill, his gift is silver;

He who gives only in his will, his gift is copper."

When we delay a gift, it turns sour; but when we give it now it is fresh as newmade bread.

*If there is goodness in life and beauty in the world to share, do it now. If there lies within you the possibility of a contribution to make the world better, don't postpone it or perhaps you'll never do it."*

PHILIP BERNSTEIN

# Men Must Be Mutual

It is told that Rabbi Asher, a great Jewish scholar, used to busy himself directly with the baking of *matzah*. His hands would become sticky, his rabbinical robe coated with flour, and his shoes smeared. One of his congregants was very disturbed that this great rabbi should leave his books and his meditations to do something that ought to be left to housewives. The congregant approached Rabbi Asher and said, "Why do you demean yourself with such activity?" And the rabbi answered, *"Kol adam tzarikh letapayl hu b'atzmo bamitzvah"* ("It is proper that every person becomes directly involved in the *mitzvah* of baking *matzah"*).

This celebration of direct action is part not only of the Passover concept but of the whole Jewish tradition of involving ourselves in the world around us. If we want flowers to grow, we must put our hands in the soil and get them dirty. If we want a better Jewish community, here and throughout the world, we must take on added responsibilities though they burden us. If we want justice in America and the world, we must not abandon our commitments to our democratic ideals. If we want our families to remain mutually loyal and helpful and strong, then we must sometimes be forthright, at the cost of unpleasantness and even personal abuse. Involvement is the road to fulfillment; it is a hallmark of being truly human.

But each of us must understand this truth not merely in an abstract general sense, but in a concrete personal way. For continuous personal involvement is the essence of a good personal life and the basis for a good society.

*Emotional isolation of man from man is the parent of tragedy.*      JOSHUA LOTH LIEBMAN

# The Power Of Pesah

Pesah comes to tell us that though a people be enslaved for hundreds of years, yet they may still know liberation. According to the most conservative historical estimates, the Jewish people lived in concentration camps and slave labor compounds in Egypt for 210 years, and yet they were eventually liberated. Indeed, the first of the Ten Commandments begins with, "I am the Lord your God Who brought you out of the land of Egypt, out of the house of bondage." This is the signature of faith, for ours is a God of freedom.

God *does* care, even though His message be slow in coming. There is a divine concern for those who are oppressed, for those who suffer, for those who are enslaved. Pesah is positive proof that freedom is yet possible. As we experience Pesah, each of us can be inspired to rededicate himself or herself to the cause of freedom. We know nothing is hopeless in the affairs of human beings and that eventually compassion and justice will prevail.

The late John F. Kennedy said it very well in one of his last addresses: "The irresistible tide that began centuries ago is for freedom and against tyranny. That is the wave of the future—and the iron hand of totalitarianism can ultimately neither seize it nor turn it back. A single breaker may recede, but the tide is coming in."

Pesah is the expression of that tide and of that hope.

*The prophets and psalmists employ the great historical event of Pesah to give reality chiefly to the religious idea of God's providence and grace. The rabbis deduce from it the two fundamental elements of man's ethical education: the notion of liberty and the notion of man's ethical task.*

MORITZ LAZARUS

# What Are We Going To Do?

The Bible must be constantly studied because it has relevance and meaning for every age and time. A very interesting World War II story dramatically makes the point. The Gestapo once conducted a raid on the offices of the Norwegian Bible Society. When they entered with drawn guns, the Nazi terrorists demanded, "Have you got any Jewish books here?" The secretary of the Society answered very calmly, "We have nothing but Jewish books here. Look around you." And he waved toward his shelves of Bibles as if to say, "and what are you going to do about it?"

The question "What are you going to do about it?" is something that touches not only terrorists but also traditional Jews. What we must do about it is study it, ponder it, and live by it. The Bible is truly a revolutionary book. We must remember that the exodus from Egypt was a revolutionary movement. But, then, it is always this way when someone reads the Book of Exodus and truly lives by it. Those who read the Bible cannot help but be touched by it. It was Horace Greeley who once observed, "It is impossible to mentally or socially enslave a Bible-reading people."

Indeed, the Bible has been a force in almost every struggle for freedom and inspiration to those who advance the cause of human rights. That is why we must continually study it. For only when we take the time to think through again and again the teachings of the Bible can we make it meaningful to our own time and our own situation. Every serious and thoughtful study of the Bible leaves us with the question: "What are we going to do about it?"

*This book of the law shall not depart out of your mouth, but you shall meditate on it day and night, that you may be careful to do according to all that is written in it.*

JOSHUA 1:8

211

# The Purpose Of Passover

Pesah activates us, it literally puts us to work. Think of all the things we have to do. We have to clean the house and change the dishes, order the *matzah* and wine, invite the family, make sure that the youngest knows the Four Questions, buy baby a new pair of shoes, and so on. The *Seder* itself makes participants of us all. Mother has to cook the meal, father has to lead the *Seder*, everybody has to sing, everybody must eat the *matzah* and all the other foods.

Aside from motivating and energizing us, the Passover observance teaches us an important lesson: All of us must participate in the great drama of liberation, all of us must share in creating a better society, all of us must move from inaction into action if we are to better the world. As one wit put it: "You may be on the right track, but if you just sit there you'll be run over."

Finally, Pesah is a way of making vivid to our senses our ancient trials and historic purpose. The *Seder*, with its symbolic foods, enables the Jew to relive and recreate his past. Israel Zangwill correctly said, "On Pesah the Jew eats history." He literally ingests the bread of affliction, and so the meaning of freedom becomes a part of the very marrow of his bones. Jews have always known what it means to suffer. The *Seder* simply presents the story of this suffering and of redemption—in a way that makes us feel it with all our senses. We hear the crackling of the *matzah*, we taste the *haroset*, we smell the sharpness of the horseradish, we feel the Haggadah in our hand, and our eyes take in the entire scene of Jews actively recreating their tradition. Through this personal involvement a Jew senses completely the meaning of Passover and the underlying message of freedom.

*The Seder nights tie me with centuries before me.*

LUDWIG FRANK

# Dealing With Death

One of the greatest fears that a person faces is death. Some people try to deny it through various means. Others try to create an illusion of immortality by building pyramids or other monuments. Jews face death realistically and treat it as a natural termination of life. Jewish tradition urges that the fact of death is good reason to learn how to appreciate life, treasure existence and make the most of each day.

Jews of the Bible faced death resolutely and learned through this honest confrontation to live with patience, courage, sympathy and dignity. They developed a sense of faith in the natural order of things and a trust in God and His superior wisdom.

An old story makes this very point. One day a peasant took his little son to a village nearby. Along the road they came to a swift stream which was spanned by a rickety old bridge. It was a bright, sunny day; the father and son made the crossing without mishap. It was dusk when they started on their homeward journey. The boy remembered the stream and the rickety old bridge and became afraid. The father, noticing his anxiety, lifted him and carried him in his arms. The boy fell fast asleep as his father carried him over the bridge and all the way home. As the sun of a new day streamed through the window of his bedroom, the boy awakened and discovered he was safe at home. So God brings us through the valley of the shadow of death.

*I, Dorothy Ruth, am in this ground*
*Roots and rich soil close around,*
*Growth, creation, taking and giving*
*So life was death and death is living.*

DOROTHY KAHAN BAR-ADON

# The Just Society

The responsibility for a just society falls not on society in general but upon the individual person. You and I, each of us, must feel a sense of personal involvement or we will not have a just society.

Recently a woman wrote that she no longer listens to the news on television. As soon as the newscast begins, she turns it off. She explained that she could no longer bear to see the pictures of the refugees in the world and then she added, "I do not want to become personally involved." One thinks of all the newspaper stories of muggings and assaults which bystanders watch without lifting a finger to help.

Well, if things that are unjust happen in the world and we do not want to become personally involved, how will we ever help to create a world of sanity and peace? If everybody adopts this attitude and no one feels a sense of obligation, then will not society revert to a jungle?

Justice results not from a casual involvement but passionate activity. It means not just feeling for the victim of injustice but actually doing something about it. It is not just reading about a social problem but rather speaking up about it. The emphasis is on pursuing a course of action which will help, no matter how slightly, to make society a little more humane, a little more just.

In the *Dialogues* of Plato it is recorded that Socrates was once asked, "When will there be justice in the world?" He answered, "When those who are not wronged feel as indignant as those who are."

*A scholar who heeds not the appeal of the oppressed and declines to work for justice on the ground that he is too busy with his studies is as one who destroys the earth.*

EXODUS RABBAH 30:13

# What Do You Average?

There is a tendency in our society to overemphasize the gifted child on the one hand, and the child who chronically misbehaves on the other. In this process, somehow or other, the average child—and let's face the fact, most of our children are average—is being overlooked. One teenager said it very well: "These days you have to be either a genius or a kook to be noticed."

This young person was not far from wrong. While we help the gifted child use his gifts, and while we are concerned with the disturbed child, we should nonetheless not overlook the normal child who deserves our attention and help as well.

Elizabeth Morris, a teacher in Cahokia, Illinois, donated $5,000 of her hard-earned money to set up a scholarship fund for financially needy "C" students. She did this because she recognized that two-thirds of all classes are made up of "C" students, and they have something to contribute. This viewpoint is supported by a report entitled, *Your Child's Inner Life*, which points out that a child with an average rating may be good at collecting plants or making doll's clothes. There may be a slumbering future scientist or top fashion designer who will never be awakened if his parents go into a defeatist slump over his average work.

It often happens that students who do only moderately well in school go on to substantial achievements. But the main reason to show concern for the average child (and adult) is not because they might potentially be more than they are, but simply because they are in themselves worthwhile human beings.

*God made the small and the great, and cares for all alike.*
THE WISDOM OF SOLOMON 6:7

# There Ought To Be A Law

At one period in his life Mark Twain was involved in some complicated legal difficulties. A friend tried to convince him that with a little cleverness he could save himself a great deal of trouble by subtly evading the law. But Mark Twain refused to take this way out, saying, "Honor is a harder master than the law."

There is a definite link between law and ethics. Force alone can never insure the observance of laws. If law does not have its source in a moral commitment, it ceases to have meaning.

An obvious example is the widespread violation during the 1920's and 30's of the Volstead Act, a law that prohibited the manufacture and sale of liquor. People all over America disobeyed what was essentially an unwise law.

In this context it is interesting to note that since the year 70, the Jews have had no police system to enforce Jewish law, which is known as *halakhah*. But so great was the loyalty of the Jewish people to the Torah and to those who interpreted its laws that the Jewish legal system has remained intact until this very day. From the year 70 until 1948, the founding of the State of Israel, Jews had no political power with which to enforce their laws upon their own people. Yet Jewish law was upheld and maintained because Jews revered the source of the Torah and respected the laws of our people.

This kind of commitment and respect is vastly more powerful than courts and jails and punishments and fines. When people believe and are committed to honor and to law, then society is a good place in which to live.

*A law is something which must have a moral basis, so that there is an inner compelling force for every citizen to obey.*
CHAIM WEIZMANN

# The Will And The Way

Many people conclude that there are absolute limitations on the amount of food and energy available to us to solve our problems. We look at the sea and all we see is water. But beneath it and way down deep, there are untold acres of edible material. We look at the sky and we see the clouds or the blueness. But way out there in space is a limitless supply of energy. If only we were willing to invest in deeper research, we could find a way to harness the potential for productivity for all the people on this planet.

A congregant walked into a minister's study, and was most cheerful and happy. The minister was surprised by the congregant's attitude, because for the past few years the congregant had had severe financial difficulties. He had invested in land in which he hoped to drill to find minerals. Unfortunately, it had turned out to be nonproductive. The minister said to him, "I am happy that you are happy, but how come the sudden change?" He said, "Reverend, we just struck a rich deposit on the land." Then he went on to say, "Do you know how it happened? I was ready to quit and suddenly the foreman said, 'Let's dig down deeper and see what happens.' I replied, 'All right, we have nothing to lose and everything to gain.' And after a week of added drilling we hit a fabulous vein. It pays to dig deeper!"

If only when we were willing to quit, we would have the drive to go a little deeper. What untold wealth there lies for us in human relationships and in the physical world if we have the push to go beyond the first few layers.

*All is possible to him who wills.*    MINHAH HADASHAH

# To Remain Human

Elie Wiesel, the spokesman of the Holocaust, has written an article entitled, "To Remain Human in The Face of Inhumanity," a proper Jewish response to hate and anger. In the article he describes the scene of the liberation of his concentration camp. Only a few thousand inmates had survived the horrors of the death camp. When the first American jeeps appeared at the gates, there were no outbursts of joy. The inmates just did not have the feeling to rejoice or even the energy to cheer. Some of the survivors were Russian prisoners of war. They grabbed some jeeps and machine guns, and they raced to Munich and opened fire at will. That was their first gesture as free men. They needed vengeance before they needed food.

But what did the Jewish survivors do to prove they were free? Wiesel tells us, "Believe it or not, they held services." They would have been perfectly justified to seize weapons to express their rage. It would have been their right. But, instead, they chose to recite the most ancient prayers, for they knew this was morally right. They chose to be human, and acting as authentic Jews they chose to forswear vengeance even in the face of astounding grief and provocation.

And what is the message of this historic occurrence? Is it not the message of the heart of Jewish tradition: to remain human in the face of inhumanity, to assert that it is possible to find some goodness even in a world gone mad? This is the miracle of Jewishness. When it is put to the ultimate test, it will practice restraint and reaffirmation of the dignity of man. And if others do not recognize that they are children of God, at least we will.

*Self-control and understanding, righteousness and courage, there is nothing in life more meritorious than these.*

WISDOM OF SOLOMON 8:7

# Training For Jewish Survival

A group of American Jews once had a very interesting experience in Israel. The group had the unique opportunity of visiting the main Israeli air base near Beersheba. They went through the classrooms, watching instruction classes at the airfield from the beginning sessions in the Piper Cubs to the advanced work with Phantom training jets. As they were leaving, they saw the air cadets running around the courtyard piggyback. Each young man was carrying a fellow trainee on his shoulders, and they were laughing as they ran.

One American turned to an officer and said, "I suppose they are enjoying time out for a game." The officer replied, "That is not a game; it is serious training for survival." He went on to explain that a Phantom jet carries two crew members—the pilot and the navigator. "If they should have to bail out, the statistical calculation is that through the eject or the landing, one may break a leg or his back. The other man will have to carry him through the desert or the hill country to safety, and it will not be easy for it will be dead weight." Then the Israeli officer added a striking sentence, "Every man knows that his survival depends on his brother carrying him as a burden, but every man also knows his brother will do it, for he would do the same if he had to."

The strength of Israel is exactly that each man is prepared to carry his brother. The power of any people is the willingness to accept the concept of brotherhood, and to bear burdens for society. The success of any society is in direct proportion to the degree of responsibility that its members are ready to assume.

*Israel is collectively what every survivor is individually: A No to the demons of Auschwitz, a Yes to Jewish survival and security—and thus a testimony to life against death on behalf of all mankind.*    EMIL L. FACKENHEIM

# The Three C's

Part of the reason we suffer so much in human relations is our unrealistic view of human nature. We tend to see and judge people in absolute terms, as if they had to be models of perfection. From the Jewish point of view (which incidentally coincides with practical experience), every man is a mixed bag of emotions. The human being is capable of good and bad, is aggressive and passive, hating and loving. Somewhere along the line, our controls may slip, our worst side comes out, and others are hurt in the process. This is why we all need to forgive and to be forgiven.

How wise we would be if we would learn to get off each other's backs. Just as there is no need for parents to be excessively demanding, so there is no good reason for children to be overly provocative in dress or speech. If older people tend to seek and pressure for more conformity, it is equally true that younger members of our society are often insensitive and indiscriminate in condemnation and harsh criticism.

But we can recover a sense of peace and balance if we wish it. Consider for a moment that we in America have learned to live together with different religions. The hates of yesteryear between churches and synagogues have largely disappeared. So why can't we also learn to get off each other's backs in relations between races, in negotiations between business and labor, in contacts between students and society? Why continue living with self-inflicted suffering when we can have the satisfaction that comes through the three C's—common sense, consultation and compromise.

*Rabbi Joshua ben Korcha says: It is meritorious to compromise.*    SANHEDRIN 6b

# The Mutual Trust

Despite the rapidity of our movements, despite the personal turbulence we encounter, in the midst of all of our change, if we have a tradition we will be secure and safe. Of all the world's peoples, Jews are the most experienced with challenge. From the time of Moses until today, Judaism has always been a risky faith. But those who have kept the faith have learned that the faith keeps them.

We are all involved in Israel in a deeply personal way. Its problems and its promise are as much ours as any resident of Israel. Our destinies are intertwined and we know it. We wonder as we see the headlines what is going to happen there. We sometimes ask if its leaders really know what they are doing. The answer to this concern is that we must continue to keep faith with our Israeli brothers, and that faith will keep us together as a strong people.

An American Jew who was visiting Israel decided to attend an Israeli night club in which the performers spoke and sang only Hebrew. At one point a comic came out and everybody began to laugh at his jokes. The American joined wholeheartedly. His tour guide turned to him and said, "You don't know Hebrew, so how do you know it is funny?" The American Jew replied, "I trust my people!"

This is the attitude we must maintain. We must trust our people and we must keep faith with them, for ultimately that faith will keep world Jewry strong.

*Jews of different countries regard and love one another as members of the same people because they remember that the ties that bind them did not begin yesterday; they are four thousand years old. This sense of history alone is a great and uplifting thought, inspiration to respect this bond and hold it dear.* PERETZ SMOLENSKIN

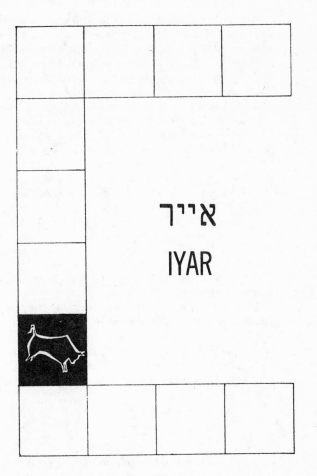

אייר

IYAR

# The Evidence Of God

We can neither prove nor disprove the existence of a Supreme Being. For every argument on one side, one can find an equally convincing argument on the other side. Ultimately, faith cannot be completely demonstrated. It is not illogical; but, on the other hand, it cannot be proven absolutely either. It is simply that as you live and experience and think and feel, you either know in the very marrow of your bones that there is a God, or you do not.

There is an old story of a traveler who once crossed the desert with a devout guide. The traveler marveled at the faith of the old guide, who several times a day took time out to pray along the way. "Why do you pray to someone whom you cannot see?" asked the traveler. "How can you be sure that there really is a God?"

The old guide did not answer immediately, but the next day as they journeyed the guide answered with another question. "Last night as we slept in our tents we heard a noise. How do you know that camels passed by?"

The traveler was quick to reply. "Because this morning I saw the footprints of the camels."

The wise old guide smiled knowingly. "Likewise do I know there is a God. When I see the beauty of the fiery sky, when I drink from the cooling waters of the green oasis, when I behold the stars in the heavens above, I know that these things were created by a Master Craftsman. I know there is a God, because I see His footprints everywhere."

*As a house is impossible without a builder, a dress without a weaver, a door without a carpenter, so the world cannot be without a Creator.*    MIDRASH TEMURAH, CHAPTER 13

# Honesty Is Human

A recent visitor at a hospital observed a startling change. As he walked down the hall, he noticed a nurse wearing a nameplate with the initials R.N. after her name, which means Registered Nurse. She was dressed in a bright orange linen dress and did not wear the traditional nurse's cap. The visitor said in jest to the nurse, "I suppose with all the experiments going on that this is your new uniform." She replied, "As a matter of fact, it is and the purpose is to make us look human."

She then pointed out that all the nurses on the floor were wearing street dresses in bright colors. She further informed the curious visitor that the experiment was based on the theory that patients would relate better to human beings than to technicians, and that in hospitals the simple and direct human approach is the best.

This might be one of the most important lessons people have to re-learn today. The emphasis is on "re-learn," because simplicity and directness have always been the most effective way to communicate.

Would it not be wise if we could learn to relax all of our pretensions and become persons? Why be clever when we can communicate in honesty? Why be estranged from the world when we can share personally in helping human beings? To achieve this, all we have to do is to express ourselves honestly.

*Let your Yes be a real Yes and your No a real No.*
SEDER ELIYAHU RABBAH 23

# Remember The Helper

A library becomes a library only when people take out books and read.

A school is just a building until teachers and students enter and learning takes place.

A synagogue is only a structure unless people come and worship there.

All these examples indicate the great potential that we can discover in the world if we know how to relate to it properly. In a sense we are partners of God in the constant process of creating a better and more beautiful world.

A delightful little story that illustrates this thought concerns a flower show at which a new variety of rose was awarded one of the coveted prizes. The modest rose culturist who had grown it stood on the platform to receive the award while at his side the chairperson extolled the loveliness of the blooms.

"How perfect this flower is, with its vermillion petals and its exquisite scent. See what surpassing beauty God has created!"

The rose culturist nudged the speaker gently and whispered, "Remember, I helped!"

Our job is to help God, our faith, our families, and our friends. The world is filled with the promise of greater and better things, but it is up to each of us to help realize this potential.

It was beautifully put by the late Rabbi Joshua Loth Leibman when he said, "Carbon atoms form charcoal when related in one way and become diamonds when related in another."

*Whoever would change people must change the conditions of their lives.*                                    THEODOR HERZL

# The Ways To Civilization

The ancient rabbis raised the question: "What constitutes a civilized human being?" After considerable discussion, they formulated what is known as *sheva mitzvot b'nai Noah*, "The Seven Requirements for Being a Civilized Man." Or to broaden it, the seven attributes that distinguish a humane society. The following is the list:

1. Worship of one God.
2. A refusal to commit violence.
3. A refusal to steal.
4. A rejection of obscene language.
5. Condemnation of sexual immorality.
6. Kindness to animals.
7. A commitment to settle disputes by law and to promote justice.

One sees here a close relationship between reverence for God and reverence for man. A good person is also a just person. Religious people also respect other people.

There is the story of a learned but ungenerous man who said to Rabbi Abraham of Stretyn, "They say that you give people mysterious drugs and that your drugs are effective. Give me one that I may acquire the fear of God."

"I don't know any drug for the fear of God," said Rabbi Abraham. "But if you like, I can give you one for the *love* of God."

"That's even better!" cried the other. "Just give it to me."

"It is the love of one's fellow men," answered the Rabbi.

The real way to find God is through human beings. The path to the Divine is discovered in devotion to humanity.

*He who renders true judgment is a co-worker with God.*
MEKHILTA TO EXODUS 18:13

# Israel Is

A father once owned an enormous amount of land, and he decided to bequeath it to that one of his three sons who could best manage to run it. He gave each son $5,000 and he said, "Do what you wish with it. And in one year I will ask you for an accounting."

A year later, he called his sons to him for the reckoning. The first son said, "I spent all my money and I had a good time." The second son said, "I took my money and I hid it in the room so nobody could get at it, and so I still have it all." The third son said, "I invested my money, and now I have the original sum plus all the interest and profit I earned from it."

The father then said, "The third son shall head the family because he knows how to use the original deposit so that it will yield its benefits."

Applying this anecdote to the land of Israel, which has had so many different occupants over the years, we can ask to whom does the land belong? And we can answer: to the ones who have used it properly.

This is the great truth about Israel. The invaders throughout history abused the land, carried away its wealth, and plundered the soil without regard for the future. Then the succeeding generations let the sands come in and block the productivity of the soil; they permitted the swamps to fester and sicken; they ignored all that the land might yield. But when the *haluztim*—the Jewish pioneers—returned to their ancestral homeland, they drained the swamps, they irrigated the desert, they reforested the land and reclaimed it. It was almost as if the land had waited for its beloved children to return to it.

*The Land without a people waited for the people without a Land.*
ISRAEL ZANGWILL

# Now Or Never

We should not delay in giving our words and ourselves to others. Many of us, called to serve on boards and committees and to assume other responsibilities, often think, "I've really had it. It is enough!" Or, "I will do it some other year." But this is not the right attitude. You say you will do it later, but you may have even less opportunity to do the job in the future. Do it now, and you will find your life more worthwhile.

There is a story about the famous Jane Addams, who was responsible for building Hull House, the first settlement house, in Chicago. Jane Addams, the first person to do something positive for slum areas, set a shining example for all of us. And her life's work began in a very simple and telling way. She was walking through the slums one day, and was terribly disturbed by what she saw. She began to think about whom she should contact, and how she should organize to begin to help the poor, and who might be the chairman of such an effort. It would be difficult to find someone; for, after all, who would assume such an awesome responsibility? As she walked on a bit further, she suddenly decided, "I will take it on myself." She did, and she not only helped clear the slums, but she also made a great name for herself in American history. Because she did not let her chance go by, because she assumed her responsibility as soon as she saw it, she was able to do great things, and she was in turn endowed with greatness.

*Hillel said, "If not now, when?"* AVOT 1:14

# What's In A Question

The life-style of Judaism is dominated by a questioning approach to life. The Talmud is built on an attitude of constant inquiry, and the word "why" is to be found in Talmudic literature at least 10,000 times. A large portion of later Jewish literature is called "Responsa," which is a collection of responses to questions asked of the rabbis. Traditionally, when one asks a Jew, "why do Jews answer a question with a question?" the Jew replies, "Why not?"

But, if we think about this a little more, we will find that the question technique is the basis of all learning, as Socrates, who used questions to teach, well knew. Questions are also the inspiration for all research. A scientist goes into a laboratory and says, "Why do things happen this way?"

George Washington Carver was one of the greatest scientists of the South. He discovered approximately three hundred ways to use the peanut for food and industry—discoveries that helped to save the South economically. Once a child asked him how he came to make all these discoveries. He replied simply: "I put a peanut in my hand, I looked at it, and I asked, 'Mr. Peanut, what are your secrets?'"

If all of this could come from a simple question asked of a peanut, what could happen to us if we used the same approach? What if we took a leaf and asked, "What can you tell us?" What if we asked a person a question and triggered a new way of thought in his mind? And what if we asked of Judaism: "Is there a new way to express our feelings about our own faith?" What if the whole world asked: "Why can't we have peace?" What if? What if?

*Never hesitate to ask where the acquisition of virtue is concerned.*   ELIJAH BEN RAPHAEL DE VEALI SABA

# Beyond Babel

According to the general intrepretation, the building of the Tower of Babel was undertaken because people had become arrogant. They challenged God, almost as if they wanted to take His place. In order to frustrate their plan, God confused their language, "so they did not understand one another." Because they now spoke different languages and did not understand each other, the rabbis explained, if one workman asked for mortar, another might hand him a brick; then the first, in his anger, would throw it at his partner. As a result, quarrels were frequent, and eventually the Tower just fell apart.

This interpretation teaches that whenever communication fails, disaster is imminent. So today, the United Nations is rapidly becoming a Tower of Babel and we fear for its collapse. It is not simply that its members do not speak the same language literally, for after all they use a sophisticated instantaneous translation system. But it is rather a lack of understanding of each other's motives and a lack of communication in trying to achieve peace.

Conflicts in the human family, whether it be in the individual family or the family of nations, occur when there is misunderstanding. If only each member of the family would seek to understand the other, then instead of throwing brickbats, bricks would be used to cement human relationships. If each nation were seriously concerned with creating harmony and could communicate this feeling through word and deed, then surely the United Nations would not be a Tower of Babel, but a monument to brotherhood.

*Without understanding, there is no knowledge; without knowledge, there is no understanding.*    AVOT 3:17

# The Core And The Rind

The Talmud tells a truth in the following one-sentence parable. "He found a fruit; he ate the core and threw away the rind" (Hagigah 15b). The point of this parable is that in each situation of life we must learn to extract that which is essential and meaningful and discard that which is unnecessary or harmful. What is good, we must accept and enjoy; what is wrong, we should reject and discard.

One Thanksgiving week, a teacher asked her class to draw pictures of things for which they should be most thankful. Some drew pictures of turkeys, others drew pumpkins and fruit and yet others sketched Pilgrims. But one little boy drew a picture of a hand. The teacher was puzzled and she asked the class what it might mean. Some suggested it was God's hand, others thought it might be the hand of the farmer, and still others speculated that it might be the hand of the corner policeman. She finally turned to the little boy and said, "What does it mean?" And he replied: "It is your hand, teacher. Everytime I needed you, you held out your hand to me. You hold my crayon to guide it, you turn my page when I cannot find it, you pat me on the head when I deserve it, you touch me when I need it."

This is the core of life. People need to touch and be touched, to find that they are real and that the world is real. We all need to hold somebody's hand sometime or other in our life. We all at some time or other need guidance, help and a little pat on the head. This is the core of living. Be thankful that there were hands held out to help you; be grateful for the times you can help others, for this is the core of life.

*As one hand washes the other, so must one person help another.*
                                                        PETER MARTIN

# Do It Yourself

It is important not only to "do it yourself" but to *be* yourself. In all of life we find that people who put on false faces and false fronts end up being failures. But a person who is himself, who accepts himself, who speaks the truth about what he believes and who takes responsibility for himself—that person eventually makes his mark in the world.

Pope John XXIII was one of the great men of our time. When he first assumed the papacy he often had serious problems. He reported that he would lie awake half the night thinking, then suddenly he would decide: "I must ask the Pope what to do about it in the morning." Only then could he fall asleep. But shortly afterward, he would suddenly awaken with a start, fully aware, and he would think, "My God, I *am* the Pope!" It was during such moments that he made the great decision to call the Ecumenical Council—a decision that changed the world and our lives.

We will wander about all of our days and we will evade all of our decisions until the moment we come to the understanding that "I am the person who must do it myself"—the ultimate moment when we accept the responsibility that everything good in the world begins in oneself. And so we might pray:

"O Lord, let there be righteousness and charity
in the world,
And let it begin with me.
Let there be prayer and dedication in the world,
And let it begin with me.
Let there be promise and new hope in the world,
And let it begin with me."

*Every single person is a new thing in the world, and is called upon to fulfill his particularity in this world.*

YEHIEL MICHAEL OF ZLOTCHOV

# The Illustrious Immigrants

Professor Oscar Handlin, a lifelong student of American history, once wrote: "Once I thought to write a history of the immigrants to America. Then I discovered that the immigrants *were* American history." The fact of the matter is that—except for the Indians—every person in the United States is either an immigrant or the descendant of an immigrant.

Beginning with the first group of 102 Pilgrims who settled here, immigrants have played an indispensable role in the shaping of America. Eighteen of the signers of the Declaration of Independence were non-Anglo-Saxons and eight were themselves immigrants. And in this document the important sentence, "All men are created equal," was written by Philip Mazzei, an Italian immigrant writer. We celebrate a day honoring the first 102 immigrants, but what about the 44 million immigrants who came after them? They have enriched every phase of American life, and we can never really honor them enough. The following are only a few illustrations.

We all know that Alexander Graham Bell invented the telephone, but few of us are aware that he was born in Scotland. John Ericsson, who invented the propeller ship, came from Sweden. Phillis Wheatley was one of the first women in America to have published a volume of poetry, and she was a black woman who came off a slave ship from Africa. Irving Berlin created some of our greatest popular music, and he was of Russian-Jewish background. Albert Einstein of Germany and Enrico Fermi of Italy brought with them to America the essential knowledge of nuclear energy.

*Culture is always a product of mixing.*    FRIEDRICH HERTZ

# Renewal

In all of life we see the process of renewal. What is a wedding anniversary except the celebration of a relationship and a recommitment to its ideals? What is a birthday? It is the marking-off of a period of time, celebrating it and then dedicating ourselves to use and to make the most of the time to come. What is a *yahrzeit*, the anniversary of a death? Is it not a time to remember and to recall the best moments of a person's life and then to incorporate those moments into our lives for inspiration and comfort and hope? All these give testimony to the process of renewal.

Actually, we are doing it all the time without giving it a great deal of thought. Urban renewal is a part of every city with a progressive program. Teachers receive alertness credits when they take new courses. Every time we vote we reaffirm our confidence in the democratic system. All of this is the process of renewing, revitalizing, and recreating.

A teacher once asked her class, "Can a leopard change its spots?" All except one tiny tot agreed that a leopard cannot change its spots. "So you think that a leopard can change its spots?" inquired the teacher. "Yes," said the boy. "If he gets tired of one spot, he can always get up and move to another spot."

We must always be prepared to move from our present positions to see better things. For by being visionary, by dreaming, by anticipating and by renewing we can create ways not only to relieve our present problems but positively to improve the quality of life itself. What was done once can be done again and can be done even better.

*Then said Samuel to the people: "Come and let us now go to Gilgal, and renew our allegiance to the kingdom. . . ." And all the people of Israel rejoiced greatly.*    I SAMUEL 11:14-15

# A Religious Diet

The practice of *kashrut,* the maintenance of the Jewish Dietary Laws, is one of the finest ways to civilize a person. The observance of kosher disciplines has as its fundamental purpose to control our predatory killing instinct and to replace that instinct with reverence for life.

The laws of *kashrut* prevent wanton slaying of animals and restrict our consumption of meat to a certain few. Only a *shohet,* a duly trained and authorized person, may take the life of an animal. This technique of controlling aggression and violence is unparalleled in any other culture. Moreover, the restrictions against mixing meat and dairy products and other kindred regulations school our appetites and discipline our gluttonous impulses.

An old Yiddish tale expresses this concept perfectly. Once in the *shtetl,* the European small town, a Jew fell on hard times. Desperate, he decided to become a robber. He went to the edge of town and hid, ready to leap on the first traveler. Soon, one of his friends appeared. The would-be robber raised his knife and said, "Give me your money or I will stab you." The friend laughed, "Don't be silly." "I mean it," said the robber, "I will plunge this knife into you." "But you can't," said the friend, "I know that knife and it is a *milchig* (dairy) knife."

*Kashrut is a systematic means of educating and refining the consciences of those who observe it from early age to death, which continues in every age and in every country wherever there is a Jewish family and a Jewish home.*

SAMUEL H. DRESNER

# The Today Show

Some things have to be done today and we must not put them off for tomorrow. In fact, in certain instances if we do not do things today, there will be no tomorrow. Consider the natural world. Some fruits, if not eaten today, will spoil by the morrow. In a similar way certain human expressions must be fulfilled today or they will spoil by tomorrow.

What is the use of visiting someone after he or she has recovered from an illness? What is the use of saying, "I'm sorry," the day *after* a quarrel? These things should be done on the day itself.

Doing things now can prevent as well as heal. Making an appointment for a physical examination today may enable you to live tomorrow. Saying "I love you!" today may insure a relationship for tomorrow. As Benjamin Franklin wisely observed, "One today is worth two tomorrows."

It is necessary to prepare today for tomorrow. Isn't that why we have insurance policies and make Social Security payments and invest in mutual funds? Ought we not also to make plans to insure a good life for tomorrow? For example, middle age is the time to think and plan for a retirement which will be fruitful. Now is the time to begin a habit of study that we may enjoy its benefits in the future. Now is the time to be thinking about our environment, to be concerned about peace, to be interested in Israel, for only in this way will we insure our survival as human beings, as Americans and as Jews. Yesterday is on this side of the bank, tomorrow is the other side of the bank, and the bridge that joins them is today.

*When you make an offering unto the Lord . . . complete it on that day. Do not leave any part of it for the next day.*
LEVITICUS 22:29-30

# Everyone Has A Name

If we are to have harmony in our daily lives, we must realize that nowhere is it more important to strive for understanding than within ourselves. We tend to think in labels and talk in cliches. When we are confronted with a challenge, we pigeonhole people according to our prejudices and classify ourselves into causes to suit our own convenience. So we become insufferable in our self-righteousness. "We" are admirable; "they" are to be admonished. "We" are good; "they" are evil. "We" are the true believers; "they" are the misguided. But all the while we miss the prime understanding of human uniqueness. I am a person and they, too, are persons. I have feelings and they have feelings.

This story of a young man and his father is an authentic expression of this Jewish ideal of regard for human uniqueness. One day when the young man was sitting with his father and eating lunch in their place of business, a regular customer came into the yard. The son, looking out the window, saw him and then remarked to his father: *"Pa, a goy shteht in yard* ("Dad, there is a gentile in the yard."). The father turned to him, looked him in the eye and said evenly, *"ruf aym nisht kein goy, ehr hat an namen"* ("Don't call him a gentile, he has a name").

People have names and feelings. People have personalities and identities. But the people of the world too often forget this truth. And our forgetfulness exacts a heavy toll from us. To see others as human beings with personalities and names is to help humanize the world and bring it healing and happiness.

*Why did God create but one person from whom all are descended? So that no one should be able to say, "My father is better than your father."*    SANHEDRIN 37a

# The Sabbath Is Significant

*Shabbat* is the only holiday mentioned in the Ten Commandments. *Shabbat* is a weekly holiday which is symbolized by the lighting of the candles by the woman of the household, by the reciting of the *kiddush* by the man of the home, and by the whole family sitting about the table as a unit. Unless there is a *Shabbat* there is no assurance that at least once a week there will be a *family* meal. Moreover, unless we rest on the seventh day, we do not appreciate the work of the other six days. Unless there is one day of release from the burdens of the world, we become machines and not human beings. Machines are never free to do what they want to do; only people are. Therefore, the Torah tells us: On every seventh day be human and not a parasite, be yourself and not a "yes person," in short, be a Jew.

The *Shabbat* was created by God, the Torah tells us, for even the Almighty rested on the seventh day from the labors of creation.

A Chinese parable tells of a man who went to market with a string of seven large copper coins on his shoulder. Meeting a beggar, the man gave the beggar six of the seven coins. But the beggar, instead of showing gratitude, slipped up behind the man and stole the seventh coin.

Many people accept from God the gift of six days to do their labor and then, instead of being grateful, steal from Him the seventh—the Sabbath Day. Devoted Jews, however, have always been grateful for the privilege of a *Shabbat*, a day of rest, and for the way it helps preserve life. And so it was written, "More than Israel has preserved the Sabbath, the Sabbath has preserved Israel."

*To observe the Sabbath is to bear witness to the Creator.*
MEKHILTA TO EXODUS 20:13

# The Soft Sell

There is a false but widespread belief that the way to get something done is to exert pressure, the way to change people's minds is to force opinions and the way to succeed is through driving aggression. But pressure only produces counterpressure, force creates resistance and those who drive hard often lose their sense of direction and end up in the very opposite place from that which they sought.

The proper approach was long ago noted in the Book of Proverbs (15:1): "A soft answer turns away wrath." In other words, the Bible is telling us to use the "soft sell." We do not have to go around pushing people, shouting at the top of our lungs or otherwise forcing the issue. All we really have to do is to state our case quietly, make our point simply and be firm but gentle.

In considering Biblical history, whom do we remember: The Egyptians who persecuted and punished, the Canaanites who fought and destroyed, or Moses who majestically intoned the Ten Commandments? In the medieval period, whom does history honor? The Borgia family who robbed and pillaged, or Michelangelo who patiently painted the great ceiling of the Sistine Chapel? In modern times, who will be the hero of our age: Joseph Stalin who murdered and oppressed, or Albert Schweitzer who brought medical attention and quiet love to a whole continent?

Kindness never ends in a moment but continues to do its work. As there is a chain reaction of violence and hate, so there is a chain reaction of thoughtfulness and consideration. To perform one *mitzvah*, to do one kind thing, to say one good word, is like tossing a pebble into a quiet pond and watching its waves spread far and wide.

*A wise person must be soft-spoken with all.*

MAIMONIDES, YAD, DE'OT 5:7

# Here And Now

The Ten Commandments are very lovely and very lofty, yet they are couched in general terms. But, Judaism in its method and its wisdom applies these ideals in specific ways. The Torah portion each week leaves the lofty heights of Sinai and brings the moral law down to the valley of daily decision.

For example, the Bible gives us a detailed analysis of the laws of interest, a specific description of what constitutes false testimony and gossip, and even the laws on responsibility for property loss through fire, neglect and so on. All of this indicates that religion is not just a vague sentiment, but rather a specific ethical guide.

We tend to think that religion belongs in a synagogue or a church. We call this institution a House of God, but isn't a home where morality is practiced also a House of God? Isn't a hospital where people are healed and compassion is practiced also a House of God? Isn't a school where we advance knowledge and teach responsibility also a House of God? In fact, we might very well ask, isn't wherever people dwell in decency also a House of God?

Religion will serve its true function when it enters the experience of our daily lives. We tend to associate religious thought with heaven, when we really should understand that morality belongs to the here and now.

If religion is to have meaning in our time, it must be concerned about all the practical problems people face here and now.

*Better one hour of repentance and good deeds in this world than all the life in the world to come.*    AVOT 4:22

# Spiritual Dynamite

During the second World War the Nazis discovered that in Holland the underground was hiding dynamite between the covers of Bibles. Therefore, they forbade the opening of the Bible under penalty of death. In many homes the people rushed to their bookshelves thinking that some members of their family were using their sacred books for this explosive purpose. At an internatinal religious meeting, the president of the World Council of Churches recalled: "In Holland the people thought that the Bible must contain dynamite since the Nazis were so anxious to destroy it. So they dusted off the covers and reopened the pages to find the dynamite and they found it. Anybody who opens the pages of the Prophets will discover the explosive power of great ideas."

Our own country was founded on the solid bedrock of prophetic teaching of the Bible-carrying Puritans. In many rural areas in America, people still give their children Biblical names like Zeke, after the prophet Ezekiel, and Amos and Jonah. And in sophisticated New York City the United Nations building bears a text from the phrase from the Prophets (Isaiah 2:4 and Micah 4:3), "They shall beat their swords into plowshares and their spears into pruning hooks; nation shall not lift up sword against nation, neither shall they learn war any more." Every American Pesident has quoted liberally from the Prophets; and, clearly, one cannot be an intelligent American without a profound understanding of the place of the Prophets in the American purpose.

*We can string together, like pearls, the words of the Bible, and they are as thrilling as on the day when they were revealed in flame on Sinai.*    LEVITICUS RABBAH 16:4

# The Wonder Of It All

The excitement of wondrous living can add zest to every age and stage of life. The poet Archibald MacLeish sang of it on the day he turned sixty:

Now at sixty what I see,
Although the world is worse by far,
Stops my heart in ecstasy.
God, the wonders that there are!

As Socrates wrote centuries ago, "All philosophy begins in wonder." Why were we not content merely to eat and drink like other animals? Why must we always search and question? A modern philsopher, Alfred North Whitehead, said it this way: "Philosophy begins in wonder. And, at the end, when philosophic thought has done its best, the wonder remains."

A teacher once reported that when he began to teach a creative art group he learned a very valuable lesson from a very young child. He had been introducing a group of young students to the world of paint and color. He walked over to a five-year-old who seemed somewhat hesitant and began to say, "Now if you mix these two colors you will get. . . ." At this point, before he could finish the sentence, the child interrupted, "Don't tell me! I want to *surprise* myself!"

Don't let the sense of surprise and wonder go out of your life. Develop an expanding sense of wonder at the world, at yourself, at humanity, at God. The world will never starve for wonders—only for the want of wonder.

*Be open-eyed to the great wonders of nature, familiar though they may be. But people are more wont to be astonished at the sun's eclipse than at its unfailing rise.*
ORHOT TZADIKIM 15c

# Ironing Out Our Differences

In the Bible it is written, "You shall build an altar to the Lord your God. It shall be an altar of stones in which you shall use no tool of iron" (Deuteronomy 27:5). The reason is that metal represents murder and warfare. It is from metal that we make a knife or a sword and in our day it is from metal that we construct the gun and the cannon. Therefore, the removal of metal from the Sanctuary of God is a sensitive way of reminding us that we should eliminate war from our midst. It is a symbolic reminder perpetually that war is not honorable, and that aggression and arms are not noble. They have no place in a house or a world of peace.

On Veteran's Day the bands play, men wear their caps in a jaunty fashion, and stride down the street. The children see all this and are impressed. But wouldn't it be far better to take them to the Veterans Administration Hospital and show them what the other veterans of war look like? It takes 20 years or more of peace to make a person, but it takes only 20 seconds of war to destroy a human being. We will never have peace until we understand the terrible destruction that warfare leaves in its wake.

A wonderful story might well make our point. A boy said to his mother one day, "Mother, every time I look at Grandfather's sword, it makes me want to be a soldier and fight." The mother said, "Well?" And the boy said again, "But when I see his wooden leg I cool off."

The quotation from Deuteronomy is exactly in the spirit of this story. In the Sanctuary of the Temple the very construction of the altar symbolizes the rejection of war and the yearning for peace. We are reminded that war is hell and peace is heaven.

*Food and drink may abound, but if there is no peace they are as naught.*                SIFRA, BEHUKOTAI

# A House For God?

If we want God to dwell among us, we have to make room for Him. We have to recognize Him, we have to make time for Him, we have to find a way to relate to Him.

A cub reporter, given an assignment by an editor to cover a flood in West Virginia several years ago, called in his story during the wee hours of the morning. The budding writer, impressed by the prose that was used by foreign correspondents, filed a one-sentence lead: "God sits brooding tonight in the West Virginia hills." The editor immediately sent a return message: "Forget the flood! Interview God!"

Sometimes we become so involved in the world we forget to summon the presence of God. To hear the call of God, one must be within listening distance. To neglect the regular attendance at a House of God is to break an appointment with God. To forget to perform the *mitzvot*, the daily good deeds, amounts to canceling a contract with God.

The problem that we have in making God real is that we continue to think about Him in old ways. While we have grown intellectually, we have not applied any of this knowledge to thinking about God. We still cherish the notions about the Almighty that we acquired as children. But God is not a place, God is not a person, God is not a promise—God is a presence! God is very real and very near to those who want Him. He is as near as the air we breathe, as close as the beat of the heart.

*God does not die on the day when we cease to believe in a personal deity, but we die on the day when our lives cease to be illuminated by the steady radiance, renewed daily, of a wonder, the source of which is beyond all reason.*

DAG HAMMARSKJOLD

# To Life!

Several years ago a novel entitled *In Vivo* described the world of research. This is how the title was derived: *In vitro* means "testing in glass." *In vivo* means "testing in life." Research begins by observing what happens in the test tube, but the researcher never knows what will work until he introduces it into the bloodstream of a living thing. For everything that happens, happens *in vivo*, in life.

This is important to understand so that we participate every moment in the possibilities of life. If a person is to live, he or she has to become completely and entirely alive—alive in body, senses, mind, and will. This is not only a Jewish idea but is the essence of all religion. God gave us life to enjoy it, to use it, to share it, to feel it, to think about it, and, in the greatest sense, to help others to achieve the full potential of their lives.

The Jewish word for life is *chaim* and it is usually found in the plural. That is because life alone is only half a life. We have to learn to join our lives with others in love and thus to find our fulfillment. We love another person, and then we build a family, and the family finally gives us our deepest satisfactions. We join with others because we love liberty and when we help others to find their freedom then we know our life has not been in vain. But all of this life-enhancement is achieved not by passively sitting on the sidelines but rather by active involvement with the lives of others.

The dedication of a novel once began with the inscription: "To my friend who long ago did what I hope every reader of this work will do. She fell in love with life."

*Be happy, be healthy, long life! And if our good fortune never comes, here's to whatever comes. Drink L'Chaim, to Life.*                    LYRICS FROM *FIDDLER ON THE ROOF*

# Just So

A major ingredient of a sound society is a passionate concern for justice. Indeed, the concept of justice may very well be the most important contribution of Judaism to Western thought. The Hebrew words for justice, *tzedek* and *mishpat*, occur 670 times in the Bible. Justice is one of the great demands that the Biblical faith makes on us. One can hardly read the literature of our people without being overwhelmed by the Jewish preoccupation with fair dealing and fair treatment.

This zeal for equity is summed up in one verse in the Book of Deuteronomy: *tzedek, tzedek, tirdof*—Justice, justice shall you pursue. Rabbi Simhah Bunim, a Hassidic rabbi of the last century, raised the question why the word justice was repeated twice. He answered his question with the following insight: "This is to teach us that justice should be pursued only through justice. It can be established only through just means." Rabbi Bunim makes the fundamental point that ends do not justify means. In order to attain a just goal in our society, we must use just ways. Any other approach will only bring us disaster.

It is not enough, therefore, to seek ends that are good and just. We must also make sure that the means are in keeping with the ends. For to hurt some people in order to benefit others is abhorrent to Jewish tradition. As it has been said, "justice is the passionate concern to wipe the tears from every face in the world"—which means that everyone is regarded as holy.

*For the Lord of Hosts is exalted through righteousness, and God, the Holy One, is sanctified through justice.*

HIGH HOLYDAY LITURGY

# Not To Decide Is To Decide

Most of us in our daily living choose to ignore the decisions that are open to us. We think we don't have to make a decision yet about sending our child to Hebrew School. Time slips away, and suddenly our decision is made for us by the child who announces, "I'm not going!" So, he or she has chosen and, by default, we have not.

Some Jews say, "Well, it doesn't matter what I believe. I don't have to make a commitment about a synagogue. What I feel about God really doesn't matter." And then, one day, we find our life ending without a faith, without a synagogue, without a God.

Consider this story: Once upon a time Satan asked his helpers to propose ways of defeating a revival on earth that was then occurring. One suggested, "I would tell the people that there is no God, no devil, no heaven, no hell; and that they should eat, drink, and be merry, for tomorrow we die." "You need not go," said Satan. "No one would believe you."

A more shrewd assistant said, "Let me go and tell them that the Bible is a good book, but that it is only partially true. I would tell them that there is a God and a heaven but no devil and no hell; and that, no matter how they lived, they would be eternally happy."

But Satan said, "Only a minority would believe that."

Finally, the shrewdest said, "I would tell them the Bible is all true and that they must make their choice between God and Satan, but that there is no hurry."

"Good," said Satan. "You have the system."

*Elijah stepped forward and said to the people, "How long will you sit on the fence? If the Lord is God, follow him; but if Baal, then follow him."*   I KINGS 18:21

# The Chain Of Compassion

God desires all people to be filled with compassion and mercy. The Hebrew word *rachum* is the root word of the Yiddish expression *rachmones*—a word that cannot really be translated. Often as children we heard the phrase reiterated in our homes: *hob rachmones*. Once we heard it, we knew what it meant. It meant more than just being merciful. The closest we can come in English is the notion of compassion—feeling the passion of another human being, knowing what it is like to be in another's shoes.

A rabbi who was regarded as very pious was invited to dinner. A serving maid brought each guest a pitcher of water for the ritual of washing the hands. All the others at the table used the water freely, but the rabbi did not. He simply wet his fingers and no more. His friends were surprised and perturbed, but the rabbi explained the action by saying: "When you washed your hands, you were concerned with the ritual requirement. When I washed my hands, I was concerned about the serving girl, poor child. She has to go to the well, draw the water, and carry it to the house. Can I practice piety at the expense of her strength?"

Each of us, every day, can find simple ways to be compassionate. By being just a little more thoughtful, we can bring more *rachmones* into the world. For, after all, what is the world but a machine unless we supply the human touch? What does it mean to be created in the image of God unless we reflect His greatness? There is a chain reaction of mercy. Mercy begets more mercy, and compassion generates more compassion, and the chain reaches all the way to heaven.

*Every time that you are compassionate, the Compassionate One shall have compassion upon you.*

TOSEFTA BAVA KAMMA 9

249

# Moderately Successful

Dr. Morris Chafetz, psychiatrist at Harvard University and head of the alcoholism clinic at Massachusetts General Hospital in Boston, recommended that we ought to teach children how to drink alcohol. We should start them young with small doses, he said, so that later on they would learn to avoid the hazards of the improper use of alcohol and, at the same time, would discover the technique of controlling their desires and their impulses. In the long run, he argued, a training program in the use of wine and liquor would help reduce alcoholism and related diseases.

Immediately, everybody praised this idea as a very daring approach. Actually, it is neither new nor daring. Jews have been given regular training on every Sabbath and every holiday for thousands of year in the wise, balanced and healthy use of alcoholic beverages.

Here we have a fundamental insight into Judaism. Jewish thought emphasizes that people's desires are not to be shunned or denied, but rather to be controlled and channeled. Jews were given dietary laws in which some foods were permitted and some were forbidden. Jews were trained to enjoy a good meal on *Shabbat* but to avoid certain foods and to refrain from eating on certain days.

Sex, as well, was not a taboo subject among Jews. Jews were taught that sex was to be used in the proper way and were given instruction in the meaning of love and family life. Again here we see the wisdom of a tradition and a discipline that taught its faithful from childhood on how to handle impulses, desires and feelings. Jews were instructed neither to deny them nor to give them full reign; rather they were trained to harness these impulses fruitfully in the service of a healthy attitude toward life.

*There should be moderation in all things.*

LETTER OF ARISTEAS 223

# Hope Against Hostility

History has been plagued by the belief that some differences can only be resolved by a "showdown," in which both sides face each other at high noon and blast away. Sometimes it is one nation against another, sometimes it is one generation against another, and at still other times it is one philosophy or religion against another. But, this erroneous notion of doom and the false idea of the inevitability of conflict often becomes a self-fulfilling prophecy. In all historical instances of supposedly irreconcilable differences, after the smoke has cleared and the dead have been buried, the opposing forces learned to live with each other and ultimately to help each other. The tragedy was that they did not do so in the first place.

We know that all races and all religions and all cultures can get along with each other, if they want to. Moreover, there can be peace in society if there is equal justice for all and a sense of respect for differences. But we must be willing to accept the premise that there are different ways to do things, various ways to solve problems, and that while one particular way may be fine for us, it may not work for someone else. As the great composer Brahms said after hearing an unusually fiery interpretation of his famous *Violin Concerto*: "So—it can be played that way too."

If all races and cultures learn that there are many ways to play the symphony of life, then we may yet earn the gratitude of all the coming generations.

*It is not inevitable that we march in hostile and separated hosts into the common abyss. There is another possibility of an ordered world illuminated by reason and governed by law. If we cannot yet touch it with our hands, let us at least grasp it in our vision.* ABBA EBAN

# The Highest Degree

From the Jewish point of view, it is better than any academic title or degree to be called a *mensch*. A *mensch* means more than being a person, it means more than being a human being, it really means doing that which is right, decent and proper.

In the Bible we are told that the greatest of all Jews had only one title. He was not called "Doctor," or "Ph.D." or even "Rabbi"; he was called, *haish Moshe*, "the man Moses." Moses was a *mensch*! He was a person who lived simply to do his duty, carry out his responsibilities and have consideration for others. All the abilities and talents that were given to him—and they were more than were ever given to another human being—he used for others. This is what a *mensch* does. He or she lives for others.

Education may solve some of our problems, but it may create others unless it is education for *character*. In the 1930's, Germany had the highest educational standards of any country in the civilized world and had made enormous contributions to scholarship. In order to obtain a Ph.D., or to undertake research in any field of human endeavor, one had to know German. And what did these people do with all their education? They started the second World War, perfected means of mass destruction and invented the concentration camp system. On the other hand, all over the world there are people who are illiterate but kind and gentle. These people, real *menschen*, do the drudge work in hospitals, or they clean homes, doing the labor for others. They do menial work, helpers and healers, rather than haters. Therefore, our ancestors said it well: *tov torah im derekh eretz*, "Learning is good if it is joined with good character."

*One who possesses both learning and character is like an artist with all tools at hand.*    AVOT DE RABBI NATHAN 22

252

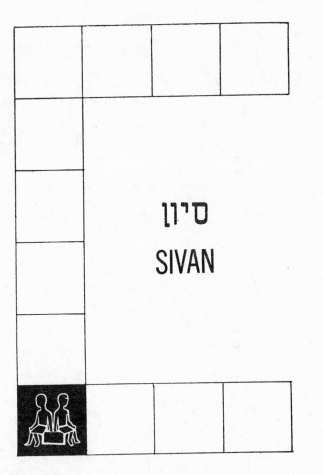

סיון
SIVAN

# Adding Life To Years

In a very famous poem, "The Rock," T. S. Eliot poses a question that goes to the heart of modern life. He asks, "Where is the life we have lost in living? Where is the wisdom we have lost in knowledge?" The answer is that we have lost a portion of life by not living, we have let wisdom slip from our hands by pursuing facts alone. We have turned to statistics when we could have used common sense. We have consulted specialists when we might have used our own judgment. There is so much around us in life that we miss if we leave our decisions to others or go only by the rule of the book.

Life is so wonderful, even with its pain and its anguish, that not to live fully is an insult to the Giver of life. It is like being given a gift by a dear friend, and then not using it.

Former Vice President Garner had lost a ten-dollar bet on a baseball game, and the winner asked him to autograph the bill. "I'm giving it to my grandson for a souvenir," he explained. "He wants to frame it and hang it in his room."

"You mean the money's not going to be spent?" asked the Texan.

"That's right."

"Well," said Garner, "then I'll just write you a check."

What is the use of having life and not living it?

*So while we are praying to God for long life, let us not forget to ask Him to help us fill that life with learning and good deeds, with decent living and worthwhile doing, with making others happy, with bringing comfort to the bereaved, with giving strength to the fallen, with helping the needy, the sick, the orphans, and the aged. Don't waste your years with nothingness. Make your years worthwhile, be they long or be they few. Don't squander the years that God gives you. Make the best of them.* ABRAHAM E. HALPERN

# What's The Good Word?

The words we use tell a great deal about us. The publishers of a dictionary recently reported that a parrot can learn about 250 words. A bright six-year-old knows about 2,500 words. A dull adult knows approximately 9,000 words. An ordinary person has a vocabulary of between 35,000 and 70,000 words. Obviously we lift our intellectual, social and moral stature by increasing our words. And how else can we do that except by reading and by recalling great words that are the touchstones of the human spirit. For stirring phrases have their place in the chronology of man. Clement Attlee once said of Winston Churchill's oratory, "Words at great moments of history are deeds."

And who will ever forget Churchill's words after the German armies invaded the Low Countries: "I have nothing to offer but blood, toil, tears and sweat." With this one sentence, Churchill mobilized all of Britain into a heroic effort.

Or who will ever forget Roosevelt's words in the heart of the Depression in 1933 when he counselled, "We have nothing to fear but fear itself." With this one sentence he unified America and inspired us to shake off our national despair.

And for us Jews the words that we proclaim twice a day, "Hear, O Israel: the Lord is our God, the Lord is One!" have been the foundation and the strength of our people. This one sentence has held us together. Committed to the concept of One God by this personal proclamation, we have withstood all the massive onslaughts of history and remained strong, firm and creative unto this very day.

*A word at the proper time, how good it is.*

PROVERBS 15:23

# Growth Amid The Desert

Recently, a new plant was discovered in the Negev, the dry and barren desert in southern Israel. The plant, named *aaronsohnia*, can grow in arid wilderness. It is this plant that made possible the resettlement of the wastes of the Negev.

The plant is called *aaronsohnia* after an agronomist named Aaron Aaronsohn. He came to *Eretz Yisrael* with his family from Russia in 1882 when he was six years old. From that moment on he developed a lifelong interest in the study of plants and trees that could flourish there. As he grew into manhood he became a soil specialist. He built the first agricultural experimental station in *Eretz Yisrael* seven miles south of Haifa. He devoted his life to developing plants and trees that would withstand drought, locusts and the many other stresses brought about by the extreme climatic conditions of the Middle East.

It was Aaronsohn's work that made possible the resettlement of *Eretz Yisrael*. Without his research on plants and trees, the early pioneers could never have settled the land. And this telling point is often missed in modern Jewish history: The Israelis did not conquer the land with guns or words or government. They conquered the land with trees. The moment they learned how to use the soil, how to care for the soil, how to plant and grow and harvest, how to blanket the whole landscape with grove after grove, they conquered Israel.

*I planted a tree in my little garden.*
*And to the soil of my garden this is what I said:*
*"You and I are bound together by this little sapling.*
*May we grow and flourish together."*

ZEV (A *KIBBUTZ* POET)

# Human Harmony

One of the ways we can achieve harmony in the human community is through patient understanding. We must understand that our young people are yearning desperately to grow up in a world free of the threat of war and the extinction of the environment. We must understand that older people do not wish to be placed on a shelf and forgotten. They, too, want "a piece of the action." We must understand that expressions of dissent are not denials of patriotism but may very well be the essence of the love of America. We must understand why people are offended when the American flag, which is an historic symbol of freedom and democracy, is deliberately desecrated.

Our Bill of Rights as Americans has become a long one. But it is interesting that there is no companion Bill of Responsibilities, and there certainly should be. We proclaim vociferously the rights of free speech but nowhere do we state the obligation to listen, to listen particularly to those with whom we disagree. But any person who proclaims that he or she can never be wrong has already closed the door on the possibility of being right.

Things that grow do not have to shout to demonstrate their value and their beauty. Similarly, a successfully growing society must learn how to harmonize its many components to produce a better life for all, and this can be done only by consciously attempting to eliminate hate and reach understanding.

*Fortunate is the one who has found wisdom and acquired understanding.* PROVERBS 3:13

# Torah! Torah! Torah!

Most people read the Bible and other related literature such as the Prayer Book for what is called "proof texts." To prove that God exists, to prove a miracle, to prove that if you say this prayer or utter that phrase you will find instant healing, or redemption, or whatever. But this approach misses the whole point of Torah, that the verses of the Bible as well as rabbinic phrases are not mystical or magical utterances but distilled wisdom. A verse from Scripture does not represent the holy because Moses taught it but rather because it expresses a fundamental insight into human behavior or a vision toward which we should strive. It is not just the source but the content as well that is important.

Two mule drivers, bitter enemies, were walking on the road. The mule of one broke down under its load. The other saw the incident but proceeded on his way. After a while he thought, "It is writen in the Torah, 'If you see the animal of your enemy lying under its burden, you shall not pass him by; you must relieve the animal of the burden.' " Immediately, he turned back and helped the other mule driver with the burden.

The first mule driver thought to himself: "My companion is really a good friend, but I had no idea." They then both went to an inn and ate together in peace.

What caused them to be reconciled? The fact that one remembered a teaching of the Torah. Indeed, let us look into the Torah, for through it we will learn to reconcile ourselves with our community, with our environment, with our very own selves. For Torah is not just a word; it is a whole way of life.

*The Torah is our life and the length of our days.*

JEWISH PRAYER BOOK

# Have Your Faith Lifted

Shavuot is known as *hag habikurim*, the festival of the first ripe summer fruits. The most ancient and most essential function of Shavuot is to remind us of the beauty of the natural world and its constant renewal, and to reawaken our faith in the possibilities in the universe, for beauty and for good. Shavuot comes to remind us that the world has summer as well as winter, the surprise of spring and the beauty of fall. Its purpose is to give us perspective. For in the last analysis, religion as well as life teaches us that what really matters is the perspective we have on our lives— in other words, our point of view.

A very wealthy man once proudly escorted an artist over his lavish estate. "You see," said the millionaire, with a lordly sweep of his arm, "I own all this land." "Yes," replied the artist, "but it is *I* who own the landscape."

The world is ours if we know how to look at it, how to revere it and how, through faith, to wait for its blessings through the hard winter into the spring that leads into the beauty of the early summer.

This is most relevant to our presence on earth. How we handle life's experiences ultimately depends on our point of view. Did we come to mourn our loss or to be warmed by the memories of what we were privileged to have? Are we constantly bewailing our lot or learning instead how to live on with faith and courage and hope? Of course we remember the pains of life, but if we have the right perspective we will also recall its pleasures. Our lives are determined by how we look at them.

*Our deeds cannot be measured except by the yardstick of the vision which brought us higher.* BERL KATZNELSON

# Death Can Serve Life

Above the entrance of the Department of Autopsies in the French Medical School at the Sorbonne the following words are inscribed: *Hic est locus ubi mors ad vitam perfecit,* "This is the place where death is made to serve life." The way religious and intelligent people ought to view death is to make it render a service to life. To be aware of death, to be aware that life has a natural end, should make us value life all the more. Grief within limits is necessary and appropriate, but grief beyond reason is a denial of God and man. To mourn excessively is a declaration that human life is one's own possession and not the property of God.

The rabbis in the Talmud ask, "Why is the water of the eyes salty?" "Because," reasoned a sage of old, "when a person weeps for the dead constantly he becomes blind. But since tears are salty, and make his eyes smart, he stops weeping." Our tears sometimes do make us blind to those who need us, who need our smiles, our unrestrained laughter, our wholesome joy. Our tears blind us to the real meaning of faith that reaches beyond this life to eternal life with God.

The torments of grief and the anguish of loneliness in bereavement often come in the wake of feeling that one has been thrust alone and afraid into a world that death made. It is at this point that one must try to make life worthwhile through study, through work, through community service, and through creative leisure. These activities reaffirm our sense that the love of someone in the past has given us the strength to move on into the future, to live in a way that brings honor to the family name and help to others.

*The Lord gave, and the Lord has taken away; blessed be the name of the Lord.*
                                                                    JOB 1:21

# The Right Response

The word charity is an essential part of the religious vocabulary. But charity is only a partial translation for the more inclusive Hebrew term *tzedakah*. Charity implies a sense of condescension or, at best, a feeling of graciousness. *Tzedakah*, on the other hand, represents both a social obligation and a religious commitment.

This responsibility of the individual to the community finds apt illustration in a Hasidic tale. A man once resolved to devote the whole day to the recitation of the entire Book of Psalms. Toward evening as he was approaching the end, a representative of the rabbi came over and told him that the rabbi wished to speak with him. The man said, "Tell the rabbi I will see him as soon as I have finished reciting the Psalms." In a little while the representative returned and said, "The rabbi must see you immediately." When the man came to see the rabbi he asked, "Why did you bother me when I was in the midst of my prayers? Could you not have waited until I concluded?"

And the Hasidic rabbi replied, "I called you because I wanted you to make a contribution to a needy family. Psalms and prayers can be chanted by angels as well, but angels cannot give charity. Only mortal man can perform such deeds for his fellows. *Tzedakah* is greater than chanting the Psalms."

The needs of human beings must be answered by other human beings, and only as we understand this basic truth about life can we create a society of worth and meaning.

*Do not harden your heart or shut your hand against your needy brother.*    DEUTERONOMY 15:7

# Perfectly Divine

It is important to understand that God is to be experienced, but that He cannot be captured in any one thing alone. We think we can contain God in a thing, and He will be with us. We put a little statue or a small box with a religious symbol on the dashboard of our car, and we think we have captured God and He will protect us. Is this not naive? For what can save us if we drive carelessly? We think we can represent Him in a religious symbol, put Him on a string, and tie it around our neck; and He will, therefore, be with us in person. Now, how can this protect us from an illness if we do not take the normal precautions of rest, proper diet and good health? Some even believe that we can put Him in a box in an Ark, or store Him up in an altar, and there He will be. We do not truly understand that these are merely the symbols of His moral teachings.

Once a Jewish carriage driver came to the great Reb Levi Yitzhak of Berditchev with a serious religious problem. He said, "Rabbi, I would like to come to the synagogue more often and be in the presence of God. But, unfortuantely my business keeps me so busy carrying others that I have little time to do this. Perhaps I ought to change my job."

Reb Levi then asked these questions. "When people come to hire your carriage do you charge everyone the same price?" The man answered, "Yes, of course." Reb Levi continued and asked, "What do you do if they are poor?" And the driver responded, "Oh, I don't charge them at all." And Reb Levi answered, "My son, you are already in the presence of God, and you don't know it."

*Where people gather for worship, where judges sit as a court, and where even one person engages in study, the presence of God is there.*                    BERAKHOT 6a

# Suppose They Gave A War

Each of us is the only person who can give others a peaceful and sane society. We can turn away from violence and commit ourselves to human values.

A story found in Greek literature is told of Pyrrhus, one of the great warriors of antiquity. In an interval of leisure while preparing to invade Italy, he was conferring with his favorite advisor Cineas. Cineas asked what they would do if they conquered the Romans.

"Sicily is near," replied Pyrrhus. "We will invade that rich island."

"But will we stop there?" gently asked Cineas.

"If heaven smiles," Pyrrhus said, "that will be but the preliminary to greater enterprises. We shall conquer Macedonia."

"And then?" Cineas asked quietly.

Pyrrhus smiled, "Why, then, we shall sit at ease and drink cool wine and gladden our hearts with talk."

"But," Cineas said at last, "what stands in our way *now* for us to enjoy these privileges of ease? We have them at hand, *without* bloodshed and trouble and without imperiling others."

We can have the good life now, so why fight? We can help hunger in America, rebuild cities, strengthen our economy, clean up our natural environment, and create new programs of research to solve our most troubling illnesses, so why dissipate our energies? We can have peace, so why have war? As Carl Sandburg, the great American poet, once wrote, "Just suppose they gave a war—and nobody came." Just suppose!

*Great is peace for it outweighs everything.*

NUMBERS RABBAH 11:16

# Possibly

In the Book of Numbers we read (14:19), "Forgive the sin of this people." And the next verse continues, "and God said, 'I shall forgive as you have asked.' " Exactly what was the great sin the people had committed? It was not worshipping the Golden Calf. It was not being contrary or rebellious to the word of God. It was rather in what occurred when the first scouts returned and reported on the Promised Land. The scouts said: "It is a beautiful land. But you will never be able to possess it because the obstacles are too formidable for you. You are not worthy; you cannot do it." And because the people accepted this evaluation of themselves, they sinned and they suffered for it.

We learn from this text that the real sin is the loss of self-confidence and self-esteem, and the resultant failure of nerve. When a person or a group loses the sense of worth, truly, they become unworthy. But a patient and thoughtful re-examination of our lives will restore our sense of worth; when we regain our confidence in self, we recover our faith in the meaning and purpose of being human.

Someone once asked a child what he wanted to be when he grew up. The boy's quick reply was, "I want to be possible." "Possible?" said the visitor, perplexed. "Yes," said the little fellow. "Every day my mother tells me I'm impossible."

We have to increase our feelings of self-worth by focusing on our possibilities. We must begin by believing in ourselves. It is a matter of faith—faith that we ourselves can solve our problems.

*The strength of Judaism consists in this, that as soon as one period of history comes to an end, another begins. A new idea replaces the old, fresh forces come into play, and the result is continuous progress.*    NACHMAN KROCHMAL

# The Reality Of Israel

Who would have thought there would be a State of Israel, and that it could survive? Yet today there is an Israel, and it not only survives but thrives and grows.

Why has all this come to pass? Simply because Jews took seriously God's promise to Abraham that the land of Israel is theirs in perpetuity. Jews reckon their experience not in days or years but in centuries. They are the children of history, and everything they do is seen from the perspective of the ages.

An article by a Christian minister who visited Israel concludes with this: "Look at those mountains," I said one day to a Jewish companion, pointing to a barren range of hills to our left. "There's nothing you can do with those."

"Those hills," he replied, "were once beautiful with figs and olives. We shall make them beautiful again."

"How will you do it?" I asked.

"We shall terrace them," he said, "as they were terraced in the old days. Those slopes are not mere sand and rock. There's soil there still. And the soil that has been washed away into these valleys, we'll carry it back, basket by basket, shovelful by shovelful, until the hills are green again."

"You can't do that," I cried, "not in a hundred years!"

Then came the bravest words I heard in Israel: "What's a hundred years to a Jew?"

Indeed it is because Israel's seed endures that the state has survived. This is in keeping with God's promise to Abraham that Israel will endure to the end of time.

*The Lord said to Abram, "Raise up your eyes and look into the distance ... all the land you can see I will give to you and to your descendants forever."*   GENESIS 13:14-15

# Listen To This

Most of us proceed on the assumption that the way to establish a relationship with God is to pray. Well, this is only a half truth, because if we do not keep still how do we know what God has to say? If all we do is talk, how can God get a word in edgewise?

Occasionally, someone asks: "Why doesn't God speak to us the way He spoke to Moses?" They should be reminded that Moses went up to the top of the mountain and said nothing for forty days and forty nights. So, perhaps, God is speaking to us but we are not listening. The Almighty may use feelings rather than words. His messages are everywhere in the universe, but often we are just not prepared to receive them.

It is appropriate to cite an incident that begins the spiritual life of the Prophet Samuel. The boy Samuel is asleep in the sanctuary of Shiloh when the call of God comes to him for the first time. Aroused from his sleep by the sound of his name, Samuel assumes that it is the aged priest, Eli, in the nearby room who has called him. Dutifully, he rises from his bed and goes to Eli and says, "Here I am, for you called me." "No," Eli replies, I did not call you. Go lie down."

Once again Samuel hears his name and he rushes to Eli. Again the boy is told that he was not called. When this happens a third time, the old priest tells the boy Samuel that if he hears the voice again he should reply, "Speak, O Lord, for your servant listens."

Perhaps, the time has come for us—in our world, in our homes, and in our private consciences—to say: Speak, for your servant listens.

*Hear, O Israel.*                    DEUTERONOMY 6:4

# Have Compassion For All

Compassion means "to feel passion with." Only as we feel the passion of other people, their angers and their loves, their disappointments and their dreams, their hates and their hopes, can we really be of service. It is our willingness to be involved in experiences of encounter with others and our inner selves that will make for the compassionate society. We must be willing to put ourselves in someone else's position. This is what sensitivity really means, and it is ultimately a religious affirmation.

A very interesting illustration of this sympathetic identification with the feeling of others is seen in this true story: One sunny May day in Central Park a blind man was seen tapping for attention with his cane. On his chest was a sign: "Help the Blind." But no one paid much attention to him. A little farther on another blind man was doing better. Practically every passerby put a coin in his cup, some even turning back to make a contribution. His sign said: "It is May . . . and I am blind."

Think of the person who loses a job and how he or she feels. Think of a child in a ghetto and what makes him or her react the way he or she does. Consider our brothers and sisters in Israel who time after time have been let down by the world, and you will begin to understand their siege mentality and their mistrust of the politicians of the world. If you were an unemployed person, if you were a child of the ghetto, if you were an Israeli would *you* feel any differently? When we come closer to the feelings of these people, then surely we will come closer to understanding and helping them.

*Have compassion for all, not only people but all living things.*            PATRIARCHS, ZEBULUN 5:1

# Every Man A Judge

The seventeenth verse of the twenty-fourth chapter of the Book of Deuteronomy tells us, "You shall not deny the rights of the stranger." And for this counsel the Bible adds a very interesting reason: "For you shall remember that you were a slave—a stranger—in the land of Egypt."

Now, it is interesting that here the Bible appeals to people to be careful of the rights of others not on the basis of a moral code nor even of a belief in God but rather of personal experience. What it is saying is: How can you be unfair to others when you understand the pain and the suffering that come in the wake of being treated unjustly yourself? How would you feel if this happened to you? Use your own self as the basis for dealing with others.

This mode of human thought, putting one's own feelings at the basis of one's actions, can be very important in our dealings with others. For example, when we criticize minority groups and their actions, have we forgotten how we felt when *we* were in the ghetto? We often are harshly critical of teenagers. But, then, have we forgotten what it means to be a teenager ourselves, having to face all the dilemmas of a growing person? Very often we will pass judgment on some act of human behavior and, yet, we may have forgotten that in a period of personal stress we once did the very same thing. All of this is implied in this Biblical verse.

In fact, it was well said in an American Indian proverb: "Never judge a man until you have walked several miles in his moccasins."

*The gateway to compassion is a passion for understanding.*
SAMUEL M. SILVER

# No Room For Hostility

It is important to understand that there is a basic difference between anger and hostility. Anger can be a legitimate reaction, and sometimes the only reaction to a situation, but when it turns into hostility it can hurt someone needlessly. If people are hurt, can one realistically expect them to be quiet and not give vent to their feelings?

Now, think for a moment. Do you expect anyone who is discriminated against, who is unemployed, who is impoverished, not to feel angry? If a bus load of teenagers were blown up by a terrorist's bomb, would parents sit back and accept it placidly? If we have suddenly sustained the loss of a dear one, is it unreasonable to expect some sense of outrage at the cosmic order?

There is a revealing incident about a little boy who was very troublesome one day during recess at his school. Some girls had been teasing him, and in a rage he chased them through the playground, pulling their hair, and knocking them down. After recess, the teacher said, "I want you to apologize to these girls for losing your temper."

"All right," the boy replied, standing up like a man. "Girls, I'm sorry I lost my temper." But as he sat down he heard some girls giggle. He jumped up again, "But I didn't lose all of it!" he warned.

The point is that there is some anger in all of us, and we must accept it and recognize it as part of being human. We cannot react to provocation with complete indifference and still remain human beings. But, at the same time, we must not let our anger get out of hand and hurt innocent people.

*Devote time each day to studying yourself . . . ferreting out your weakness, working at self-improvement, purifying your immortal soul.*          ISRAEL SALANTER LIPKIN

# The Education Of A Jew

Our young people are continually turning to us and asking us for guidance and direction. They want to know, and with good reason, how they can apply Judaism to everyday living.

A delightful story makes this point very well.

A Jewish chaplain was on a Boeing Air Force jet taking off from the Yakota airport in the Far East. As he sat in his seat he removed his Air Force service cap, and put on his *kipah* and his *tallit* in preparation for prayer. An Air Force sergeant in the next seat looked at him with obvious curiosity. The Jewish chaplain turned and trying good public relations said, "Do you know what this is?" and he pointed to his *kipah*. And answering his own question, he continued, saying, "It is my parachute."

"But, Sir, the Air Force sergeant replied, "it is too small for a parachute."

Then the chaplain showed him his *tallit* and the fringes of the *tzitzit* and he told the sergeant, "This is my rip cord."

The sergeant scratched his head, looked at him in a puzzled manner, and said, "Frankly, Sir, that is not what my rabbi told me before my Bar Mitzvah."

The time has come to stop kidding the kids. We must tell our young people what it means to be Jewish in terms of hardship, obligation and responsibility so that they will earn its rewards of dignity, achievement and fulfillment.

*If you do not let your son grow up as a Jew, you deprive him of those sources of energy which cannot be replaced by anything else. He will have to struggle as a Jew and you ought to develop in him all the energy he will need for the struggle. Do not deprive him of that advantage.*

SIGMUND FREUD

# Make Waves

One of the purposes of ritual in religion is to move us to *do* something. Meditation, prayer, study have as one of their goals inspiring informed action that will help other people and improve the lot of society.

When we are involved in life itself we find that not only are we carrying out the will of God but we ourselves become happier in the process. For example, don't we feel better after we visit someone in the hospital? Are we not ennobled when we participate in a program for community improvement? When we actively help the underprivileged, do we not feel a sense of satisfaction? When we comfort the bereaved, do we not emerge as better people? A simple thoughtful action to make life a little pleasanter for someone else may become for us an act of therapy. The deepest satisfactions in life are not only what we learn but, more important, what we do.

Take this charming story, for example. It was a beautiful spring day and a grandmother had promised her four-year-old granddaughter to take her for a walk along the edge of the river. But cooking and other household chores kept her busy inside the house. The little girl waited patiently for a long time. Finally, she could hold out no longer. She took her grandmother's hand and pulled her along. "Stop working, Grandma," she said. "Let's go outside and get some use out of the world."

The world is here to be used, to be enjoyed. But to accomplish this, we must be willing to move. People say: "Don't make waves." But sometimes we must make waves, tidal waves of purpose and affirmation.

*He shall bring it with his own hands and then he shall lift it as an offering before the Lord.*          LEVITICUS 7:30

# Contract With God

One of the fundamental statements in Jewish theology is the concept of the covenant. In Hebrew it is called *brit*, and it refers to the agreement which God made with Abraham. If we translate this basic concept into our own lives, we can understand that every life involves a contract with God.

If life is a contract or covenant with God, then we might consider what is the element that is basic to a legal binding agreement. Essentially, a contract involves mutual responsibility. This means obligations on both sides to help each other, and in some way each party gives something to the other.

When God gives us life, He fulfills the first obligation on His part. Then, in turn, *we* are obliged to use this life with wisdom and understanding and to benefit others as well.

We might be reminded of the story of two men who were dining together in a restaurant. After a time they got to discussing politics, and their voices rose with passion. When it looked as if they might come to blows, the owner came dashing up and warned, "Gentlemen, leave politics alone, and eat and drink."

"Nonsense!" said one of the diners. "If a person thinks only of eating and drinking, what distinguishes people from cattle?"

And the owner replied, "Paying the bill, sir."

To turn to a more serious view, we must understand that we have to pay the bill of life. That is our part of the contract with God.

*The Lord God made a covenant with us . . . not just with our fathers but with us who are alive this day.*

DEUTERONOMY 5:2 f

272

# For The Public Good

We must be willing to subscribe to the principle of public law if civilization is to stand. Laws are meaningless unless people are willing to support them. What good is a law if no one will observe it? You remember what happened to the Prohibition Law? It became a mockery in our land, because people did not believe in it. The Roman Empire was based on the concept of law. Because the private citizens would not observe it, the Roman Empire fell apart. We must not permit this to happen in contemporary society.

We obviously cannot legislate people's feelings. They go deeper, and are more profound than the legislative process. We can, however, use legislation as a standard-setting device to show people what society believes. Some people, fortunately, will always have a more rigorous morality than the law demands. As a matter of fact, they are usually the ones who help to create new legislation. There will also always be some people whose morality is far below what the law requires, and for them laws must exist. Legislation thus stands for a compromise moral situation. But it does serve as a very definite standard-setting device by which to guide public morality; and to insure that, whatever our morality, we observe certain minimal standards of law and justice.

A teacher once was lecturing his students on the theme of how they should play the game of life. After the lecture was concluded, one puzzled student raised his hand and asked, "But how can we play the game when we don't know where the goalposts are?"

Public law may not tell us how to play the whole game, but at least it represents the goalposts of our society. This is an important step as mankind inches its way along the road of progress.

*The law of the land is the law.*                    GITTIN 10b

# The Soul Of The Synagogue

An elderly Jewish woman used to worship in her old synagogue regularly. Her children, who lived in a new suburb that boasted of a new suburban synagogue, continually urged her to spend the holidays with them. They proudly pointed out all the beauties and glories of their synagogue. She finally agreed to attend a service with them. At the conclusion of the service, the children asked their mother what she thought of their synagogue's striking and beautiful architecture, what she thought of the wonderfully comfortable seats, the air conditioning, the marvelous cantor and choir, and the eloquent rabbi. Of course, the mother agreed that it was all very beautiful. She had but one minor comment: *alles is shayn, ober men ken nisht vaynen dorten,* "Everything is beautiful, but there is no place to cry."

This is, indeed, the heart of the matter. The synagogue must be a place to shed tears for the tragedies of life, to cry out against the injustices of the world, to rage against the perils and pains of life, but it must also be a place to cry out in joy over the good things life gives us. Tears of happiness for the marriages that are celebrated, the children that are born, and the milestones that are reached. It must be a place to proclaim what we have achieved in justice and responsibility. All of this must find expression in the synagogue.

Unless the synagogue is also a place *tzu vaynen,* to cry out our heart's hopes and our soul's griefs, then we will not have succeeded as Jews. For if we do everything else but we have not been moved to speak from the heart in the sanctuary of God, then our religious efforts become worthless.

*The synagogue is the one unfailing wellspring of Jewish feeling. There we pray together with our brethren and in the act become participators in the common sentiment.*

MORRIS JOSEPH

# When The Past Is Present

We must continually remind ourselves that we are the product of many generations. We were molded by the glorious history of our people, and we owe them due recognition.

If we have achieved something in Jewish life today—the State of Israel, a magnificent Jewish community, great advances in Jewish learning—it is due basically to our heritage. The Bible, Rabbinic literature, the Jewish medieval writings have laid a strong moral and intellectual foundation for us.

A young man was recovering in a hospital from an accident. One day, his surgeon remarked to him that he was quite fortunate, and perhaps he ought to offer a prayer of gratitude for his recovery. The young man replied with some sacrcasm, "Yes, doctor, my folks were all religious Jews, all the family way back; but I do not take much stock in that sort of thing." The doctor thought for a moment and said, "You have inherited stock, and very valuable stock. Do you know why you are making such good recovery from your accident, why the bones knit, and the wounds heal so rapidly? It is because those ancestors of yours bequeathed to you good, clean blood and a sound constitution. If I were you, I would not sell their stock short."

We must all remember that we come from a great heritage. We were given a stock that is priceless. Therefore, the question should not be "Can we be proud of our ancestors?" But rather, "If our ancestors were alive today, would they be proud of us?"

*My guidelines are good and I have a beautiful heritage.*
                                                        PSALMS 16:6

# To Be A Person

Several years ago, in his moving drama entitled *Incident at Vichy*, Arthur Miller described the hatred and cruelty inflicted on a group of victims. In the last scene one of the characters confronts the wrongdoers, saying, "I know about everything that happened but you do not understand what I am trying to do. It is not your guilt I want; it is your responsibility I am seeking."

Responsibility comes from the word "response." We must learn how to respond to one another, to try our very best to be sensitive to the needs and feelings of each person. We must respond to the needs of our community, and they are great. Anyone can stand up and read a catalogue of the sins of our times; but, then, we are not being fully helpful until we also begin to cite the responsibilities of our times.

According to Jewish tradition, two rabbis once debated the question: How do we know when the night ends and the new day begins?

The first rabbi said: "The night ends and a new day begins when you can tell the difference beween a blue thread and a purple thread."

The second rabbi said: "The night ends and the day begins when you can see the the face of your neighbor."

Soon it will be dawn again. Let us begin to look for the faces of our neighbors, and in facing them honestly and directly we will find a sense of fulfillment and responsibility. It is easy to heap guilt on oneself for duties neglected and promises ignored. It is harder—but so much better—to dare to keep faith with our best selves.

*When we appear before His throne, God's first question will be: "Have you dealt honorably with your fellow men?"*

SHABBAT 31a

# The Art Of Love

Love can be expressed in many ways. One significant way can be found in the following incident.

Dr. Michael DeBakey, the Houston, Texas, heart surgeon who has pioneered in the creation of mechanical organs and hearts for the human body, recently received a letter from a teen-ager who asked: "Does a plastic heart have love in it?" Dr. DeBakey wrote back the following: "Yes, a plastic heart does have love in it, a very great deal of love. The love in a plastic heart is the love of many people who love other people and don't want them to die. So these people work all day and often all night to build a heart that will make people live longer."

What we often forget is that all we do all day long for others, even in its remotest sense, is an expression of love. It is important to remember this in spite of the problems that beset us, despite the destruction and violence in our midst that find expression in so many ways. It is a strange thing that hate makes headlines but love rarely is placed on the front page. That is because hate is often sudden and a shocking occurrence; but love is a quietly enduring lifelong concern.

The late Henry Luce, who was the founder of *Time* and *Life* magazines, met on one occasion with the editorial staffs of the magazines just prior to their summer vacations. This is what he said in his concluding remarks: "Be ye troubadors of the Lord. Soon all of you will be leaving on vacation. When you are away, stop and think about what you really love, what things you live for, and what things you would die for."

*We need love and creative imagination to do constructive work.*
                                                    PAULA OLLENDORF

# The Meaning Of A Mistake

We learn by living. Although it is obvious and trite, it is a most fundamental principle in learning. There really is no growth within the world or within ourselves until we test ourselves in the college of hard knocks. There is no such thing as instant wisdom. It can only come through process and pain; through probing and patience. Wisdom is gained by thrusting ourselves full force into the process of living. While we can acquire knowledge from books and information by listening, we can learn only by living. To be sure, living means risk, and it means the possibility of being hurt.

This brings to mind a wonderful story of a very successful businessman who was addressing the Chamber of Commerce on the subject, "The Secret of Succeeding in Business." His formula was "good judgment."

After the speaker was finished, one of the members of the audience came up to him and asked, "How do you acquire good judgment?" The successful businessman replied, "Through experience." But the questioner persisted, "How do you get experience?" And the businessman replied with a smile, "Through bad judgment."

The only way to learn is to make mistakes, and the only way to find out whether we are right or wrong is to test ourselves in the process of living. To be willing to experience is the most important will of man. This is a hard lesson to learn. It is hard to learn in our own lives, and it is hard to learn as parents. We seek to shelter our children, to hope they will be spared pain; but we must realize that if they learn through mistakes, these are no longer stumbling blocks but stepping stones.

*I learned much from my teachers, more from my books, and most from my mistakes.*   BERAITOT DE RABBI YITZCHAK

# H-O-P-E

We are beginning to understand that it is enthusiasm that helps lift life out of the ordinary and makes it mean something. If you play life cool, you may freeze. But, on the other hand, play it hot, and—even if you get burned—you will at least shed warmth over the world.

While we properly abhor riots, illegal demonstrations, and those acts which are destructive in their outcome, we must not lose sight of a significant insight. Expressions of intense feeling are not signs of hopelessness but rather hopefulness. The classic clincal description of depression is listlessness and apathy. The first sign that a person exhibits upon coming out of depression is usually concern with something outside of one's self, and even when this concern is in rage, it is usually a good sign.

So, also, the best way to relate to others is by being concerned and feeling rather than being cool and aloof. As Jews, we know that it has been the care for other Jews in peril that has enabled us to survive as a people throughout our history. As Americans, we are finally beginning to understand that only as we are concerned about our community will our communities and our cities sustain periods of stress.

A radio station recently broadcast an appeal for hope. The announcer said that this was a new program based on the letters "H-O-P-E," and it stands for "Help Other People Everywhere." Hope is a way to keep the spark of enthusiasm alive. The word "enthusiasm" comes from the Greek words *en theos*, which means "God in you." May God be in you in everything you do, every day of your life.

*Whatever task lies to your hand, do it with all your might.*
ECCLESIASTES 9:10

# The Courage To Be Happy

The ancient rabbis properly understood that a wealthy person is one who is satisfied with his possessions and that happiness is an attitude toward life. One who is content to live with modest means is truly rich and one who can count his or her blessings is profoundly happy. It all depends on one's viewpoint.

In a clubhouse following a round of golf, some men were discussing their game. The low scorer was very upset and the high scorer was particularly cheerful. This was rather unusual since their attitudes should have been exactly reversed. A visitor was puzzled by this, so he walked over to the amiable golfer and asked him to explain this apparent contradiction. "Well," he said, "it's very easy to understand. He shot a 77 and is miserable because he remembers his five bad strokes. I scored at 105, but I am delighted because I recall my five good strokes. It all depends on how you look at the game."

This is true also of the game of life. It is not important whether we go the course of life in par or not. All that really matters is whether we enjoy the game as we move along. There will be roughs and traps, but eventually we will land on the green. Whether we find it pleasurable depends on our point of view. For the true estimate of experience is not what happens to a person—it is rather what a person does with what happens to him or her.

When the Speaker of the House, Sam Rayburn, celebrated his fiftieth year of service to Congress, he remarked that he hoped to be around a few years longer. His words were, "I like this world better than any other world I've ever lived in." He had the courage to be happy.

*This, too, is a virtue: to be happy.*              LUDWIG BOERNE

# Mercy And Compassion

In religious literature the admonition to be merciful and compassionate is usually addressed to the individual person. This provides us with the insight to understand that these very qualities are essentially personal. If we sincerely seek to apply these values, we should see people instead of problems, companions instead of causes, and human beings instead of humanity.

This approach is illustrated in the career of a very successful lawyer who was well known for being able to get reduced sentences for the accused criminals that he represented. When asked the reason for his success, he replied: "In speaking to the court, I never say 'my client,' or 'the defendant'. I always say 'Tom Jones' or 'Mary Smith.' "

When we filter our thinking through our own personal experiences, then and only then do we acquire real mercy and compassion. When we consider the plight of someone, we must not think of it in terms of the poverty problem or of generalized social action or justice; but rather we must see this person as a mother, a father, a sister, a brother, a child. The world's problems are only statistics until we break them down to family units and translate their meanings in terms of daily living. When we do these things, we restore meaning to the terms "compassion" and "mercy." There is a poem that makes this very point.

> "Give me a theme," the little poet cried, "and I will do my part."
> " 'Tis not a theme you need," the world replied, "you need a heart."

*You must pattern yourself to be like God: Just as He is merciful and compassionate, so you be merciful and compassionate.*                    SHABBAT 133b

# Of Men And Fences

Because the roofs in the Middle Eastern countries were generally flat and used for many purposes, the Bible urged that fences be placed around the edges to prevent a child, or even an adult, from accidentally falling off.

The rabbis carried this thought into the spiritual realm and urged the building of a *seyag la torah*, "a fence about the Torah." The purpose of this restraint was to prevent a person from being tempted to violate basic laws. Thus many minor laws in Judaism have the purpose of serving as a "fence" to keep the individual from falling into major errors. There are many instances in Jewish teachings of an individual being counseled to refrain from an act not because it is wrong in itself, but rather because it might lead to further wrongdoing.

John Sherman, a Senator from Ohio at the end of the nineteenth century, came home from Washington during an election year. When asked why he did so, the reply was, "I have come home to look after my fences." From this statement has come the phrase "to mend one's fences." This subtly reminds us that it is important to be careful and thoughtful about relationships that could deteriorate and become harmful. We must always be aware that prevention of a harmful act is part of the process of thoughtful living.

Robert Frost wrote in his poem *Mending Wall*, "Good fences make good neighbors." And great teachers of ethics have always known that discipline and forethought are the preconditions for a moral life.

*When you build a new house, you shall make a fence for your roof, so that you do not bring guilt on your house if anyone should fall from it.*                    DEUTERONOMY 22:8

# To Serve God In Purity

Man's service of God ought to be without concern for gain or advantage. To expect a reward for a good deed is to act as if there could be a bargain between God and man. This view is not only a distortion of the reason for serving God but is also based on a selfish desire. The performance of a responsibility or a kindness gives one a sense of inner fulfillment that is enough purpose for the act itself. It is sufficient for the responsible person to do what is right simply because it is right.

This brings to mind the parable of a man who met a woman carrying a pan of fire in one hand and a pitcher of water in the other. The puzzled man asked the woman why she was carrying these objects. She replied that her purpose was to burn paradise with the fire and to quench the flames of hell with the water so that people may serve God purely for the love of God.

This symbolic legend expresses the Jewish ideal that service to God is sufficient in itself. To the mature religious person, virtue is its own reward. With this in mind, when we perform any virtuous act we must endeavor to do so for the right reason. Notoriety and acclaim for the performance of acts that serve God and people only detract from their true meaning. Perhaps this is why the Talmud wrote: "The greatest charity is that which is done in secret" (Bava Batra 9b). Those who express their devotion to others and their love of God by performing good deeds quietly and without ostentation truly are those who sustain the world.

*Do not be like servants who serve the master in order to receive a reward, but be like servants who serve the master not on condition of receiving compensation.*    AVOT 1:3

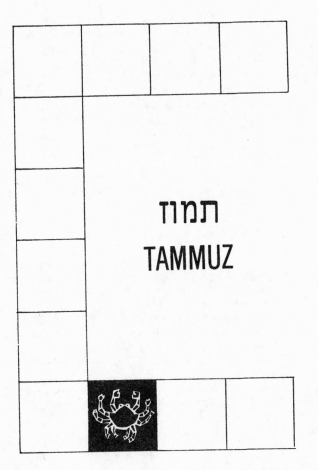

תמוז
TAMMUZ

# The Faith Behind "Amen"

The Hebrew term for faith is *emunah*. *Emunah* is quickly recognizable in the more common form of *ahmayn* or *amen*, the word that often concludes a prayer. The phrase was first used by Psalmists and is still part of the prayer structure of the religions of the western world.

When we say "amen," we are in fact affirming our faith in God. We are demonstrating our willingness to accept the ways of the world, even though at any given moment they may not be so pleasing. It is a willingness to suspend judgment until we have greater perception, greater experience and greater knowledge of the world.

"Amen" is an agreement to conform to the ways of nature and accept all of life as natural. It is natural to laugh and to cry. It is natural to be angry and loving. It is natural for the trees to bloom and to shed their leaves. It is natural for human beings to be born and to die. In all these there is no need to be fearful or to be anxious.

If one lives in good faith with God, one will accept all events as a part of life. All the things that happen to us must be accepted as part of the larger statement of good faith. There is no great feat in accepting a relationship when it is easy and profitable. But it is something to fulfill the terms of a relationship when it taxes and wearies us, when we must pay the full price of the emotions. Faith on a full stomach may be simply contentment; but if you have it when you are hungry, it is genuine.

A man once said to a clergyman, "You must have great faith." "No," the clergyman replied, "I don't have great faith. I have a little faith in a great God."

*Wait for the Lord; be strong, take courage, and wait for the Lord.*
                                                    PSALMS 27:14

# Open Lines

It is a paradox that in this world of improved and instant communication we are terribly distant from one another. Somehow we have not learned how to approach one another in love and how to keep near to one another by communicating our true feelings. Yet, on those occasions when we do open communication and draw near to one another in speech and in deed, we find life endowed with meaning and fulfillment.

Dr. Kalman Yaron, a high official in the Kol Yisrael broadcasting industry, happened to be in Ramallah on the last day of the Six-Day War. On his way to the radio station, he came across a young Arab holding a white flag. The Arab, his face trembling, asked if he would send a telegram to his sisters in San Francisco with just two words, "Family living." Dr. Yaron said he would and refused to take money for this good deed.

Some months later he once again met the Arab, who kissed him and thanked him for what he had done. He became a friend of the Arab's, and the two families celebrated the civil New Year together. The Arab then told Dr. Yaron that one night he had a nightmare. He had dreamt that the walls between East Jerusalem and West Jerusalem, between the Arabs and the Jews, had sprouted up again. The Arab awoke in a sweat with one thought, "Maybe they will forget to cut the telephone lines between Yaron's house and ours."

Maybe if the nations of the world, the cultures of the world, and the people of the world did not cut themselves off from one another, we could live in peace and find our lives more satisfying and more worthwhile.

*Your deeds will bring you nearer or your deeds will make you more distant from one another.*      EDUYOT 5:7

# A Common Sensing

When an American rabbi returned from a trip to Israel, some of his congregants wanted to know what had been his greatest religious experience there. He said it was coming across a group of kibbutzniks building a road through the middle of their kibbutz where no road seemed needed. Puzzled, he asked the workers about it. They explained that one of the children had been stricken with paralysis, and the only way they could keep him with them on the kibbutz was to build a road for his wheelchair from his living quarters to the dining hall.

This expression of the compassion of Judaism is truly the soul of Israel. For to care for one's own in a dedicated manner is the first lesson of our ancient culture as taught in the Torah. To see sanctity not in stones or relics but in such an act of humanity as a whole community's concern for one handicapped child, requires neither saintliness nor intellectual insight but a quality that we might call spiritual common sense.

This kind of *sekhel* (common sense) was revealed again when Golda Meir summoned an international meeting of Jews in Jerusalem on the theme of "The World Jewish Conference on Human Needs." Few other ethnic, religious or political groupings have issued a similar summons in all of history. Mrs. Meir truly gave voice to our commitment in saying, "Only a people with a fantastic dream have the will power to fight for its realization." World Jewry must keep hold of this dream and not lessen its drive for mutual welfare until every human being can walk with freedom, self-respect and dignity anywhere on this earth.

*A ruling derived from common sense is also designated by the rabbis as "Words of Torah."*    ZEVI HIRSCH CHAJES

# Every Person An Astronaut

On July 20, 1969, a boot size 9B placed a footprint on the moon and changed the life of human beings forever. In order to achieve this staggering feat, three astronauts were crammed together for eight days during which they traveled nearly 500,000 miles. Aside from the physical strain, the psychological pressures on them were enormous. Yet the most amazing feature of the entire enterprise was the fact that they got along so well under such unbelievable tension-laden circumstances. Everyone did his job, no one spoke a harsh or angry word, and even when the heartbeats accelerated during the final moments of lunar descent because of the extreme stress of split-second decision-making, nobody "blew his cool."

Why did they perform so well, emotionally as well as physically? It was because they had been trained to perform their functions well. It was because they had learned to live with each other, accepting each other's differences and making allowances for individual moods and personality variations. They were committed to mutual harmony and they were determined to keep that goal ever before them.

In a similar way, we who live on this spaceship called Earth must realize how much our own security and peace is dependent on everyone else's. In the small satellites of our families we must avoid collision courses by adjusting to one another. As we travel in the orbits of our daily lives—in schools, in jobs, in community gatherings, in friendship circles—we must make room for one another and avoid disastrous confrontations. Each of us is enclosed in a module called "self," and we must learn to navigate it if we are to avoid the craters of discontent and rocks of irresponsibility so we may land safely on our own Sea of Tranquility.

*The measure of progress is cooperation.*    EDWARD A. FILENE

# Suffering Is A Teacher

In a drama entitled *A Play For The Leisure Class* there are only two characters: a moden man who has just died, and an angel of the other world. The deceased gradually comes to himself and a shining angel is before him asking, "Can I do anything for you, sir?" "Well," the man wants to know, "what can I have?" "Anything you want," is the angelic reply, "the only restriction is that we do not permit pain or suffering or struggle here."

The man's requests are all instantly realized: thirty years taken off his age, luxurious quarters, cars, clothes, everything he desires. But soon the man says, "I am tired of all these luxuries. I want challenge and purpose and work." "I am sorry," the angel says, "but all this involves effort and struggle, and that is out of the question." The man shouts, "But I want pain and suffering and life. I can't stand this everlasting bliss. I'd rather be in hell!" The angel steps back and asks, "Just where do you think you are, sir?"

Challenge as a teacher is true of nations as well as of individuals. The American nation has matured far more in the last forty years than in all of its history. The casualties of two World Wars, the suffering in the Great Depression, the stalemate in international conflicts, the horrible threat of atomic destruction have brought us to a maturity of outlook. There is finally today a recognition of America's responsibility to help the underprivileged nations of the world and advance the cause of peace. The trials of the twentieth century have made us grow into an acceptance of pain as a part of life and our responsibility to help relieve it as a prelude to peace.

*If life is what you seek, meditate on challenge, for struggle is a great teacher in the school of life.*

YALKUT, PSALMS 67, QUOTING PROVERBS 6:23

# Jewish Valuables

There are as many interpretations of Judaism as there are Jews. Yet most can agree on the elements which constitute the essence of our tradition. It is the convictions and the customs of Judaism which mark our life style and shape our identity. All else is but a variation on these themes.

While Judaism does not adhere to a rigid theology, yet it embodies certain beliefs about life, certain prescribed standards for living. The moral and ethical code of our way of life was first stated in the Bible and then interpreted and applied by generation after generation of Jews. The Ten Commandments continue to guide us, as moral truths that express the highest wisdom known to human beings. In sum, human experience, as gathered throughout the centuries, can be found in the Scriptures. Its verses constitute the distilled wisdom of living. The fact of the matter is we cannot break the Ten Commandments; we can only break ourselves against them.

There is the story of the young girl who sat next to a rabbi at dinner. Being at a loss as to what to say, she asked: "Have you read the latest hit novel? The rabbi answered, "No." The girl retorted: "You'd better hurry up. It has been on the best seller list for several months." The rabbi then asked the girl, "Have you read the Bible?" She replied, "No." He then said, "You'd better hurry up. It has been on the best seller list for several thousand years."

Thousands of years of Jewish experience, of records of individual lives of Jews, and the history of Judaism are ample testimony to the abiding worth of Jewish values.

*Torah represents the accumulated literary and spiritual heritage of the Jewish people through the centuries.*

ISRAEL S. CHIPKIN

# The Family Foundation

Occasionally we forget what the family is really for. It is for love, for mutual help, for understanding, for growth, for building the kind of attitudes that will make self-respecting and responsible human beings. Every smoothly functioning society knows that the family comes first.

In England it is the custom for the Prime Minister to report to the sovereign head of the nation on the affairs of the Empire. This is traditionally done through a formal visit by the Prime Minister every Wednesday evening at 6:30. The day after Queen Elizabeth was crowned and assumed her royal office, she received a call from Prime Minister Winston Churchill informing her that he would be coming by to present the report on the state of the Empire at 6:30 on the coming Wednesday evening.

Queen Elizabeth replied, "Oh, no you won't, because at 6:30 I will be putting the Princess to bed." And then she added by way of explanation, "There are many people to whom you can report on the state of the Empire, but the Princess has only one mother. You are welcome at any other time, sir."

From the Queen on down to the average father, to every child we must renew our commitment to the centrality of the family. Every Jew knows that the first act of a Jew when he or she moves into a new dwelling is to put a *mezuzah* on the door. With that one act we make our house not just a home, but a secure sanctuary where on every holyday, every Sabbath, and indeed every day we can experience the joy of family life.

*A home is the total contribution of love on the part of each person dwelling in it. It is the sanctuary where the real presence of family life and family love dwells.*

SOLOMON ROODMAN

# Rightside Up!

A book was recently published under the title *Good Lord, You're Upside Down!* The heroine is a fashion photographer. She uses a large camera placed on a tripod, and she drops a cloth over her head as she looks into the viewfinder. One day, one of her friends happens to take a look through the camera's viewfinder, and is shocked to discover that from the viewer's point of view the entire scene is reversed. This is the regular position of the camera, but the man, taken aback, says, "Good Lord, you're upside down!"

Actually, one of the problems of our society is that we view the world in the wrong way and our values are upside down. We seem to have a distorted view of life. If a house is blown up, it receives front page news; but if a house is built, nobody really cares. All we see in the headlines and in article after article is war, hate, destruction, and all the things that people do to hurt other people. But all the things that people do to help other people rate only a short mention, if anything at all.

A minister who was in the process of completing his new religious structure once wrote that he went to the building site and met a member of the Board of Directors, who was carefully scrutinizing the rising sanctuary. The minister asked with concern, "What's wrong with it?" The Board member responded with a smile, "I wasn't looking at what's wrong but *at what's right with it.*" This is the way we have to look at life—with its right side up!

*Life is good and a gracious gift of God. To love God one need not hate the world. Life should not be feared or condemned or renounced, but sanctified and enjoyed through wholesome living in which the whole of man— body, mind, and soul—are fulfilled.* ABBA HILLEL SILVER

# The Capacity To Give

The essence of giving is to give openly and freely without strings attached. Only when we give this way will we bless our lives and those to whom we give. If you give a child a gift and say, I am doing this if you do thus and so, then it is not a gift. It is a bribe. If you contribute to a charitable cause and add the note "providing you spend it in this specific way," then it is not a gift. It is a manipulation. If we say to God, "I will pray and I will keep Your law if You guarantee health or wealth," that is not a service of the heart. It is rather a bargain.

How do we give openly and freely? The ways are many. Sometimes we give money, sometimes we give service and sometimes the nature of the gift distinguishes its true meaning. The poet brings a poem, the farmer his corn, the painter his pictures, the businessman his income, a laborer his labor, and the child his sincerest efforts and devotion. But whatever it is, it must be done in love and it must be an honest and real part of ourselves.

John Wesley once preached a sermon in which he declared: "Get all you can."

An old man exclaimed, "Amen."

"Keep all your can."

Another "Amen" from the old fellow.

"Give all you can."

And the old man mumbled, "What a shame to spoil a good sermon."

If we give all we can to others and we raise our hands openly with generosity, then surely we will bring blessing into the lives of others and in turn find our lives blessed.

*The generous person will be enriched; and the one who waters will himself be watered.*    PROVERBS 11:25

# The Law Of Return

This has been called the Age of the Uprooted, the Century of the Homeless Man. The refugee, clutching his or her child and pitiful belongings, is its symbol. Attitudes toward the refugee have varied from warm welcome to outright rejection. In the State of Israel, for example, the official and unofficial policy has been one of openness and hospitality.

The profound humanitarian impulse of the Jewish people as well as their sense of responsibility toward their fellow Jews has created a policy of unlimited help to those wishing to return to the "land of their fathers." Even going beyond extending freedom and protection, Israelis—supported by Jewish communities throughout the world—have provided housing, medical care, education, vocational training, and practical aid to the new immigrants and their families.

In general, this approach has not only been deeply religious and responsible but also has brought to Israel additional human, cultural and creative resources. All of this is part of the redemptive process of modern Jewish history in which Jews, suffering from outrageous persecution, are given the opportunity to rehabilitate themselves as free people. The principle of the Law of Return was enshrined in the Israeli Proclamation of Independence: "The State of Israel will be open to Jewish immigration and the ingathering of exiles."

This law, because of its profound expression of Jewish feeling, is certainly to be accorded the status of *mitzvah* in every sense of the term. Those who help in its observance are truly fulfilling the commandments.

*Every Jew has the right to come to this country for the purpose of settling in Israel permanently.*
LEGISLATIVE ENACTMENTS OF ISRAEL, SEC. 163

# A Heartening Effort

We cannot force or legislate enthusiasm and commitment. These are matters of the heart and one must feel them from the inside or they will not matter and, ultimately, will not endure. Democracy in general, and Judaism in particular, is built on the premise that the citizen and the private person will be moved enough by the concerns of the community to share, to participate, to be involved.

We can speak all we want about the urban problem, but it does not make any difference until we are personally involved. We can say all we wish about Israel but, ultimately, only as we individuals are personally committed will Israel stand strong. We can talk about peace in the world from here to eternity but it will never come to be until each person is willing to participate. In fact, if we want to make a contribution of a lasting nature to anything it has to be through our own personalities and our individual life styles.

It is told of a poor but friendly cook, who was well known in the neighborhood, that whenever a neighbor became ill she brought in meals to be helpful. One day, she brought in a plate of hash. After the family ate it, one of the children turned to her and asked her how she succeeded in making such good hash. The woman answered, "The meat is nothing; the salt and pepper is nothing; but when I throw myself into the hash that is what makes it what it is."

When we are willing to throw ourselves into programs, into community actions, then the world will begin to change. For it will reflect us and what we are willing to offer from our hearts.

*And they came, the men and the women, all those whose hearts moved them.*
EXODUS 35:22

# Middlescence

Middle age usually begins when we awaken one morning and look into the mirror and discover that our hairline is receding a bit too fast, or the number of wrinkles is multiplying; or the newspaper print is growing smaller, or someone says, "You look well—for your age." Then comes the acid test. Either we panic and think, "O, dear God, my life is half over!" or we straighten up proudly and proclaim, "Thank God, I made it! So far, so good."

Middle age maturity means that we have developed the capacity to accept our responsibilities and duties, and that our ideals and values are yet worthwhile and attainable. It also means that we have learned that the world is not our personal catering firm and that there are other people in the world who have rights equal to our own, that the truth is not black or white but gray.

Middle age should be a time of contentment. It is a time when we still have the need to satisfy our sexual feelings, but there is no need to prove ourselves sexually. It is a time when we have learned who are our true friends and who turned out to be faithless. It is a time when we have already experienced the pain of the loss of some of our dearest ones and so we treasure even more the love of those who remain. It is a time to be tolerant of the idiosyncrasies of others because we find that we each have our own *meshugas*, eccentricities, as well.

Indeed, the prospect of middle life can be a very hopeful one and all the fears we imagined about it turn out largely to be myths. Today, fifty is not the beginning of the end, but the end of the beginning. The middle years can be the best years if we continue to move but not to rush.

*Much experience is the crown of age.*     BEN SIRA 25:6

# 'Tis Of Thee

In America today we have a long way to go to create a just society, but we are haltingly moving in the right direction.

That we should have criticized ourselves so devastatingly as we have in these recent years must be seen as a sign of fundamental good health. We know from studies and experience that the sick patient is on the road to recovery the moment one is aware that he or she is ill. One of the reasons we had a sick society during this past decade is that our expectations were too high, even as our commitments were too low. Because we had illusions about our liberal selves and underestimated the severity of our problems, we immediately felt disillusionment when we failed to solve them quickly. What we now need are clear social goals that are idealistic yet realistic, challenges that are advanced yet attainable, programs that are inspirational yet practical. But, above all, we need the commitment to help us overcome our present "compassion fatigue," so that we do not tire of responding to human needs and so that we can retain the drive and the perseverance that has always been a virtue of Americans.

A kindergarten class that was studying the pledge of allegiance to America was asked by the teacher, "Tell me, what is your country?" One little tot replied, " 'Tis of thee."

Yes, America, 'tis of thee. It's your country and mine. If every person cares as much about his country and its citizens as about himself or herself, then we will create the climate for a compassionate society.

*The fundamental American tradition is to create a dynamic country with freedom to move, to change, to work; with opportunity to learn, chance to rise in the world; with a duty to keep the free spirit of the country free.*    GILBERT SELDES

# Cheers

We all have problems, we all have pressures, and we are perpetually beset by challenging situations. But our faith teaches us that despite it all, if we hold fast and make the most of life it can be worthwhile at any age. All of life, whether we be three, thirteen, thirty-three, sixty-three or ninety-three, can contain wonder, amusement, achievement, and excitement.

A young man reported that when his grandfather was in his eighties, his routine was as follows. He would get up every morning, look at the newspaper, have one quick drink of liquor, and then sit down to breakfast. One day his grandson said to him, "*Zayde* (Grandfather), for years I have wondered—why do you start the day looking at the newspaper, having a drink, and then having breakfast?"

The answer came as follows. "*Mein kind* (My child), I get up in the morning and I open the newspaper to the obituary page. If I don't see my name, then I take a drink and say '*Lechayim*' (to life!)."

What we must do is to retain our zest for living, our determination to enjoy life to the utmost, and our desire to make the most, even of the least.

God gave each of us the gift of life. What we do with this life is our gift to God.

*Happy is the person who finds wisdom, and the one who obtains understanding.* PROVERBS 3:13

# Finding God

The principle of learning by living can even be applied to knowledge and understanding of God. One can read the Bible through and through, and never really know God. This can only come about through the process of living and experiencing.

Every woman who has given birth to a child and then looked upon the face of this child for the first time understands that there is a God. Every man who in the darkest hour of his life has thought himself abandoned and a failure, and has found a friend who has come to him with an offer of money or friendship or just plain understanding and sympathy, has learned that there is compassion in humanity. Every young person who has gone out into the world and found some adult who took an interest in him or her has understood that there is a spirit of dedication and willingness to help in this universe of ours.

These are the experiences that turn us to God. Not just literature or prayers or rituals, although they are important; but rather the experiences of and with men, women and children living and learning about life itself.

*God, where shall I find You*
*Whose glory fills the universe?*
*Behold, I find You*
*Wherever the mind is free to follow its own bent,*
*Wherever words come out from the depth of truth,*
*Wherever tireless striving stretches its arms toward*
*    perfection*
*Wherever men struggle for freedom and right,*
*Wherever the scientist toils to reveal the secrets of*
*    nature,*
*Wherever glorious deeds are done.*    SABBATH PRAYER BOOK

# The Mystique Of Joy

There is an insight into happiness which we tend to forget: We cannot make anyone else happy without becoming a little happier ourselves.

Once, a well-dressed man was walking in a park. He suddenly came upon a little boy who was leaning against a tree, sobbing his heart out. The boy pointed to the top of the tree and said, "My kite is caught up there and I don't know how to get it down." Without hesitation, the man climbed the tree and rescued the kite. The boy smiled up at the man and said, "Thank you." And the man smiled back, "You're welcome." Here was a double miracle. The boy was happy and the man was also happy. It was unimportant that the man tore his jacket or nicked his hand on a branch, because inside he had a feeling of satisfaction. He brought joy to someone else, so he was filled with joy. Lord Byron recorded this feeling a century ago when he wrote: "All who joy would win must share it! Happiness was born a twin."

Many people think that money automatically brings happiness. This, of course, if the greatest myth of all times. It just is not so! While money can make life a little easier, it can never buy happiness, because ultimately happiness is not having what you want, but wanting what you have. Happiness is in people, not things. Moreover, happiness must be shared. It is contagious to all those who touch it. You have to travel within yourself in order to reach it, because the city of happiness is located in the state of the mind. And this always includes others.

*Happiness is a perfume which you cannot pour on others without getting a few drops on yourself.* LOUIS MANN

# The High Cost Of Hate

Often in our conduct of daily affairs we tend to forget the fundamental truth that we all belong to one another. Though each of us is unique, let us not ever forget that we are all a part of the human race. We are simply branches sprouting out of the main trunk of humanity. Hurt one and we are all hurt, love one and we all become enhanced.

The potential for good or ill in a single act is dramatically illustrated in the life of Dr. Albert Sabin, whose oral vaccine was responsible for the widespread prevention and almost complete eradication of the dread disease of polio. But there is something else about this man that few know.

There was a scar over his left eye that was about a quarter of an inch above the eye itself. As he once explained to a group of doctors: "This scar is a part of my own personal heritage as a Jew. I got it as a child raised in a small Jewish town in Poland. Some Christian children threw stones at me because I was Jewish. Had the stone been a quarter of an inch lower, my left eye would have been blinded. Since I do not see with my right eye, if the stone had struck my left eye I would be totally blind today."

Now, just ponder for a moment what would have happened to us all if Sabin had been unable to look through a microscope. That one tiny act of hate, of flinging one stone, could have resulted in the maiming and the death of thousands of children because the oral vaccine might have been discovered years later than it was. One tiny expression of hate could have harmed all humanity. That is why each of us in his own way must discipline himself or herself when it comes to expressions of anger, of prejudice, of violence, of sheer hate. When we hate we harm our own selves in the process. It cannot be otherwise. It has never been otherwise.

*Even the great are demeaned by hatred.*　　　SANHEDRIN 105b

# Security Can Be A Snare

The desire for security places many roadblocks before us: Don't risk, don't stick your neck out, don't experiment; for all these involve possible pain and failure. But where would the world be if people did not go beyond their needs for security in a search for a better tomorrow? Look at the astronauts! They could have had security, but instead they have risked a great deal to help mankind progress. And what about Moses? If he had remained a simple shepherd, working for his wealthy father-in-law, unwilling to risk abuse, pain, and the terrible stress of leadership, would we be a great people today? Would we even be a people at all?

We know that all through history people who have relied on money or material possessions alone have ended up disastrously. They were robbed of their will to achieve even as their children were denied the opportunity to advance. When money and things become everything in our eyes, they are in fact worth nothing.

The story is told of a man who was aboard a sinking ship. Together with all the other passengers he was given a life preserver. This particular traveler had some gold bars with him. He was so anxious to save his fortune that he slipped the precious objects into his belt. Unfortunately when he hit water, the weight of the gold treasure dragged him down to the bottom.

Security is important, but it isn't everything. Money is important, but it isn't everything. Comfort is important, but it isn't everything. Be sure that you are not a slave to your lowest desires but their master.

*It is proper to command money, not to serve it.*
                                    LEON OF MODENA

# A Sense Of Balance In Life

A socially concerned woman was walking in the slum area of town to investigate the housing situation. As she was absorbed in her viewing, she was jostled by a drunk who was passing by. The lady scolded the drunk and said, "If I were in your condition I would shoot myself." The inebriate retorted, "Lady, if you were in my condition you would miss." Too frequently, we get into a mental state where we lose perspective and thereby miss the meaning of life.

If you have a headache today, remember you did not have one yesterday and you probably will not have one tomorrow. If you are, experiencing illness, have you lost sight of the possibility that tomorrow might be better? Even if you have loved and lost, at least you have loved. Some people do not have even that memory.

Whatever our condition, we must not lose our interest in joyous living. It is important not only to take pleasure, but to make pleasure. We must learn to break up the day, the week, the year with lifts all along the way. Coffee breaks help ease the tension of the day; a pleasant, leisurely lunch now and then makes a nice bridge to the afternoon; a refreshment before dinner enables things to go smoother; a sincere prayer before bed eases the transition into tranquil sleep. Reading a good book does wonders for one's morale, attending a stimulating lecture raises our vision beyond ourselves and, on a deeper level, a perfect observance of the Sabbath gives us, after all, the pause that refreshes. And what is the use of life without vacations, without trips, without pleasure to balance effort and hard work? Indeed, what is life without a sense of balance?

*It is good that you should take hold of this, and from that withhold not your hand; for the one who reveres God will experience everything.*    ECCLESIASTES 7:18

# Studying The Matter

Judaism is unique in that of all religions, it alone has made a ritual of study. For example, according to our tradition one can study a passage from the Talmud, and then following it, recite a *kaddish*, which means study in itself is considered a worship experience.

Teaching is not trivia; it is a Divine Commandment. And what is the essence of the Jewish faith? A Torah Scroll, which is really a book. And what is an Ark? Nothing more, or indeed less, than a bookcase. Training people to respect a bookcase has been the genius of Judaism!

The modern Jew must understand that Judaism will survive only through learning. We must learn more about the world, more about our physical and biological environment, for the world can be beautiful if we take the time to learn to make it so.

A pretty young college girl walked into the professor's office the day before final exams, batted her eyelashes, and said nervously, "Oh, Professor, I'll just do *anything* to pass this course!"

"Anything?" asked the professor.

"Oh, yes, just anything. I'll do *anything* to pass this course!"

The professor sat back, thought for a minute, then asked, "Even *study?*"

Many of us say we will do anything to save our souls, to be religious, to help. But, then, maybe we ought to begin to demonstrate the seriousness of our commitment by "even studying"—studying ourselves, studying the wisdom of the past generations, studying the world, and studying new ways to improve our life.

*Study is worth as much as ritual sacrifice.* MENAHOT 110a

# Wonder Bread

The ancient Rabbis taught: "A loaf of bread on the table is a greater miracle than the parting of the Red Sea," the point being that what recurs daily in the world is truly more miraculous than a single historic event. If we pause and consider a moment, we will surely appreciate all the forces that are necessary in order to produce a piece of bread: the earth and its soil, the rain and its water, the farmer and the reaper, the baker and the distributor. There is one brand of bread that is known as "Wonder Bread." Actually, every kind of bread that we eat is in a sense "wonder bread."

In the history of all religions, bread is treated with reverence. In Judaism we use *hallah* for a Sabbath meal, and there are set rituals concerning it. This goes back to the days of the First Temple when there were exact requirements as to the way bread was to be used in the service itself. And bread still occupies a high significance among the traditions of our people. When a family moves into a home, our first gifts traditionally are bread and salt. On Passover we open the service by saying, "Come, share our unleavened bread." On Rosh Hashanah, on the first night, we eat bread covered with honey. Thus we recognize that bread is, indeed, the staff of life.

All of this was beautifully expressed by Daniel Berrigan in the following words: "When I hear bread breaking, I see something else; it seems almost as though God never meant us to do anything else. So beautiful a sound. The crust breaks up like manna and falls all over everything. And then we eat; bread gets inside humans."

*Praised are You, O Lord our God, King of the universe, Who brings forth bread from the earth.*

TRADITIONAL JEWISH PRAYER

# My Pleasure

We are often caught in the trap of obsessive work. And so during the moments when we take our pleasure, we are often plagued by a sense of guilt. So we defer our enjoyments for "later on." We say, "I'll take up gardening after the children are grown." Or, "I'll do community work after I retire." Concern about this pattern is shared by many critics of contemporary civilization. A worthwhile book by Walter Kerr, the eminent drama critic and author of several plays, is entitled, *The Decline of Pleasure.* His whole thesis is put in the following quotation from his introduction.

"If I were required to put into a single sentence my own explanation of the state of our hearts, heads, and nerves, I would do it this way: we are vaguely wretched because we are leading half-lives, halfheartedly, and with only one-half of our minds actively engaged in making contact with the universe about us."

A fussy train traveler was finding much trouble in placing her belongings. She put bundles first on the seat, then on the floor. She opened and closed windows, adjusted shades and fidgeted about like a nervous hen. When her husband protested, she said, "I want to get fixed so I can see the scenery with comfort." But he shook his head. "We are not going far, and the scenery will be all over before you get fixed to enjoy it."

Many people go through life "getting fixed to enjoy it"— while life passes and is gone.

*Who is happy?*
*The one who sees a blossoming world*
*And gives it a personal blessing.*        BERL KATZNELSON

# The Wages Of Religion

"You shall not coerce your neighbor. You shall not commit robbery. The wages of a laborer shall not remain with you until morning" (Leviticus 19:13).

One might wonder why the Bible is so exercised over a delayed payment. What if a man's pay is delayed overnight? Does it justify the use of such strong language as "coerce your neighbor . . . commit robbery"? We know that in our society few employers pay their employees before the end of the week. In the case of corporations, payment for services rendered may not occur until weeks or even a month. Therefore, what is the reason for the Biblical excess?

Perhaps the Bible contains such a strong condemnation to emphasize that any delay in doing what is right is a form of oppression and injustice. If in the Biblical economy the laborer, who lived from hand to mouth, had to go to bed hungry, his children unfed, then the Bible was justifiably concerned.

Dr. Abraham Heschel, in a collection of essays entitled *The Insecurity of Freedom*, makes this point about the difference between the pagan outlook and the teachings of Judaism. The pagans believed in the words of Cicero, "The gods attend to great matters; they neglect small ones." In Judaism, God is pictured as being concerned about the smallest detail that might affect a human being. Judaism's emphasis is on the conduct of the marketplace, the behavior in the home, and the welfare of all men—every person.

*The teaching of Judaism is the theology of the common deed. The Bible insists that God is concerned with every-dayness, with the trivialities of life.*

ABRAHAM JOSHUA HESCHEL

# Jailbreak!

Justice Felix Frankfurter once addressed an audience of doctors at the Harvard Medical School. He began his address with this striking question: "Have you broken out of jail lately?" He went on to explain that people allow themselves to be imprisoned in mental and spiritual cells with very stout walls, and there is no communication with the outside world.

The truth is that people with closed minds are living in a kind of jail. One of the ways we confine ourselves is called "habit." We do the same things, we live the same way day after day, and thereby deny ourselves the freedom of new experiences, and the excitement of doing things differently.

Some workers take the same route to work day after day. They would not think of changing their route for anything short of a street detour. They deprive themselves of new and varied sights.

Some men and women wear the same style of shoe year after year. They fear that if they change the design they may appear different to their friends.

Some people choose the same color every time they purchase a new car, thus denying themselves the opportunity of a change of pace.

Some of us retain the same circle of friends. We deeply fear to break out and make new friends. In this way we deny ourselves the pleasures and excitements of experiencing new human beings.

So the question still remains, "Have you broken out of jail lately?"

*Do not depend entirely on habit; use your own judgment.*
MOSES KREMER

# God Is Not Alone

The Bible tells us, "Isaac sowed in that land and reaped a hundredfold the same year and the Lord blessed him" (Genesis 26:12). What we find here is both a person's work and God's blessing. It brings about a hundredfold increase precisely because man and God are working together. That man needs God, we already know. But here God also needs man. If we think about this very carefully, we find that real progress is made when both forces operate in harmony.

It is interesting to contemplate that God stores the hills with marble, but it takes a Michelangelo to sculpt a beautiful statue. God fills the earth with metals, but it takes a Frank Lloyd Wright to fashion them into a home. God stocks the forests with wood, but it takes a Stradivarius to make a violin. Everywhere we go, God blesses human beings with abundance. Where they use nature wisely, it is with restraint.

Ultimately, the destiny of the world in many ways is in our own hands. It is not enough to pray; we also have to take practical measures to build a better world and create a healthier environment for human habitation.

In a contemporary poem, a rabbi wrote that there is no point in only praying to God to end starvation, despair, or disease—for all these are in people's Godgiven power to accomplish.

*Therefore we pray to You instead, O God,*
*For strength, determination and will power,*
*To do what we can,*
*To do what we must,*
*Then we will find our reward a hundredfold,*
*And then truly we will discover that*
*We have been blessed by the Lord.*                    JACK RIEMER

# The Art Of Living

One of the great problems in contemporary life is that we have forgotten how to take and give pleasure as ordinary human beings. We have become disoriented in our search for happiness, and we are out for "kicks." We look for gratification in the pornographic movie, the erotic book and the delusionary drug. And after our experiences with them are over, we end up with an emotional hangover. We seek satisfaction in the bizarre and far-out, and all we find is sickness. That is because we are looking for happiness in the wrong places. Fulfillment is not way out there but right in here. It is nowhere but inside ourselves.

Happiness is ultimately to be found in our own attitude and approach to life. To grow your own flower, to make your own dress, to raise your own child, to love your own spouse, to do your own homework—all these bring a joy greater than any jag or fleeting fad can give. Happiness is not in things, it is in thoughts. It is discovered by being involved in life itself.

Artur Rubinstein, one of the greatest pianists of our time, says: "I'm passionately involved in life: I love its changes, its color, its movement. To be alive, to be able to see, to walk, to have houses, music, paintings—it is all a miracle. I have adopted the technique of living life from miracle to miracle. What people get out of me is this outlook on life which comes out of my music."

Life is like a piano. The discord is there; the harmony is there. Live it correctly, and it will bring forth beauty. Live it falsely, and it will bring forth ugliness. The way we *use* life is all important.

*We are all artists in life.*                    JOSEPH JACOBS

# The Power Of A Person

One person, by force of his or her personality, can be the pivot of a whole society. Hitler turned a whole nation into an overwhelming force for hate. Gandhi directed a whole people toward nonviolence and peace. In the family as well, often one person can make the difference between harmony and strength on the one hand or discord and despair on the other.

When we think of the power of one person, we can recall that Frederick the Great once sent this message to one of his generals: "I send you against the enemy with 60,000 men." When the troops were counted they numbered only 50,000. The general sent a letter of protest and complaint that there must be a mistake. "No," replied Frederick, "there is no mistake; I counted *you,* my general, as 10,000 men." Every person, by virtue of what he or she is, can count for a great deal; and, thus, realize the greatest potentialities for good or evil.

In the morning newspaper we read all about the problems of the community, the nation and the world. If we really felt deeply about them, we would probably never get to the second cup of coffee. But if we ourselves do not feel deeply about certain things, how then can we blame others because they did not feel deeply about us and ours?

When we do begin to feel strongly about certain events, we can actually determine their course. That is why advertising agencies, business firms, community organizations and television networks constantly survey our attitudes and our desires. Aldous Huxley expressed it all very well in a phrase he used in *Brave New World:* "When the individual feels, the community reels."

*One human being is worth as much as the whole creation.*
AVOT DERABBI NATAN, CHAPTER 31

# The Pursuit Of Peace

According to an old Indian fable, two holy men are walking down a road together. They come at length to a high wall which blocks their view. Out of curiosity, they climb up a tree to see what lies behind it. What they see is a lovely garden, more beautiful than anything they have ever seen before. Both holy men are entranced with this vision. Suddenly, on an impulse, one of the men leaps over the wall into the garden in the hope of staying there forever. The other is tempted to follow. But, instead, he stops and thinks. After gazing long at the peace and beauty of the garden, he climbs down the tree on the outside of the wall. Then he walks back along the dusty road to the village to share with the people there the beauty of the vision of a peaceful life that he has seen.

We can see the garden as a metaphor for our beautiful philosophic writings, humanitarian ideals and religious teachings. The world can be a beautiful place in which to live if only we try to understand human harmony and to share our visions:

To understand that all nations can live together and share in an era of unprecedented prosperity.

To understand that each of us personally has a stake in healing a shattered segment of America.

To understand that our wives, our husbands, our children, our relatives, our neighbors, everyone we know, are persons and have a right to be as they are and live as they live. With this kind of understanding we can fulfill the ultimate vision of mankind, which is more important than power, than wealth, than fame—and that is peace.

*Other commandments are performed when the occasion arises, but of peace it is written, "Pursue it."*

LEVITICUS RABBAH 9:9

# The Simplicity Of A Symbol

The purpose of a symbol is to remind us of our highest goals and values. In American life the flag should remind us what America stands for—not jingoistic flag-waving but the great ideals of democracy and freedom with responsibility. In Judaism as well, the symbol serves an important purpose. The *tallit*, for example, is a reminder of our obligations to ourselves, our faith and society. The symbol must never be worshipped for itself but rather for what it represents.

During the first World War, a Jewish soldier suffered from what was then called shell shock. All the members of his unit had been wiped out except him. Miraculously, he escaped but with slight injury. But because of the severe shock he developed amnesia. All kinds of treatment were applied to him but none was successful. He gave no sign of recognizing anyone or anything.

One day, a Jewish chaplain was visiting him. As the chaplain spoke to him, he saw the soldier form a word with his lips. He finally managed to say the one word, "Jewish." Beginning with this association, he began the road to full recovery. What had happened was that the Jewish chaplain had on his lapel the insignia of the Ten Commandments. The soldier recognized this great and enduring symbol of his faith, and along with this recognition came his memories of being Jewish.

Our symbols help us bring meaning and purpose to life.

*The Lord spoke to Moses, saying: Speak to the Israelite people and instruct them to make for themselves fringes on the corner of their garments throughout the generations. . . . That shall be your fringe; look at it and recall all the commandments of the Lord and observe them.*

NUMBERS 15:37-39

314

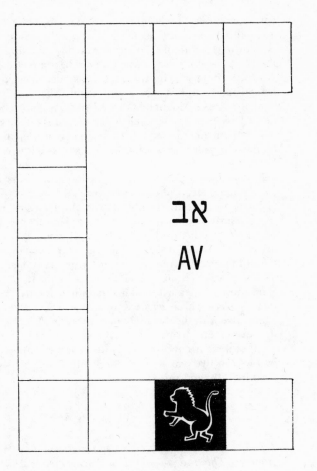

אב

AV

# The Adventure Of Life

Life in current literature is described in one of four ways: as a journey, as a battle, as a pilgrimage, and as a race. Select your own term, but in every case the need to see it through is the same. For if life is a journey, it must be completed. If life is a battle, it must be finished. If life is a pilgrimage, it must be concluded. And if it is a race, it must be won.

In the Rocky Mountains just a little way into Independence Pass, there is a very narrow section. It is on the side of a mountain, and on one side of the road is a sheer cliff and on the other side a deep fall. Usually, the pass is littered with fallen rocks. Upon reaching this spot, the traveler usually hesitates a bit. This may have inspired someone years ago to erect a sign there, reading: "O, yes, you can! Millions have!"

Think about your own life and you can, I am sure, match this reassuring experience in many ways. How many women sometime or other during their first pregnancy have wondered if they would really be able to give birth and then raise the child properly? And yet they did. How many men on the eve of marriage have entertained a 'moment of panic about supporting a wife and maintaining a family? And yet they did. As world citizens, we doubted whether we would be able to live with the threat of nuclear warfare. We don't like it, but we are living with it.

All of these instances are only the merest examples of the way we can live year after year—not only courageously, but meaningfully and purposefully.

*Life is an adventure because we are always faced with a frontier. The line of our attainment merely shifts the frontier forward and defines the next task against which we must pit our strength.* BEN ZION BOKSER

# The Third Is God

All of us without exception need to feel at home in the world, and for the religious person this sense of belonging demands a close and warm relationship with God. People whose philosophy of life includes a simple but personal relationship with God, live with a feeling of security. When we know we belong to God and He belongs to us, we can go about our way surmounting every obstacle and dealing effectively with the problems and challenges we must inevitably face.

Those of us who must face the greatest stresses know the value of a deep faith in God.

Thus Lord Moynihan, a great British surgeon, when he had finished operating before a gallery full of distinguished visiting doctors, was asked how he could work with such a crowd present. He replied: "It's not really such a crowd. Actually, there are just three present in the operating room when I operate—the patient and myself." "But that is only two," his questioner commented. "Who is the third?" Moynihan responded, "The third is God."

Wherever we go, whomever we meet and in whatever we do there is always the presence of God with us. When properly understood, this presence becomes a source of inspiration and strength. When we relate to God, then we know that we belong in the deepest sense possible.

*Where can I escape from Your spirit?*
*Where can I flee from Your presence?*
*If I ascend to heaven, You are there;*
*If I descend to Sheol, You are there too.*
*If I take wing with the dawn*
*To come to rest on the western horizon,*
*Even there Your hand will guide me,*
*Your right hand will hold me fast.*　　　　PSALMS 139:7-10

# Everyone's Responsibility

An employer interviewing an applicant for a position said to the candidate, "For this job I want a responsible man." The applicant announced, "Then you want me. Everywhere I worked, whenever something went wrong they said I was responsible."

By responsibility we mean the ability to respond as one human being to the needs of another human being. For example:

Being able to understand the confusion of youth in search of values, the concerns of those in middle age who must bear the economic burdens of society, and the anxieties of older people about retirement, loneliness and purpose in living.

Being able to empathize with those who are ill in mind and body, those who are bereaved, those whose marital problems disturb and distress them, and those who must face the world alone.

Being able to appreciate the fact that all mankind—black, yellow, white, red, whatever—has fundamental needs. That men and women need respect, love, something meaningful with which to identify, and an atmosphere conducive to creativity. This is so whether a man or woman finds himself or herself walled in a frustrating ghetto or living in the comfort and warmth of the suburbs. All human beings have these desires. Then, quite simply, our basic concern ought to be that as individuals and as a society we do not become unresponsive, uncaring and unsharing.

*O that I might burn bright*
*To be the light in my brother's night.*          YEHOASH

# Be What You Are

To a devoted Jew the most basic expression of one's being is one's Jewishness. In order to be true to ourselves as Jews we must freely express our Jewish feelings. We must speak with great honesty about who we are and why we are.

Bernard Berenson was the greatest art critic of the Italian Renaissance. Until his death he was the symbol of sophistication in the Western World. But few knew that he was a Jew born in the Lithuanian Ghetto, who came to Harvard as a former Yeshiva student.

In his 89th year Bernard Berenson wrote this:

"How easy and warm the atmosphere between born Jews like Isaiah Berlin, myself, Bella Horwitz, when we drop the mask of being *goyim* and return to Yiddish reminiscences and Yiddish stories and witticisms! After all, it has been an effort (no matter how unaware) to act as if one were a mere Englishman or Frenchman or American; and it is something like a homecoming . . . to return to 'mother's cooking.' "

What a pity that this great intellectual needed 89 years of his life to learn that it is best to be what you were born to be. How easy and warm it is to come to *shul* and share the fellowship of Torah and prayer. How comforting it is to be oneself with fellow Jews. How lovely it is to say a *yiddish vort* and not have to translate. When we do all these things we know we belong and no power can ever take from us the security of this feeling.

*The Jewish genius is not of the kind that plants its seed, and leaves it for the silent centuries to assimilate it and mature its fruits. It needs living hearts for its soil and the whole world's only wide enough to provide them.*

ISRAEL ABRAHAMS

# Days Are Scrolls

The most basic problem of humanity is not educational but spiritual. The human mind does not need to be stuffed, it just needs to be opened—opened to the wonders of living. Because life leaps up like a geyser for those who drill through the rock of indifference, inertia and insensitivity.

This search for life also should be the essential purpose of all our prayers. Prayer is not a statement of human greeds, but an honest expression of human needs. Prayer is not a shopping list in the supermarket of the universe. We should not pray, "Help me to win!" but rather, "Help me to live!"—to live and forgive, to live and believe, to live and give, to live and love.

The mood and meaning of this thought can best be found in a little story that carries a large message. A traveler once came to a small midwestern town. He was intent on learning all the details about the regional history. As he was approaching the local city hall, he came upon some boys at play. On an impulse, he stopped one of the boys and asked, "Tell me, son, have any great people been born in your city?" The lad thought for a moment and he replied, "No great people have been born in our city. Only babies."

The boy was right. Babies become great human beings only by striving and living creatively. And our days are like our lives. It is within our power to make them great. For this reason hope and faith fill our hearts; confidence and trust possess our minds; cheer and goodwill dominate our spirits. A new day can lift the spirits and awaken the hope that if the past was bad, the future will be good, and if the past was good, the future will be even better.

*Days are scrolls: write on them what you want to be remembered.*
                                            BAHYA IBN PAKUDA

# Inspiration and Perspiration

Most of us think that genius is something that just happens, but this is not really so. As someone once defined it, genius is 5% inspiration and 95% perspiration.

At the age of 75, Mischa Elman gave a recital at Carnegie Hall in New York which drew rave reviews from the critics. But few people realized that Elman, who made his debut at the age of seventeen, still practiced his scales four hours every day at 75; and the dancer Fred Astaire at 65 continued to practice a minimum of six hours every day when he was preparing a new routine.

So when people ask, "Why does a child have to go to Hebrew School five or six years in preparation for a Bar or Bat Mitzvah?" you can tell them about Mischa Elman or Fred Astaire. There's no shortcut. Excellence and achievement require enormous preparation.

Likewise, people often ask, "Why do we have to keep all the rituals and traditions in order to be Jewish?" The answer again is that it takes an enormous amount of spiritual discipline and exercise in order to become a proficient Jew.

Becoming a fine human being demands years and years of concentration on doing what is right and proper. Rich achievements are no accidents. They result from long, hard work and the patient accumulation of experience, learning and doing until we arrive at our goals.

And so we must practice, practice, practice. A good Jew must practice Judaism every day of his or her life. A good citizen must practice democracy every day of his or her life. There is no easy path to the heights of excellence.

*The prophetic spirit rests on a person only after one has made an effort to receive it.* ZOHAR, GENESIS 77b

# What Money Cannot Buy

Several years ago a group of businessmen met for dinner. They began to discuss money. One successful and aggressive businessman made the statement that money can buy everything. In fact, he wrote out a check for a thousand dollars and told his dinner companions that they could have it if they could convince him that there were four desirable things that money could not possibly buy.

One man called the waiter over, took his pencil, and on the back of the menu listed four things that money could not buy. They were: a baby's smile, youth after it is gone, the love of a good person, entrance into heaven.

Without another word the businessman handed his friend the check.

Yes, it is important to understand what money can do, but it is just as vital to comprehend what money *cannot* do.

Therefore, we must rethink our goals, and we must learn the skill of knowing how to spend wisely and well our time and our money. For just consider these few items:

We spend more money on eye make-up than eye research. That is because we are interested in how we look rather than how we see.

We spend more time watching TV than reading books. That is because we would rather be tranquillized than think.

We spend more energy in making money than in making life worthwhile. That is because we are more concerned with our finances than our feelings.

We must learn instead how to spend our money with good judgment, our energy intelligently, and our time wisely.

*Surely there is a mine for silver and a place for gold which they refine. But where shall wisdom be found? And where is the place of understanding?*              JOB 28:1, 12

# Pray Tell Us

We must have a means by which to measure man and man's activities. Without such a measure our morals are indeed lost. It is the Prayer Book and the call of the prophets that are the moral guides for our activities for the entire year. As we review our experience as individuals, as a nation, as members of the wider circle of mankind, we must give honest account of ourselves, and a sincere evaluation of what was done and what was left undone. We do this by measuring ourselves against our religious tradition. For without guides, we are surely lost in the maze of the modern world.

Not long ago two Israelis were traveling in the Negev area on a surveying expedition. During the night a heavy sandstorm blew up, and they sought shelter within a cave. When the storm subsided the next day, they left the cave and found that great havoc had occurred. Not only were their tracks covered, but trees were uprooted, some streams had changed their courses, and even large rocks had been tumbled from their accustomed places. All the landmarks they could have used were gone. One of the Israelis shouted in panic, "We are lost! We are doomed! Without the landmarks to guide us how can we ever find our way back to civilization?"

His companion calmly took out his surveying instruments, looked at the sky, and said, "No, we are not lost; as long as we have stars in the sky to guide us, we shall get out." And they did.

This is precisely the meaning of prayer. It is a summons to see the stars above us and beyond that, to see God, our guide on the straight paths of integrity and honesty.

*You don't have to pray loudly; just direct your heart to heaven.*                                        RABBI HIYYA

# Masada Will Not Fall Again

Masada is a rocky outcropping in a stony desert in Israel a half mile from the western shore of the Dead Sea. It was held by Jewish zealots following the fall of Jerusalem in the year 70. In the spring of the year 73, Flavius Silva brought up the Tenth Roman Legion and surrounded Masada with massive strength to crush the last pocket of Jewish resistance. The night before the final assault Eleazar ben Yair and his 960 followers decided to take their own lives rather than have the Romans conquer them, have their women mistreated and their children condemned to slavery.

When this site of Masada was excavated by Professor Yigael Yadin and his co-workers, the excavators found scrolls, some grain, a synagogue, a *mikvah* and even the bones of the slain lying exactly in their places for almost 1900 years—a deeply moving store of artifacts. Among the most significant and astounding finds were some jars of grain marked with the words "priestly tithe" and shards with the inscription of the letter *tav* for *terumah,* which means "contribution." These finds indicate that the inhabitants of Masada reserved a part of their very precious and dwindling food supply for a contribution to the poor and the Temple. In the face of certain death, they still set aside a portion of their grain for donations to the Sanctuary and to the Jewish people.

But that one act gave meaning to their death and assured their spiritual survival. They have survived through us; through Israel that lives on in their fierce determination; through Jews who vow that centuries of Jewish sacrifice, heroism and idealism will find fulfillment in our time.

*Masada will not fall again!*

OATH OF ISRAEL DEFENSE FORCES

# The Finest Light

When it comes to marriage, often men try to find a beautiful girl. But does it necessarily follow that a girl with a model's face and a model's figure will become a model wife? Sometimes we look at a man and he looks gruff and gross and we think that he must be an ignorant boor. But when he opens his mouth, he reveals a gentle manner and a sensitive soul.

Thomas Aquinas, the founder of medieval scholastic thought, was called by his contemporaries, "the ox," because he looked like one, but his mind was one of the greatest in the history of philsophy. Abraham Lincoln was called "the ape," because of his gangling arms and his gross features. And we all know how fine and subtle was his nature.

This question of the short view vesus the long view is illustrated by the work of Claude Monet, one of France's famous Impressionist painters. He was particularly known for the way he could bring fresh color and appearance to a painting. Very often he would paint a portrait a dozen times at different hours of the day. He would start at dawn and continue until sunset. At the end of his day's work, he would select the best portrait of all of those done of the same person. One day, one of his students asked: "Master, why do you keep doing fresh images and tiring yourself?" Monet replied, "I like to paint a person in his finest light."

We, too, should look upon every person many times, in many circumstances, so that we can ultimately see him or her in the finest light.

*The one who is understanding and just fills the world with kindness.*                                              SUKKAH 49b

325

# No, Too, Is An Answer

A man slipped on the escalator and started sliding to the bottom. Halfway down he collided with a woman, knocking her over. Together the two continued to the bottom.

When they reached the main floor, the woman, still rather dazed, continued to sit on the man's chest. He looked at her with an air of resignation. "Madam," he said politely, "I'm sorry, but this is as far as I go."

As in the story, so in life. There are certain things in which we can go only so far. We can go only so far in work and in play, in eating and in drinking, and even in grieving and mourning. We must understand that there are limits to everything we do in life. Learning to live with limits is learning to be mature. Understanding the words "no" and "not" is an important part of a good and wise life.

This was well illustrated in the following episode.

A secretary was once being taken to task by her employer because she left the word "not" out of a letter.

She began to pout under the scolding and said, "After all, it's only one little three-letter word."

The indignant boss roared back, "So you think one three-letter word is not important, do you. Well, where do you think we would be today if the word "not" had been omitted from the Ten Commandments."

Learning the word "not" is an important religious experience.

*We can unite in firm negation of idolatry and find perhaps more of a common faith in this negation than in any affirmative statement about God. Certainly we shall find more of humility and of brotherly love.* ERIC FROMM

# Chaos Or Community

Scientists tell us that at one time in history two types of living creatures inhabited the earth. There were the soloists and those who lived in societies. Large and powerful beasts, like the dinosaurs, seemingly invincible and indestructible, arrogantly kept to themselves and nursed a deep hatred for one another. It was these animals which perished. Species like the ants, the birds, and the bees, who formed communities, interacted, and divided their labor for their mutual benefit, have survived for countless ages.

The real keynote of civilization is "community." For unless we have a shared sense of belonging and a strong pull of commitment to community, all the officials and the laws in the world will not help us. Community in the truest sense of the word is what makes for a peaceful society. This means a willingness to trust one another, a desire to help one another, a true concern for the welfare of one another.

An American businessman expressed it well in these words:

> We have two choices as to which way we can go. We can divide into camps and shoot it out, or we can try to find common grounds so that we can grow together again. One course is easy but blind; the other course is hard and slow but is the path of wisdom. One course leaves all the thinking to someone else; the other requires deep, painful thought in a never-ending search for answers. One course will bring bloodshed, destruction and ultimate crushing of freedom—the crushing of the human spirit; the other course can bring peace.

*Either fear or fellowship . . . either chaos or community.*
TAANIT 23a

# Easy Summer Living

Summer is the time when we should withdraw from some of our involvement with our families and our community, and be a little more thoughtful about where we are going in our constant activity and why we want to go there—a time for making mid-course corrections in our voyage through life.

Moreover, we need time just to sit and rest and give our minds and our bodies a chance to catch up with our frenzied activities as we enjoy the lazy, hazy, crazy days of summer. And as we turn to summer, we return to a sense of the glory and grandeur of the created world.

There is a wonderful story of an angry gentleman who walked up to a ranger in beautiful Yosemite National Park and asked, "Where's your golf course?" Told there was none, he demanded sharply, "What are you supposed to do around here? Look at the scenery?"

What are we supposed to do in the summer? We should look at the scenery—both outside and inside us. The message of summer is to relax our grip on life and to revel in the beauty of the world. Summer is the time to travel, to cultivate flowers, to enjoy the warm waters, and also the time to sit still and look inside ourselves and upward to the sky.

Richard Hovey, an American poet, expressed our feelings with these words: "I am tired of four walls and a ceiling; I have need of the sky, I have business with the grass."

*Be still and know that I am God.*                    PSALMS 46:11

# Food-Forbidden and Favored

The rabbis of the Talmud explained the prohibition against eating certain foods as a safeguard against becoming spiritually and psychologically ill. They pointed out that what goes into a person's mouth is just as important as what comes out of it. Consuming too much alcohol, too many drugs, too much food has dangerous consequences.

Just as certain foods are harmful, others play an important role in well-being and memories. Studies on early learning conducted at Yale's Child Study Center and studies of our personal and cultural history conducted at Harvard support this idea by showing how tastes and smells conditon certain forms of thinking from early childhood onward.

This can be illustrated by the story of a woman who was once having tea at a friend's house. The hostess served a variety of crackers. The guest picked up one cracker, took a bite and joyfully exclaimed: "Why, this is the cracker I have been wanting for years! We had it every morning in the first grade with our milk, and I never ever forgot its taste."

All of us remember the foods of our childhood with many associations. The ancient rabbis with great wisdom understood this well. That is why on Pesah, with every bite of the cracker known as *matzah*, a Jew tastes freedom. That is why every Shavuot, with a bite of a *blintz*, a Jew savors the freshness of the Torah. And the lack of food on Yom Kippur makes the point by helping us remember the taste of the first food after the fast, so that we know what it means *not* to have food, even as we are taught to appreciate food after hunger. Clearly, the prohibition against certain foods and the seeking out of other foods play an important role in the development of spiritual feelings.

*You shall not make yourselves unclean with them and thus become defiled.*　　　　LEVITICUS 11:43

# All In The Family

All of us have a deep need to belong to a family. It is through this need and by this need that we develop a sense of security in the world. But, we must understand that a family is much more than a group of people sharing the same biological lineage. A *real* family is a group of people who love one another . . . who are devoted to one another . . . who work for one another. Within their circle is cooperation, understanding and comradeship. Each member of a family strives to make all the other members happy—and in doing so finds happiness for himself or herself. All of this was well expressed in this poem:

> The family is like a book—
> The children are the leaves,
> The parents are the covers
> That protecting beauty gives.
> At first the pages of the book
> Are blank and purely fair,
> But time soon writes memories
> And paints pictures there.
> Love is the little golden clasp
> That binds up the trust;
> Oh, break it not, lest all the leaves
> Should scatter and be lost!

The time has come for us to realize that we must draw closer to our families for we all need each other so much.

*Ideally, the Jewish home is holy and sanctified. There is religion in the home, there is learning in the home, values are taught, character is molded. In the home there is security, protection, beauty, warmth, serenity and inspiration. The home generates a feeling of being wanted, of being needed, of being loved.*    HILLEL E. SILVERMAN

# The Chain Of Love

The verse in the Bible containing the classic statement on love for others (Leviticus 19:18) ends with the words: "I am the Lord." The reason for this is that the most important way we can express our love for God is to learn to love His creatures—our fellow human beings. If we hate a person, do we not also hate God? For every person was created in the image of God.

Love is not a divisible thing. It is rather a chain reaction that leads us on to higher forms. We fall in love with a stranger, and then we marry the stranger and the stranger becomes our spouse. Then through the love of another person, we learn how to love a family. From the love of family we come to learn love for a community. From the love of a community, we reach the stage of a love for the world. Then in and through the love of the world, we learn to love God. By the first act of love of one person, we eventually bring God and the world together. This is not something we do accidentally but in a positive, deliberate way. We must choose before we can begin to love.

A Hasidic teacher once put a theoretical question to his pupils. If a Jew arises from his bed in the morning and has to choose in one moment between two ways, the love of God and the love of his neighbor, which should take precedence? The answer the teacher gave was that it is written in the Bible, "Love thy neighbor as thyself, I am the Lord." There we have stated the proper order and choice. We should love human beings before God. But, the point really is that true love of God begins with the love of people.

*The love of people is at the same time a love for God. For when we love one, we necessarily love one's handiwork.*
JUDAH LOEW

# Listen While You Work

At one point in his career a judge seemed to become so efficient that he arrived at his judicial decisions very quickly. When asked how he was able to do this, the judge replied, "I listen to the plaintiff and form an opinion."

The questioner then asked in amazement, "Don't you listen to the defendant?"

And the judge answered: "I used to, until I found that it gets me all mixed up."

But actually it is precisely because we *refuse* to listen to both sides that we are becoming all mixed up in daily living. In the family, often no one seems to be listening to anyone else. The generations cannot communicate with each other and there seems to be no way to bridge the gap. Adolescents quarrel with their parents and these parents are in a state of tension with *their* parents.

Everybody is talking and nobody is listening. But did you ever stop to wonder what really is bothering the teenager in our society? Is it so easy to grow up in a world filled with the fear of the unknown or the knowledge that it will take years and years to be trained for a profession? On the other hand, if you are a teenager, have you ever quietly sat down to try to understand your parents' needs? Is it so easy to make a living in a competitive society? Is it a light thing to contemplate the awesome responsibilities that rest on the shoulders of every parent? Nor can the older person be understood until we attend to the voices of those who cry out in loneliness and in fear of growing old and unwanted. There *is* a bridge to the generations, and that bridge is called listening.

*You shall hear the small and the great alike.*

DEUTERONOMY 1:17

332

# Scripture As Sensitivity

When we remember our historical experiences as slaves, we call to mind what it means to be treated unjustly and unfairly. As we recall the moments of our pain, we begin to understand that it is not right to cause pain to others. There is good psychological logic in what the Bible teaches. As you would not want to be hurt, do not hurt others. If you never allow yourself to forget what it means to suffer, then it is unlikely that you will consciously visit suffering on others. Here, then, the Torah teaches us a very valuable lesson about human relations. And this is important for when people rise to greater freedom or wealth or power, they tend to forget what it was like before.

As we look at the lessons of history, we find that this is really the nature of political persecution. The French Revoluton promised liberty for all. Yet, the minute the revolutionaries came into power they proceeded in the Reign of Terror to chop off the heads of everyone who disagreed with them. The Russian Revolution promised an equalitarian, classless society. Yet when the workers' party came into power it proceeded to persecute all other classes. The American Revolution was fought on the basis of the principle of political freedom for all. Yet, a country so dedicated nevertheless closed its eyes to the enslavement of its black minority. In all these instances, had the visionaries remembered the original painful conditions that inspired them they would not have hurt others when they came into power.

The Biblical verse below reminds us that we must keep our sensitivity to oppression alive and alert.

*Remember that you were a slave in Egypt.*
                                    DEUTERONOMY 24:18

# The Question Mark

It is human to doubt. Of all God's creatures, the human being is the only one who asks, "Why?" Why is there evil? Why can't people get along together? Why must I believe in God? These are questions that we should not be afraid to ask. For only as we question can we learn more about the nature of belief and commitment. Judaism has never feared —and, in fact, quite openly welcomes—doubt. It is precisely one's faith in God and the universe that gives us the strength to doubt.

A motorist whose engine was knocking badly pulled up to the curb in a Vermont village and asked two pedestrians, "Is there a mechanic in this town?"

"Yes," one of the pedestrians replied.

"Well, what's his name?"

"Ephraim Hawkins."

"Ephraim Hawkins, eh? Where's his place of business?"

"116 Chestnut Street."

"And how do I get there?"

The native doing the talking directed him, and the motorist drove off.

"Eph," said the other pedestrian, "why didn't you tell that man that you are Ephraim Hawkins?"

"Well, Cy," drawled Ephraim, "it's like this: he didn't ask me."

If you don't ask, you will never learn; if you don't keep asking, you will never test and strengthen your faith. But if you doubt, your determination will develop your faith, and if you keep on asking, then your quest will lead to more satisfying answers.

*What is man after all but a question? To ask and only to ask, to ask honestly and boldly, and to wait humbly for an answer is the reason we are here.*    RAHEL LEVIN VARNHAGEN

# The Final Count

Our era puts great emphasis upon images. Rarely a day goes by in which we do not read the way a television or movie star is trying to change or improve his or her image. Politicians dye their hair to present more youthful images. Advertising campaigns are mounted to give an institution or a product a better public image.

In the Bible, on the other hand, we find almost no such emphasis. Thus God's candidate to bring the Israelites out of slavery and eventually to lead them to Mount Sinai to receive the Ten Commandments was not a silver-tongued orator. Indeed, according to the Biblical description, Moses lacked self-confidence, experienced grave doubt and had a very severe speech problem. Is this the kind of an image a leader should have?

But in later history the wisdom of God's choice was seen in its true perspective, for Moses became great because he had character, commitment, compassion, and a great concern for his cause. Thus what the Bible is really teaching us is that images are just illusions; and, ultimately, it is character that counts.

Real people really matter in this world and are the ones who influence others and move the world. Images that are graven are only one-dimensional, flat, and of very little lasting impact. Therefore, we can learn from the Bible that in the last analysis, the product—not the package—is what really counts.

*Truth can stand, falsehood cannot.*　　　　　SHABBOT 104a

# Don't Crowd Yourself

There are occasions when we must assert our convictions no matter what the group believes. There are times to stand up in a quiet but firm way and say, "I won't go along with the crowd."

A very relevant Aesop fable tells of a father and a son who were taking a donkey to the fair. As they were walking, some of the villagers said, "Look at the foolishness of the men. One of them could be riding the animal." At this point, the father told the son to mount the donkey. They traveled for a little while and they came upon a group of farmers. The farmers muttered, "Look at this generation which has no respect. The son rides but the father walks." The son then dismounted and the father got on the donkey. A little while later, they met some more people who criticized them and said, "Look at the thoughtless parent! The father rides and the son has to walk." They then decided that both of them would get on the donkey. As they neared the fair grounds, they met some more people who said, "Look at that poor little beast! Two men weighing it down." They then both dismounted, tied the animal's forelegs and back legs, slipped a pole between them, and began to carry the donkey. They came to an old bridge; and when they were in the middle, the pole suddenly broke under the weight of the beast and the animal fell into the water and drowned. The father looked at the son and said, "My boy, let this be a lesson to you. If you seek to please everyone, you will ultimately end up pleasing no one, and you will be destroyed in the process."

*Do not side with the multitude to do wrong.*

EXODUS 23:2

# Happiness

Some people think that happiness is a dry martini. Others believe that happiness is a warm puppy. To a young girl, happiness can be finding the right pair of shoes to go with a special dress. To a teenage boy, happiness is getting a driver's license. To almost all of us, happiness is coming out of the dentist's office with no cavities. Yet, this is a rather trivial view of what real happiness is all about. Judaism teaches that happiness is doing a *mitzvah*, performing a good deed. All these definitions provide ample evidence that happiness is not a set formula but rather the way one looks at life.

A visitor to Israel happened to come upon a group of North African Jews who were working hard and sweating in the hot sun. Laboring on a plateau in Jerusalem, they were engaged in the arduous and boring task of breaking stones by hand as they sought to clear a piece of land. Although they were working hard, the workers appeared to be enjoying their work. The visitor was curious about how anyone could be happy working in the hot sun, breaking large rocks into smaller pieces. So he approached them and asked them why they seemed so happy. One of the workers replied with pride, "We are helping to rebuild the land of Israel." It became clear then to the traveler that they were happy because they found meaning in their work. The ultimate happiness comes in doing something that is meaningful to oneself and to others.

*Our children should be fitted for bread-winning, but they should be taught that bread-winning is only a means, not the purpose of life and that the value of life is to be judged by the good and the service to God with which it is filled.*

SAMSON RAPHAEL HIRSCH

# Becoming A Volunteer

Gunnar Myrdal, the internationally-respected Swedish economist, once did a study of the American character. In it he writes: "The American's purse is more open for charity than that of people in other nations. It should not be forgotten that America had, and still has, the world's most generous and best organized private charity. Every call for charity from abroad, to relieve the victims of earthquakes or other calamities, has always met with a much more generous response in American than in other countries. America's work in poor lands has been magnificent over several generations."

There are many ways for Americans to continue this great tradition. The United Way and many national and international campaigns give the opportunity to do so. In religious circles we have ample means to express our generosity.

A social worker who passed a certain bar every night on her way home noticed that one of her former clients seemed to haunt the place. One evening, as he came staggering forth, she spoke to him.

"Tell me," she said, "what makes you drink like this?"

The man waved his arm in good-humored fashion. "Why, nothing *makes* me do it, Lady," he replied grandly. "I'm a volunteer."

The spirit of volunteerism is the heart of America. If this spirit is maintained, and, indeed, increased by each succeeding generation of Americans, then we shall have succeeded as Americans and as human beings.

*If you feed the hungry from your own plenty and satisfy the needs of the wretched, then your light will rise like dawn out of darkness and your dusk will be like noonday.*

ISAIAH 58:10

338

# How A Hurt Can Help

We often hear of the conflict of generations, of the lack of real communication between parents and their growing children. If the truth be told, it is a two-way problem. The older generations need to be appreciated even as the younger generations need to be understood.

One wonders how many homes would be strengthened if we could repair the failure of understanding and create a bridge through which there will be a steady two-lane flow of ideas, feelings, and convictions.

In our daily work it is important to understand the people about us. Often we misjudge actions because we do not realize what motivates them. At other times we become resentful and hostile only because we misinterpreted a statement. To understand another does not mean that one has to agree with all that he or she says or does. It only means to see for a little while through other eyes.

There is a graphic illustration in the following story: Once a five-year-old boy was screaming in the playroom and when his mother ran into the room she found the baby pulling his hair. The mother tried to comfort him and said, "Never mind, your baby sister doesn't understand that it hurts you." She hadn't been out of the room for a minute when more shrieks sent her running back. This time the baby was crying.

"What's the matter with the baby?" she asked the boy.

"Nothing much," he replied calmly. "Only now she knows."

To understand what hurts someone can be the beginning of helpfulness.

*What is hateful to you, do not do to your fellow creature.*

HILLEL

# To Be Is To Do

According to the Jewish tradition there are 613 *mitzvot;* 248 are *asay* (positive commandments), and 365 are *lo ta'aseh* (negative commandments). If a person concentrates a whole day—and indeed his whole year—on performing 613 *mitzvot,* then he will have found himself so busy living a good life that he will not have time left for wickedness. He just does not have the energy, both physical and psychic, to squander on mischief.

Once, Maurice Samuel, one of the great students of the social and literary history of our people during the past fifty years, was giving a lecture on life in the Ghetto. After the lecture, he was asked by one of the students, "What did the people in the ghetto think about sex?" Samuel answered withbout batting an eyelash, "They were so busy having children and raising them they didn't have any time to think about sex!"

Fulfilling ourselves in living by *mitzvot* is the authentic expression of the Jewish way of life. Faith is a nebulous term, but *mitzvot*—deeds—are the concrete performance of the will of God.

This is important, because we tend to spend too much time talking and too little time doing . . . caught in a kind of "paralysis by analysis." But the whole philosophy of the *mitzvah* is, surely, to think first, but then to understand the commitment to action. A Jew knows that it is a *mitzvah* to say a *berakhah* over his food. That it is a *mitzvah* to sanctify the Sabbath by lighting the candles, by saying the prayers and enjoying the Sabbath food. A Jew knows that it is a *mitzvah* to give to charity, to help someone in trouble, to work for his community. For to be is to do.

*Happy is the man whose deeds are greater than his learning.*
SEDER ELIYAHU RABBAH 17

# Second Sight

People see what they need to see. We learn from researchers that the pupil of the eye dilates upon seeing pleasant things and contracts at distasteful things. It was shown in a psychological experiment that when coins of a certain size were shown to a group of poor and rich children, the poor children saw them as bigger than they really were, while the richer children saw them as smaller than they really were. All of us see things through our value systems.

But if we wish to see what *really* goes on in the world, we must be willing to open our minds. We must see not only ourselves, but our neighbors, our community, and the whole world. There are not just white people—there are also dark people and yellow people. There are not just Jews—there are Protestants, Catholics, Moslems, and Buddhists. There is not just America, but there are countries throughout the entire world.

Even as we open our eyes and our minds to see more about God, we must also open our hearts to care about His creatures. Our hearts must be unlocked by the key of compassion and we must be willing to be concerned about the feelings of others. Openness is the keynote—when we open ourselves to experience and to love, we make room for the Lord to enter. Therefore, we must continually make sure that our eyes are open, that our minds are open, that our hearts are open.

*The mature person who refers to God as his "loving Father" does not expect a cosmic lollipop; he is simply expressing his awareness of the world, mental, physical, and aesthetic possibilities which the Lord put within him, and which God ardently wishes him to fulfill.*

HAROLD L. KRANTZLER

# Give A Hand

Individuals who have given of themselves, especially when they were not asked, are those whose names will be truly remembered. We all remember the name of the teacher who went out of his way to help us when we had a difficult time. We all recall the friend who offered assistance without being asked when we were in financial, moral or psychological straits. None of us will ever forget those meetings when a chairperson had to be selected, a courageous word had to be spoken, a commitment had to be made and, after an embarrassing silence, someone came forward without being urged and offered to help.

Essentially, this is the history of humanity. Some people give lip service and some people give real service; some people give words and some people give works; some people give applause and some people give aid. The answer really comes in how you want to use your hand.

Consider the story of the teacher who used the system of placing gold stars opposite the names of the children who answered questions correctly. One day, she dropped the box of gold stars and they fell like confetti all over the floor. The teacher got down on her hands and knees and attempted to pick up the tiny gold stars. The children watched in fascination. Finally, the teacher looked up and said sharply, "Isn't anyone going to give me a hand?" Immediately, all the pupils began to applaud enthusiastically.

There is a time to use your hands for applause, but there is also a time for reaching out your hand to help. If you happen to be the person who sees the needs of the hour and steps forward to help, you will win the admiration of those around you and you will earn the peace of mind that comes with knowing you have served.

*Let not your hand be stretched out to take, and closed at the time of giving back.*          WISDOM OF BEN SIRA 4:31

# Right On!

A visitor to Israel was standing in the shade of a tree toward evening, waiting for a friend to meet him. On the street, which was being repaired, there was a large sandpile. The man noticed that as soon as the workmen left, all the children piled in on the sand and started to dig tunnels, build castles, and so on. These children had come from different countries and ethnic backgrounds. But it really did not matter for they spoke the universal language of play. As they were busily playing, a cat came to the edge of the sandpile and began to poke at it. One child picked up a handful of sand to throw at the cat—a normal enough thing to do. Suddenly, one little boy called out in English, "Don't do it! You'll get caught!"

Then an Israeli girl piped up with, *zeh lo yafeh*, which means, "That's not nice" or "That's not proper."

She had appealed to his nobler instincts. The boy dropped the sand and resumed playing.

We must patiently teach a concept of *zeh lo yafeh*, that certain things and actions in life are just not proper for us. It is not proper to condemn industry for polluting the atmosphere and then to turn around and litter our streets and towns with cans and paper. It is not proper to say we live in the land of the free and then permit repression or deny others the rights to their own life styles. It is not proper to boast of equal public education and then turn around and sabotage it by cutting off educational funding for needed programs, and by harshly criticizing teachers. It is not proper to proclaim we are for peace and in the same breath build up armaments. Quite simply, the proper creation of a peaceful world requires the cooperation of all people.

*It is not enough to know what is right. It is important to contend for that right.*      JACOB R. MARCUS

# Never Say "Never"

The interior of the electric light bulb is frosted in order to diffuse the light and to help make the bulb more efficient. The process of frosting bulbs was invented in an interesting way. Many years ago in the General Electric Lamp Division, the engineers used to play a joke on the new employees. They assigned the newcomers the impossible task of frosting bulbs on the inside. It just could not be done and it became a standing joke in the department.

One day, however, a young man with the improbable name of Marvin Pipkin was initiated. He promptly went to work and after a period of time he developed an etching acid which enabled the bulb to be frosted. They had forgotten to tell him it could never be done, so he took the task seriously and he did it.

All of science, all of music, all of art, all of travel, all of literature, all new discoveries and adventure happen when people forget the words "impossible" and "never."

The importance of never saying "never" carries over into our personal lives as well. All of us face daily challenges that seem impossible and problems that appear insurmountable. But, the point is that while at the moment they may appear so, in the long run they really are not so. What must be remembered is that our action and our ability to solve problems is shaped by our attitude. For once we think we can't do it, we cannot. And if we are convinced we are unable to resolve a situation, we are finished before we start. That is why in viewing the challenges in our lives one should never say "never."

*Restriction by others chains the mind; by oneself, paralyzes it.*
                                                    LUDWIG BORNE

# Tradition Is A Bridge

In the Jewish way of life, convictions and beliefs are bound together by customs, ceremonies and celebrations. Values are the bricks, and custom is the cement which holds the house of Judaism together. It is the ceremonies of Judaism which enable each generation of Jews to hand over the teachings of the tradition to the next generation.

The Passover Seder is not merely a family meal, but a way to ensure that the ideal of freedom will continue among us. Shavuot is not just a Confirmation with choreography on the pulpit, but a means to restate the moral law and to teach that Sinai touches every day of our lives. Sukkot is not only building a beautiful *sukkah,* but an ever-recurring reminder of how thankful we ought to be for the bounties of nature. Rosh Hashanah comes to tell that life is not just a random series of sensations, but is endowed with meaning and purpose. Yom Kippur is observed to teach us that we are tempted not because we are evil, but because we are human. And through sincere self-examination and honest atonement we can restore our self-respect, and begin anew.

Birth with a Hebrew blessing, Bar or Bat Mitzvah with a prophetic reading, marriage with a huppah, death with the recitation of *kaddish*—the customs and celebrations make up the tradition that tells us who we are and what we must do.

*From the Jewish heritage, I have derived my world outlook, a God-centered interpretation of reality in the light of which man the individual is clothed with dignity, and the career of humanity with cosmic meaning and a hope; a humane morality, elevated in its aspirations yet sensibly realistic; a system of rituals which inter-penetrates my daily routines and invests them with poetry and intimations of the divine.*

MILTON STEINBERG

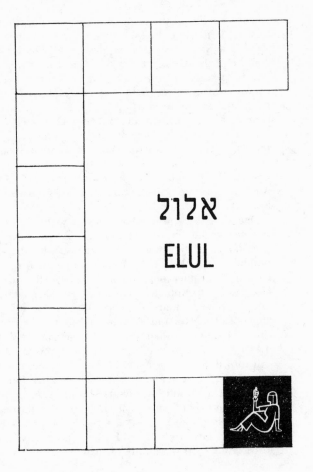

אלול

ELUL

# Come Blow Your Horn

The sounding of the *shofar* during the month of Elul tells us to look not only backward and inward, but forward as well. The *shofar* is the instrument that will herald the coming of the Messianic Age, that great time when there will be peace on earth, and all human beings as one will come to worship God. In this way the *shofar* asks us to look forward to the future with hope and assurance. It is a call for courage and a statement of faith in what lies before us.

During the war years a family in Poland was separated by the Nazis. The older boy was taken to a concentration camp and the younger one was given refuge by some very brave people. The parents were sent to a slave camp in Holland. After the liberation, the brothers went their own ways and lost track of one another.

One day, one of the boys who became a journalist assigned to the United Nations happened to be writing a letter home. In the reporter's lounge in the United Nations Building, he called out, "When does the mail depart for Holland?" Another journalist replied, "Who do you have in Holland?" The younger man answered, "My father lives there." The older journalist said, "What a coincidence! My father lives in Holland as well. And by the way, in what city?" The younger man replied, "Amsterdam." "My father lives in Amsterdam, too," was the retort. "What street?"

It turned out to be the same street, the same address, the same name. You can guess the rest. The brothers found each other after long and bitter years of separation.

How did they recognize one another? From the dwelling place of their father. So, too, when we see that all of us address ourselves to the same Father in heaven, we turn out to be brothers in the family of man.

*The shofar is a prayer without words.*   SAUL LIEBERMAN

# The Taste Of Life

"And Noah was the first farmer to plant a vineyard. Then he drank of the wine and he became intoxicated" (Genesis 9:20-21).

That Noah planted a vineyard was fine. That he made wine was good. That he tasted of it was commendable. The only problem was that he became drunk. The verse and the commentaries on it speak volumes about the Jewish attitude toward life. Judaism does not believe in denying our normal appetites. It simply urges us to be balanced in satisfying them.

In the Bible, beginning with the portion of creation through the story of Noah, we find a consistent exhortation for man to make the most of life and to enjoy life. Adam is told to fill the earth and to use it. Eve is instructed to conceive children and to enjoy them. Noah is asked to tame the animals and to cultivate the earth. All of this is a way of saying: Enjoy life, make each moment count, this is truly God's will for human beings.

Muriel Resnik was a $6,000-a-year free-lance writer until she wrote a Broadway comedy hit. Her agent phoned to report that the Resnik income would exceed $100,000 and that foreign, road-company and movie rights might make it a million dollars. Hearing no response the agent shouted, "Muriel, are you on?"

"I've just stamped out my cigarette," she replied. "The last one I'll ever smoke. With that much money to spend, I want years to enjoy it."

With all the years we have—few or many—let us enjoy them day by day, making the most of every moment—with moderation.

*Deny yourself not the good which the day brings you and let not your share of joy pass you by.*     BEN SIRA 14:14

# The Right Direction

The Bible contains a detailed listing of the various roles of those who were to serve in the sanctuary. Some were to sing in the sacred choir and others were to be carpenters. Others were to officiate at the sacrifices and rituals. Still others were to be porters and carry the tabernacle as the Jewish people traveled from place to place in the desert. All were called to serve and the work of each was regarded as equally important.

This contains an important moral lesson for all of us. Often we think that someone is superior by virtue of affluence or social position. But this attitude is contrary to the Torah which teaches that everybody has a role to play in life and that we should be judged solely in terms of whether we perform our role with competence and honesty.

In our community life some of us have to be merchants to keep the economy rolling. Some of us have to be lawyers to straighten out human affairs. Some of us have to be doctors to heal. Some have to be poets and some have to be teachers. Some of us have to labor with our hands. None is superior to another. We all belong to the holy community.

Similarly, in religious matters each religion has its own unique role to play. Isn't it possible that Catholics can show the beauty of ritual, Protestants the significance of the word and Judaism the indispensable part of the home? Isn't it possible that Buddhism can teach us contemplation, and Hinduism the need to concentrate on spiritual matters? Religion, rather than causing confrontation, should point up the uniqueness and the special contribution each of us has to make to the world.

*It is the same merit if one does more or one does less as long as one's heart is sincerely directed toward heaven.*

BERAKHOT 5b

# Second Nature

Many of us never take the trouble to study nature really closely. Most of us are woefully ignorant of the names of plants and animals and all the wonderful birds that are native to our own regions. It is therefore a great delight that many of our children are being instructed in these things in our schools. It would be even more wonderful if a city child could spend some part of the summer in the natural surroundings which are part of our heritage as human beings—the highest link in the great chain of creation.

The fact that more and more Americans are leaving the farm and coming to the city, and therefore changing us into an urban civilization, is beginning to create problems and we must be aware of them. Our loss of direct contact with nature is something for which we pay in lack of feeling and even in ignorance of our larger, natural environment.

A sentimental lady visiting a college campus paused before a huge old tree. Waxing poetic she exclaimed, "O wonderful elm! If you could only speak, what would you say to me?" The senior showing her around, a forestry student, replied, "It would probably say, 'Pardon me, I'm an oak.'"

While it is fashionable to use words like ecology and environmental, often we do not have the knowledge and understanding that makes the natural world a part of our real world. There is beauty, inspiration and wonder all about us; and, indeed, within us. But we must take time to listen and learn about nature. Only as we can identify the many elements of nature and then identify with the world of nature will we feel a sense of belonging in this world of ours.

*To be able to live in strict conformity with nature is what the men of old defined as the end of happiness.*    PHILO

# Pray Tell

No one invented prayer. Prayer is man's instinctive reaction to the world around him. It is our most profound response to personal fears and hopes, frustrations and dreams, strivings toward self-realization as human beings.

The Bible teaches that anyone can pray. Now, this seems obvious. But, in ancient ages and even in modern times, this was, and is, not taken for granted. In examining the history of religion we find that prayer was often the prerogative of the few. Among pagan cults there were prayer texts that no one could utter but the priest in the temple. In Roman culture the words were so sacred that if one word was mispronounced, the whole prayer had to be started again.

But in the Bible we find a whole new approach. Any place, it tells us, is a proper place in which to pray to God. The Bible teaches that religion is portable; it is carried in the heart and is not bound to any shrine or relic.

Moreover, Biblical prayer is the honest expression of the sensitive soul, not a set incantation. Moses speaks with God not in a fixed formula, but rather in simple sentences of his own. Beginning with the experience of Moses at the burning bush, Jewish tradition breaks with magical rites and superstition. From that experience we learn that all a person need do is think of God, and he or she is in the divine presence.

A mother put her little daughter to bed. For a short while it was quiet. Then she heard the child repeating the alphabet in a tone of voice that sounded like a prayer. "What are you doing?" the mother called out. The little girl explained, "I'm praying, but I can't think of the right words, so I'm just saying all the letters. God will put them together for me, because He knows what I'm thinking."

*Prayer, if offered from the heart and for the sake of heaven, ascends on high and pierces the firmament.* OR YESHARIM

# To Be A Jew Is To Be Strong

In each challenge to their religious, cultural or physical existence the Jews united as a people, and rose to the occasion.

Abraham was a refugee adrift in a land of blind idolatry. Yet, instead of giving way to defeat, he accepted his responsibility, rallied his followers, and created the first monotheistic faith of the Western world.

Moses was a spoiled princeling in the court of Pharaoh. Yet, instead of becoming corrupt, he united the twelve tribes and not only helped free his people but also gave them and the world a moral code by which to live.

In the year 586 before the regular calendar, the Temple in Jerusalem was destroyed, and the Jews began the long night of the exile. But instead of bowing to their defeat, they created a new place of worship named the Synagogue, and a new way to administer justice called the Talmud.

In the Middle Ages, the Jews, caught between the hammer of the Crusades and the anvil of the Church, refused to let themselves be pounded into submission. Instead, they fashioned a literature, one of whose most important books was entitled *A Guide To The Perplexed*.

In modern times, after the tragedy of the Holocaust, we did not die but were reborn in Israel. Through the *kibbutz* system we fashioned a new form of Jewish living whose creative approach to communal life is being studied and emulated in almost every contemporary culture.

Despite our profound problems, despite our catastrophic losses, we have learned that when there is striving and sharing, then Jews survive and prevail.

*To be a Jew is to be strong with a strength that has outlived persecution.*                    PHYLLIS BOTTOME

# The Cultivation Of Kindness

Kindness cannot be forced upon people. It must flow easily and naturally from one human personality to another. Real kindness is the spontaneous expression of the deeply religious and helpful soul.

There is a wonderful story of a scout master who, during a meeting of his troop, stressed the necessity of doing a good deed every day. At the next meeting he asked if anyone had performed a good deed that day. A little boy stood up and said, "Yes, sir, Joe and I helped an old lady across the street this afternoon." The leader said, "That's nice, but did you have any difficulty?" And the Boy Scout replied, "As a matter of fact, yes. She didn't want to go, but we insisted."

Kindness says, "Don't interfere in other people's lives under the pretense that you are kind." Kindness says, "Refrain from offering advice when no one really wants it." Kindness says, "Don't point up a fault when it is all too obvious anyway." Because one can also kill with kindness.

And speaking of kindness, one must also remember to be kind to one's self. Some of us are very helpful to others and willing to go to great lengths to understand them, but have not learned the art of accepting and being kind to ourselves. If you commit a wrong, can you not be kind to yourself and forgive yourself? After all, you are just a human being. Can you not be kind to your mind and read a challenging book for a change? It is time to stop underestimating your intellect. Can you not be kind to your own faith and feelings and come to the House of God for no other reason than because you need to express a sense of wonder and worship? How about making this week "Be Kind to Yourself" week—and that means being kind to your best, most worthy self.

*It is a duty to cultivate kindness.*   AARON BEN JOSEPH HALEVI

# People Of The Book

In the history of the great classic civilizations such as Greece, Rome and Israel, only Israel had a universal system of literacy. In Greece and in Rome only the upper classes and the educated teacher-slaves knew how to read and write. But, by startling contrast, in Israel *everybody* knew how to read and write because of a commandment that everyone had to study Torah. Furthermore, in the year 64 of the Common Era, Joshua the son of Gamala, the High Priest in the Temple in Jerusalem, arranged a system by which every child from age five on was to receive a Jewish education. It is also interesting to note that there was always a strong disposition among the Jewish people to see that women were also instructed.

We may perhaps gain a greater insight into the Jewish character when we realize that in the Middle Ages the great King Charlemagne could not even write his name, but almost every Jewish child could write sentences from the Torah. It is only in this century that laws for compulsory education were passed, but among the Jewish people they were enforced 1900 years ago. That the Jewish people is literate, intelligent and civilized is not a chance occurrence, but the product of a systematic commitment to learning.

Shumel Yosef Agnon received the Nobel Prize for Literature. Many honors were heaped upon the Master of Hebrew literature on that occasion. But grateful as he was for all of them, only one truly thrilled him. On the Shabbat following the announcement of the prize, he was called to the Torah for an *aliyah*. He said: "By standing before the Scroll of the Torah and saying my blessings, I felt myself fulfilled as being a part of the long heritage of Jewish literature."

*And you write this teaching for yourself and also teach it to your children.*                    DEUTERONOMY 31:19

# Our Eloquent Actions

No matter what we say, it is what we do that counts. We can talk all we want about the pornographic magazines and books that are being published, but if we did not buy them or if we opposed their distribution they would not be printed. We can talk all we want about good government, but unless we vote, ring doorbells, and take the trouble to write letters to the editor and our officials we will not change anything. In every aspect of our lives it is not inactivity, but forthright action that will determine the course of events.

> Sitting still and wishing
> Makes no person great.
> The good Lord sends the fishing,
> But you must dig the bait.

Do you remember the wonderful story of the courtship of Miles Standish? Miles Standish, an American colonist who came over on the Mayflower, was a fearless soldier, but was a coward in matters of the heart. He fell in love with a young woman named Priscilla, but he was so afraid to court her that he sent his friend John Alden to speak for him. As Alden was wooing Priscilla, in Standish's name, she sensed that John really loved her too, Because she returned his affections, after listening patiently, she advised him: "Speak for yourself, John." He did, and she married him.

Every person speaks for himself and herself. Actions speak louder than words. If you believe something very deeply then, whether in being, in feeling, or in action, as a person: Speak for yourself, John!

*Speech has no value unless it can be translated into action.*
JACOB KLATZKIN

# The Older Ideals

We all know that hardening of the arteries often comes with age. What is sad is that very often with age there can also develop an emotional hardening of the arteries. When we are young, we are interested in causes, we develop enthusiasms about helping others, and we feel a fervent desire to lessen the misery of the world. But then as we grow older, life seems to wear us down and we become indifferent to community problems, insensitive to the sufferings of others, and indecisive about committing our lives to important values.

Yet, it is so important when we are older, and a little more affluent, and a little more politically powerful, and a little more mature that we do not lose the idealism of our younger years. As a matter of fact, the gap we sometimes feel between us and the young could be lessened if they saw us as sincerely and devotedly concerned about the welfare of the world. For it is the lack of concern with enduring things, the pursuit of affluence and its pleasures that are often the targets of young people's outrage.

A father purchased a globe of the world for his little son. One night, while the news was being broadcast, the father decided he would get the globe to find the area described by the commentator. He went to the son's room, tiptoed in, picked up the globe and started out. Just then the little boy sat up and said, "Daddy, where are you going with my world?"

This is the question which members of the older community must face.

*The Jewish way in the world has consistently and unswervingly pursued the idea and technique of the good life. Not beauty but goodness is the central problem and theme of Judaism.*                        TRUDE WEISS-ROSMARIN

# Surprised By Joy

Is it right for us to ask God to grant our whims whether in weather or in material comforts or in personal desires? Is it not much more important to ask Him to help us to conform to His will? And more often than not, we do not appreciate what we already have. The virtue of religion is to teach us to enjoy exactly what we have now before we consider asking for what we have not.

There is a delightful story of Reb Mendel of Ridzin, a Hasidic leader who is known as the "Happy Rabbi." He earned this title because all day long he went about with a joyful countenance and he was perfectly happy with what he had. One day, one of his pupils decided to ask him how he was able to be so happy. He replied, 'Every day after services I go to the hospital and I ask the clerk, 'Is Reb Mendel Rodziner a patient here?' The clerk looks at the record and then says, 'No.' When I hear that I am overjoyed."

Now, isn't that exactly the point of a religious life? You have your health—not all of it, perhaps, but some of it—so be content.

You have something to eat, something to wear and a nice home. Perhaps you want a little more, but at least you have this—so be cheerful.

You have your family. Perhaps you've lost some of them—but you still have their memories—so be comforted.

*The joy of the Lord is your strength.*   NEHEMIAH 8:10

# Give And Take

Whenever we fall in love we take certain risks. However it leads we must be willing to accept the consequences and recognize that it is better to have loved and lost than never to have loved at all.

With the understanding of this principle comes a deeper perception of ourselves. It is natural when we sustain a loss, particularly when it is sudden and shocking, to ask questions. Questions like: Why was I the one to survive? Why did it happen to me? Why is it this way? No one knows all the answers, but we do know that certain occurrences are simply part of the natural world. Accidents, illness, untimely occurrences are not moral or immoral in themselves. It is sufficient to say that they happen, that they happen to all of us, and that we have to discipline ourselves to accept them.

A charming little story puts it very well: A Sunday School teacher, seeking to convey the idea of God's power, once asked her class, "Is there anything God cannot do?"

A little hand went up and a tiny voice said, "Yes, God cannot please everybody."

God's relations with us are often very subtle and we must be alert to understand them. If there be illness in the world, did God not also give us the ability to research and cure the illness? If there is suffering in the world, did God not also give us the psychological mechanism to grant us a measure of comfort? And if there is the pain of a loss, did God not also give us a memory of pleasure and the healing power of time and of our own faith to enable us to go on living?

*A vital index of our maturity is our ability to accept the closing gates that life and death impose on each of us. Though such acceptance is at times painful and difficult, it must be done lest we forfeit the opporunity to derive any happiness at all from life.*                    JACOB MILGROM

# A Kind Of Loving

An important Jewish value is *hesed*, loving-kindness. This is the rare instance when the English translation accurately expresses the essential meaning of the Hebrew. For, *hesed* is more than love and greater than kindness. Its full impact can only be revealed in the joint words, "loving-kindness." It is doing something that is simple and honest, yet profound.

To raise your child is an act of love. But to bring a foster child into your home is loving-kindness.

To visit a member of your family who is institutionalized because of chronic illness is an act of kindness. But to visit someone who is not even remotely related to you in the same circumstances is an act of loving-kindness.

Loving-kindness means the extension of our personality into becoming noble. It implies doing that which is not required of us, performing a good deed simply because it is a part of our tradition to live with others in *hesed*, in loving-kindness. And it is what the world most needs.

A famous biologist was once giving a lecture on evolution. At the end of the lecture he announced dramatically that he had finally discovered the missing link between the animal and civilized man. He had found those individuals who could be the perfect examples of that which links our ancestors to civilized man. No sooner had he finished than one of the students arose and said, "Tell us, Professor, where are they?" And the lecturer held out his hand and said, "Why, the people sitting in this room."

We are on the road to civilization but we are not civilized yet. To reach that goal we need loving-kindness.

*The highest form of wisdom is loving-kindness.*

BERAKHOT 17a

# Fear—Friend Or Foe?

To be human is to live with fear. Every infant at birth is immediately beset by two fears—the fear of falling and the fear of a sudden loud noise. Every child harbors fear on the first day of school. Every teenager is apprehensive at the first date. Every mother fears for her children. Every father fears for his economic position. Everyone worries about illness, about war, and ultimately about death. Yes, to be human is to live with fear.

Most people, at first thought, believe that fear is a negative emotion—they think of "crippling fear." Actually, fear in its early and milder stages is very useful.

What is the purpose of fear? It is simply the alarm system within our emotions that alerts us to danger and forces us to mobilize our strength. Fear saves us from disaster, and as such is a real servant to humanity.

Think for a moment. If people did not fear cancer, would they rush to the doctor at the first symptoms and hence have a better chance of survival? If people did not fear being given a ticket would they voluntarily observe traffic laws? If the great powers of the world did not fear instant and massive retaliation, do you think there would be peace? Finally, if many did not fear the judgment of God, do you really believe our society would not retreat to the jungle?

It is obvious, then, that fear is a necessary part of a healthy life.

*Everyone is frightened when confronting the unknown. To lack such feelings of uneasiness is to possess character more pure than that of ordinary mortals. It is not a sin to be frightened; this apparatus is part of natural make-up, and therefore intended by God. The sin is to run in the face of such fear.* JAY ROBERT BRICKMAN

# The Earth Is The Lord's

All of nature is revelation of the presence of God. As we participate directly in the world about us, in a very real sense we are worshipping and performing religious acts. Consider how religious a farmer is. For to plow is to pray, to plant is to prophesy, and the harvest answers and fulfills.

Obviously, we cannot all be farmers, but we can plant gardens. We cannot all work in the soil, but we can observe the natural processes in our own bodies and our own lives; and we can appreciate them. In the last analysis, we must unlearn the myth of the self-made person. We did not make ourselves, we did not make the world, we did not create the universe. It behooves us then to display humility.

The Reverend Robert Hall, an Episcopal minister in Miami, Florida, won a prize in a beautiful tree contest. He grew a perfect flowering poinciana. When he was given the award, he decided to give credit where it was due, and the minister said to the judging committee, "I accept on behalf of my Boss."

In one way or another, we all cooperate or work for the Divine Presence within nature.

Elizabeth Barrett Browning wrote:
>    Earth's crammed with heaven
>    And every common bush afire with God
>    But only they who see take off their shoes.
>    The rest sit around and pick blackberries.

Those of us who are alert can see eternity in a galaxy—or in a snowflake.

*God revealed Himself in a bush to teach us the loftiest may be found in the lowliest.*        ELEAZAR BEN ARAKH

# Speak Up And Speak Out

We must strive to be happy. We have to make an effort to bring joy into our lives and into the lives of others. We should not take good feelings for granted. We have to feel them, we have to express them, and we have to encourage others to feel good and be good, and to do good. Happiness is not accidental and it must be actually cultivated, even as joy on its finest level has to be pursued.

There is the wonderful story of Benjamin Franklin, who was well known for his wisdom and his wit. At the founding of the American Republic, he spoke many times in favor of adopting the American Constitution, one of the greatest documents of all time.

On one occasion he spoke before the Continental Congress urging the adoption of the Constitution. Following the address, a heckler arose and said, "Those high sounding words really don't mean anything. Exactly where is all that happiness you are promising us when you use the phrase 'pursuit of happiness'?"

Franklin smiled benevolently at the questioner and quickly replied, "My friend, the Constitution only guarantees the American people the right to *pursue* happiness. You have to *catch* it yourself!"

This echoes the Jewish view of life which is that it is not a vale of tears but an opportunity to do that which is joyful and in turn makes one happy. It does not mean that life is not a mixture of good and bad, of pain and pleasure, of gladness and sorrow but rather that life is to be lived with emphasis on hope and happiness. What it says in effect is that which Abraham Lincoln long ago noted: "Most folks are about as happy as they make up their minds to be."

*When one performs a good deed, he should do so with a cheerful heart.*                    LEVITICUS RABBAH 34:9

363

# To Be Human

Although a human being is partly animal, in terms of the brain there is a fundamental difference between *homo sapiens* and all other animals. A human—and only a human—can use language, can write, draw, read, and reflect upon himself or herself in a philosophic manner. To be created in the image of God implies that a human being has a mind. In the human being there is the opportunity to make moral decisions. He or she has consciousness of the existence of others, has self-awareness and has the opportunity for self-control. A person is a moral being who will be held accountable for all of his or her actions. Or, more simply, we say a person has a conscience. When a person chooses to act like an animal, he or she is a beast. But when one chooses to reflect the qualities of the spirit, then we know he or she was created in the image of God.

Inside the gorilla house in the New York City Zoo two signs hang side by side between the gorilla cages. One sign says: "You are looking at the most dangerous animal in the world. It has done more to destroy parts of the world than any other beast." Beneath the sign hangs a mirror.

Next to this is another sign which says: "You now see a creature who has achieved grandeur. This being has done more than any other animal to enhance the world." Beneath that sign there also hangs a mirror.

This is the meaning of the creation story in Genesis and the nature of the human being. As Shakespeare wrote, "What a piece of work is man, how noble in reason." for when one uses the mind, lets conscience be a guide, and understands the sacredness of human life, then he or she is acting in the image of God.

*And God created man in His image, in the image of God He created him, male and female He created them.* GENESIS 1:27

# Taking A Stand

As part of the Jewish funeral service it is traditional for the mourners to have a cut made in their garments (or in a ribbon attached thereto) and to recite a prayer of acceptance of God's will and world. The cutting is symbolic of the deeper rent within the heart. Interestingly, this ceremony can never be carried out sitting down. Mourners must stand up as they participate in the ritual. The meaning here is very clear. Even in your moment of intense grief you must stand up to life. God does not want us to take our pain and our problems lying down. He wants us to be upright, fully mobilized in will to do what must be done.

And we must stand up to life not only in moments of grief but in our daily lives—in questions of principle and especially of religious observance. We do not have to be bound by the orthodoxies of the past, nor do we have to be rebellious just for the sake of proclaiming ourselves liberals. We must be willing to stand up to the truths of life, accept what we have, and at the same time accept our faults and correct them to the very best of our ability. We must not blame others for our own inadequacies and we must be proud of what is rightfully ours.

On a very important examination day, an elementary school student went up to the teacher and said, "Can I say a prayer before we begin our exams?" The teacher, sensing that this was a spontaneous feeling and nothing formalized, decided to experiment and granted permission. The child stood up and said: "Dear Lord, if we studied please help us to pass these examinations. But if we haven't studied, well, Lord, that is just our own fault." This is an expression of standing up to life with honesty.

*Truth is God's seal.*                                    SHABBAT 55a

# Man And God

Many of us suffer because we have distorted notions about death and illness. We ought to be mature enough to acknowledge that each of us owes nature a death. It is the natural consequence of birth. We have to learn to live with our losses in an atmosphere of reality and the religious attitude of acceptance.

Moreover, organic illness is not God-ordained in an ethical sense. While we do not know everything about disease, yet quite clearly cancer, viruses and deterioration of organs imply no moral judgment against the sufferer. The only immorality about sickness is when we do not do everything within our power to prevent it, contain it and heal it. The fact is, illness is in the nature of things.

But man does question God and this story which appears twice in Hasidic literature points up the honesty of Judaism in recognizing human perplexity.

Rabbi Levi Yitzhak of Berdichev, a noted defender of this people, once urged the town's humble tailor to make his confession publicly in front of the whole congregation. This is what he said: "I, Yankel, am a poor tailor who, to tell the truth, have not been too honest in my work. I have occasionally kept remnants of cloth that have been left over and I have occasionally missed *minhah* (the afternoon service). But You, O Lord, have taken away children from their mothers and mothers from their children. So let us settle our accounts and come to terms. If You forgive me, then I will forgive You." At this point the Rabbi benevolently sighed, "O Yankel, Yankel, why did you let God off so lightly?"

It is not easy to be human. On the other hand, it is not easy to be God either. So, knowing all this, let every person learn to live in peace with his or her Maker.

*God's presence is on us and ours on Him.*   HYMN OF GLORY

# Two Is More Than One

There was a time when some among us tried to be more American than Jew and thus denied our ancestors. Lately, there seems to be the beginning of a trend toward becoming more Jew than American and some Jews wish to reconstruct the ghetto. Actually, we must understand that neither course is wise and it is not an either/or choice. Creative Jews will be those who can combine the best of both heritages. The impact of Jews and Judaism on America and their great contributions have not yet been fully appreciated. On the other hand, American democratic life and its influence on Judaism is profound and deserves a fuller recognition and discussion. It is important today to remember that each has contributed to the betterment of the other. America is better off because Jews live here and Jews are better off because they can live in America.

One of the purposes of having two eyes is to possess stereoscopic vision. This means we can see things in depth and from different angles. We have two ears so to enjoy stereophonic sound. This means we can hear the subtleties and nuances of musical sounds. In other words, we can sense in depth. The purpose of two cultures is to be able to look at life from many angles and many points of view, and with the proper perspective create a sense of deeper understanding of life.

Or put it still another way: One language constructs a fence; two languages build a gate. One view is totalitarianism; two views is democracy. One style is a bore; two styles is brilliance. For, after all, two heads are always better than one. So be proud of having a hyphen in your background.

*A Jewish culture in America can only exist together with an American culture.*
                                        MAURICE SAMUEL

367

# A Feeling For Faith

The great leaders of Judaism were able to question God and yet maintain their faith in Him. Abraham stood before God and challenged (Genesis 18:25): "Shall not the Judge of all the earth do justice?" Yet, even after this—or because of this—Abraham went on to found Judaism.

The Berdichever Rebbe had the courage (or the colossal *hutzpah*, depending upon your point of view) to demand *a din Torah mit Gott,* that God be brought to judgment because of the way He permitted the Jewish people to suffer. Yet, when he came to the end of his indictment he said: *yitgadal veyitkadash shmay rabba,* "Magnified and sancti-fied be His holy name."

Elie Wiesel, the messenger of the modern martyrs, in his early works hurls some powerful accusations against God. Yet his writings have moved many young Jews to do something about the plight of their fellow Jews and one of his books, *A Beggar in Jerusalem,* is a sensitive affirmation of the presence of God in the world in general and in the Jewish people in particular.

A thoughtful examination of the lives of Abraham, the Berdichever Rebbe and Elie Wiesel shows that the one thing they had in common was the ability to live with doubt and with unanswered questions. Intuitively, they found in their honest faith a strong spur to go on living, trusting that in the very process of living they would find solutions that were satisfying. They were not disappointed, essentially because underneath it all they had a firm foundation of faith.

There are mysteries in our lives that our reason cannot deal with—pain, death, rapture and ecstasy. It is faith that leads us through these mysteries.

*God conceals Himself from our minds, but reveals Himself to our hearts.*　　　　　　　　　　　　　　　ZOHAR, GENESIS

# A Short Distance To Go

A woman was describing to her friend an experience she had on a bus. A rather stout lady had sat down beside her, crowding her toward the window. To make matters worse, the passenger was carrying an assortment of packages which kept poking into her ribs. The friend interrupted saying, "If I had been there, I would have told her a thing or two. Why didn't you give her a piece of your mind?" To which the woman answered, in words that carried a great symbolic message, "What was the use of getting angry? After all, we had such a short distance to go together."

This statement touches on the very meaning of the passage of our lives on spaceship Earth. After all, we have such a short distance to go together; why should the journey be marked by hate and bitterness, by spite and grudges? We cannot learn from one another until we stop shouting at one another. But, on the other hand, once we have learned how to speak sincerely but softly, how to listen but also to respond, we will live more fulfilling and happier lives. For living in peace comes from the insight that in discovering how to be understanding, we, in turn, are understood.

Understanding the universe ultimately means knowing that all of life is related, all living beings have needs, all creatures are limited by time and space. In accepting these limits , we accept our common destiny and thus we learn to help one another.

*We did not all come over on the same ship, but we were all in the same boat.*                    BERNARD M. BARUCH

369

# The Melody Lingers On

The Selihot Service heralds the advent of the High Holy-days. It usually occurs on the Saturday night before Rosh Hashanah and emphasizes the music and liturgy of these sacred days. Indeed, certain feelings can only be expressed in music even as music suggests our symbolic quest to bring our lives into harmony with the rhythm of the universe and the will of God.

A beautiful legend in the Talmud says: "A harp was always suspended above the bed of King David. As soon as the hour of midnight struck, a north wind came and blew upon it and it played itself beautiful melodies. Upon being awakened, King David would begin to pray and study the Torah" (Berakhot 3b).

As the hour of midnight comes, and as the winds of chance play upon us and the lovely liturgical music is chanted, we are stirred to rise in prayer and to reflect upon our sacred teachings. The symbolism is most fitting, for the whole world can be seen as an orchestra and each of us as an instrument in it. We can decide to live in discord or in harmony. We can choose to play out our lives in futile improvising or to create a song of faith. We can begin by listening to the score of great emotions and read the libretto of a magnificent liturgy and be inspired to turn our lives into instruments of goodness. For after a genuine religious service, the song may be over, but the melody will linger on.

*Listen to the song and to the prayer.*

SELIHOT LITURGY

# Let Go, Let God Work

There are many times in life when we ought to let go. Very often, we overcontrol situations and play at being God. As parents, as community leaders, as employers, as teachers and in many roles in life we are given the opportunity of performing important tasks. But often we forget that our responsibility is to guide and not to take over. We are simply to inspire and not to overwhelm. We are to help direct without dominating. In short, there are times when we should let nature take its course.

A simple story says it very well. A farmer showed his son a large rock with a four-inch cleft. He asked the son to try to split the rock. The boy struck blow after blow and all he could do was to knock away a chip here and there. The lad turned to his father and said, "It is impossible!" The farmer than said, "Son, I will show you how to split the rock very easily." First, he threw some rich soil into the cleft. Then he dropped a pumpkin seed in it and covered it with more soil. And then he turned to the boy and said, "Now watch, the growing pumpkin will split the rock by harvest time. All you have to do is let nature take its course."

When we become involved in the lives of others, we must make sure not to become overinvolved. Most of us have a tendency, often unconscious. to impose our solutions on a situation instead of letting the people concerned find their own solutions. Yet, if we have faith we can do our best, we can rest content with our efforts, we can refrain from pushing further and then we can let natural events take their own course. In this way, we let go and let God work His purpose.

*Oh Lord, free my mind so that I may follow Your ways.*
OLD JEWISH PRAYER

# Tipping The Scales

In a small town a wealthy merchant was riding in his magnificent coach pulled by six horses on a muddy road. Because he had many horses, he had no difficulty traveling. He passed a horse and cart deeply imbedded in the mud. He watched the owner and the animal helplessly struggle to withdraw themselves and ordered his coachman to stop. They attached his carriage to the cart and then they began to drive all the horses. The cart began to move, but they were still unable to dislodge it completely. On a whim, the merchant sprang out of the carriage, jumped in the mud, and disregarding his expensive clothes, he placed his shoulder against the cart and began to push. The horse and cart were free and were soon on their way.

Many years later, the merchant died and appeared before the angels who judged whether the man was worthy to enter heaven. They weighed his good deeds against his wicked deeds, and they found he missed slightly in the balance. Suddenly, one of the angels remembered the good deed on the rainy day. So they lifted the carriage and the horses and put them on the side of the good deeds. Now the scales were exactly balanced, and they did not know what to do.

Then the angels remembered and said, "We forgot to weigh the mud that covered the man when he jumped in to help his fellow man." They took that dirt and placed it on the scale, and lo and behold, the good deeds finally tipped the scale.

After it is all said and done, we might ponder how many lives could be made more heavenly by people willing to involve themselves in the grimy, ordinary details—the mud of life, if you will.

*The test of the worthwhile life is the breadth and width of its involvement with our fellow man.*    ISRAEL H. LEVINTHAL

# The Will To Work

The meaning of our lives is determined by the work we do or the work left undone. We must understand that for all of us work does more than get us a living; it earns us our life.

Marriages may be made in heaven, but they are maintained by the hard work of people here on earth. Business begins with an issue of stock, but dividends are earned only through hard work. Problems in society may be analyzied but they are solved only through the application of sound programs and people willing to produce efforts.

In addition, work is also therapy. It is sometimes our boredom that brings on destructive behavior, while direct involvement releases our good feelings. Often people in retirement will find themselves at loose ends if they have given up their life's work without replacing it with other work, other activities or meaningful concerns. On occasion the problems that an average woman encounters in middle age arise because she has lost the will to work either in society or in the world of professions and business. Work can take many forms for a woman, whether it be volunteer work or paid employment, and a woman who has worked all of her life to raise a family cannot stifle her need to work after her children grow up. Wise women understand the truth that the bèst tranquilizer is work well done.

The human need to work applies to young people as well. Education is fine, but nothing can quite match the gratification of doing or making something worthwhile. Indeed, Sigmund Freud once wrote that the criteria of the healthy personality were the abilities to love and to work.

*Six days you shall labor and do all your work.*

EXODUS 20:9

# God Is A Verb

In the Jewish view, God is not a noun, something static and fixed for all time, but rather a force that is active and vital. The authentic Hebrew name for God comes from the verb *hayoh* which means "to be." God is existence and life made manifest in man.

God is very much alive if we act as though He lived. But, if He has no meaning in our existence and His force makes no difference to us, then it is as if He were dead. Or perhaps it is more correct to say that He is missing in action. We miss God when we are less than we should be, God is missing when we should be compassionate and we are not, when we should be charitable and forgiving and we are not, when we should be decent and honorable and we are not. On the other hand, the presence of God is with us when we practice all the Godly virtues of justice and mercy, of loyalty and humanitarianism—virtues writ large in the Jewish tradition.

Elie Wiesel, the great chronicler of the Holocaust, tells of an incident in his youth. When he was a young boy in Europe, he was taught by a very gifted rabbi. Every day the rabbi would go into the marketplace and say: "*Yidin*, fellow Jews, know who you are! Remember, Satan is loose in the world." One day, the young Elie said to him, "Rebbe, why do you go into the marketplace and tell the people to remember they are Jews and caution them about not doing what is improper? You know they will never change." The Rabbi replied: "Ah, my child, I know that. But, I keep doing it to make sure that *I* won't change."

Part of the purpose of being Jewish is to bear witness to the existence of God in the world. In this purpose, we must not change.

*He was, He is, and He will be with glory.*     ADON OLAM

374

# To Live Peaceably

The only way to have peace between nations is to have it between people. There is a chain that begins with a peaceful person and continues to a peaceful family, to a peaceful neighborhood, to a peaceful community, to a peaceful city, to a peaceful country and completes the cycle in a peaceful world. Break the chain anywhere, damage the relationship at any point, and you get ever-spreading chaos.

The Hebrew word *shalom* means more than peace; it means completeness and harmony. If we cannot have peace in our homes and in our own community, how can we ever expect to have it in the world? But, on the other hand, if we each work in our own family, if we each care for our own community and the lives around us, then will the whole earth be a beautiful, peaceful place.

There is a charming Yiddish story of an elderly Jewish woman who wanted to extend a wish to God. She wondered, "Shall I wish You life? After all, You live forever." Then she questioned, "Shall I wish You wealth? Why, You possess the whole universe." After some moments of thought she prayed: *Gott, zolst hoben naches fun deineh kinder,* "Lord, may You have *naches,* spiritual pleasure, from Your children."

If God is our Father, then we are all sisters and brothers. If all of us acted in a way to make God proud of us—living and treating each other as members of one loving human family—then this would be a real heaven on earth. So it is proper for all mankind to pray: "God, may You have *naches,* spiritual pleasure, from all Your children."

*He who loves and pursues peace, and greets and replies Shalom, brings honor to the name of God.*

DEREKH ERETZ ZUTA 11

# Fifty-Two Weeks Of Time

A notice from a popular magazine reads: "Your *Time* subscription is running out and this is the only letter we plan to send about your renewal." Inside this notice is a card on which is printed the words: "Send me 52 weeks of *Time* and bill me later." This reminder suggests that Rosh Hashanah is a time to remember to renew time itself. Rosh Hashanah, the beginning of a new year, is a time to remember the old year and, at the same time, prepare to enter the new one ahead. It is a time to subscribe once more to the finest values of mankind.

But, perhaps, even more than this it is a time to put our lives in proper perspective. One hears so often these days: Conditions in the world are bad. Well, we ought to ask thoughtfully, "Compared to what?" Compared to the Forties, when there was a horrible world war and incredible numbers of Jews were being slaughtered? Compared to a hundred years ago, when there were no vaccines, almost no anesthetics, and none of the major operations that we take for granted today? Compared to the Dark Ages of the past? Every period in history has been filled with tensions. Yet, we must also remember the achievements of each age and the fact that despite all forms of adversity, men, women and children found ways to live courageously, constructively and creatively.

This now brings us to the meaning of Rosh Hashanah. The new year is a gift to be used wisely, not a grant to be spent foolishly. Life without love is a bird without a song. Life without trust is a night without a day. Life without faith is a tree without roots. Life without hope is a year without spring. Life without friends is a sun without shade. Life without work is a bloom without fruit.

*Who gains time gains everything.*    BENJAMIN DISRAELI